SOCIAL PSYCHOLOGY

by

W. J. H. SPROTT

Professor of Philosophy in the University of Nottingham

SOCIAL SCIENCE PAPERBACKS

in association with

METHUEN & CO. LTD

SOCIAL PSYCHOLOGY

First published May 29th, 1952
Reprinted 1956, 1960, and 1963
First published in this series 1966
Printed in Great Britain by
The Alcuin Press

SOCIAL SCIENCE PAPERBACKS

are published by members of
Associated Book Publishers Limited,
11 New Fetter Lane, London, EC4

VELDA MARY SPROTT

CONTENTS

Part III   APPLICATIONS

INTRODUCTION

THE first two books to be called *Social Psychology* were published in 1908; one was written by the American sociologist E. A. Ross, the other, *An Introduction to Social Psychology*, was written by W. MacDougall. This shows that the concept *Social Psychology* is relatively new, and to this we must add the fact that the prominence of the subject is even newer. In this country at any rate students of psychology hardly thought of social psychology as a separate subject until quite recently. The work of Le Bon (1915) on crowd psychology was read and the 'psychology of crowds' was a topic which might occur in examination papers. Tarde's *Les Lois de l'Imitation* (1890) had been heard of, but in 1919 it had been relegated to the honourable and unread status of a classic. MacDougall's *Introduction* did not serve to introduce us to Social Psychology as it is now understood, it seemed rather to make us think of human beings in terms of instincts one of which admittedly was called 'gregarious'. In 1919 came Trotter's *Instincts of the Herd in Peace and War*. That book certainly invited us to take human herds seriously. Two types were distinguished: societies that resembled the industrious and peaceful communities of ants, others that were like ravenous and ravening wolf-packs. But our attention wandered, perhaps because Trotter's book was so obviously the product of war. We were called upon to condemn the wolf-like German, and that we were increasingly disinclined to do. MacDougall's *Group Mind* (1920) was a more serious proposition, but, again, it failed to inaugurate social psychology as a special discipline; the very notion of a 'group mind' was against it. Then, in 1921 appeared Ginsberg's *Psychology of Society*, a book full of learning and acute criticism. Perhaps it was too 'philosophical' for psychologists; anyway it did not place social psychology on the map.

Of course the political scientists had, by implication, been writing about social psychology, because they based their theories on a conception of the social nature of man, but psychologists did not study political science.

The sociologists in France, Durkheim and Lévy Bruhl, with their notion of the priority of societies over individuals may have prepared our minds a little for what was coming, but social psychology was a mere appendix to psychology—and was frequently cut out—until the invasion of the psychological field by the cultural anthropologists or America.

Such an account may well sound unfair; so many eminent names are left out. Bagehot, Graham Wallas, Wundt, all contributed to our knowledge of human society and the underlying psychological processes, but, regrettable though it may be, they were on the whole neglected by students of psychology.

When, in 1935, Ruth Benedict published her *Patterns of Culture* and Margaret Mead her *Sex and Temperament in Three Primitive Societies* we were presented with six short and vivid sketches of different cultures. We could not help becoming conscious of the social unit as encouraging some qualities and penalizing others. The amiable Arapesh, the suspicious Dobuans seemed so clearly the products of their different cultures, and we wondered whether we were not merely products of one among several different possible culture patterns. In taking the society as our unit we began taking social psychology seriously. 'Crowd psychology' ceased to be what 'social psychology' meant to us and the work of MacDougall, Ginsberg, Tarde, Bagehot and the rest, was reviewed from a more enlightened point of view. If societies are the conceptual units with which we deal, then we cannot but be interested in a special way in imitation as a method whereby conformity comes about, in the 'cake of custom' as a stabilizing influence, in the possibility of ant-like or wolf-like norms, and in the propriety of the 'group mind' hypothesis. No doubt we ought to have appreciated the importance of the observations made on social psychological topics before, but it seems to have required the lively stories of the cultural anthropologists to make us what might be called 'social psychology minded'.

The result of all this is that the neglected child threatens now to devour its mother, egged on to do so by its foster-parents, Sociology and Anthropology. There has, indeed, been something like a second 'Copernican revolution'. In the old days, 'conscious experience' was the centre of the psychological universe, reason guided human conduct and by means of introspection we could discover what went on in our 'minds'. Then came Freud, and with his teaching came a new perspective. Unconscious forces, instinctive or repressed, were now responsible for our behaviour; the biological 'id' was our centre-piece, the conscious 'ego' was merely the sensitive spot where the organism touched the outside world, reason was its compass and non-rational forces provided the energy. As the earth is determined in its path by its relation with the sun, so 'conscious experience' is determined by the dynamic contents of the 'unconscious'. And now the organism itself, conscious and unconscious, ego, super-ego, and all, are what they are because of the cultures in which they have developed. The culture-pattern threatens to occupy the central position; the individual is but a planet whose movements respond to the demands of social gravity.

Doubtless both perspectives are exaggerated. Of recent years we have become aware of the importance of the 'ego'. When the contents of the 'unconscious' are unravelled and the 'conscious self' accepts its predicament, then it, the 'ego', has to take charge and to make decisions. This surely means that we have to attribute to the 'ego' some kind of independent rational capacity. Psycho-analytic interest has passed from a pre-occupation with the 'id', through an analysis of the 'super-ego' to a concentration on the 'ego'.

Similarly we may run a risk if we present the individual human being as *merely* the product of his society. He is certainly that, and it will be our business to study the impact of the social environment upon him, but if we are going to say to him: 'You see how social forces influence you, how they generate in you all kinds of conventional acquiescences, now then make use of your knowledge,' we are appealing to something independent of specific social patterns though what we appeal to may require social relations for its existence.

But, however we phrase that point, the fact remains that cross-cultural investigation has shown that far more of our conduct is socially determined than we had realized, and it is by no means easy to separate 'Social Psychology' from what is usually called 'General Psychology'. It is not that 'Social Psychology' occupies so small an area that we are hard put to it to collect enough topics. The opposite is the truth. 'General Psychology', that is to say topics which must be excluded from 'Social Psychology', has shrunk so much that one may be hard put to it to decide on what is left.

Since we all must have at least the society of our mothers for the earliest years of our lives, all that can be attributed to us in our own right is a collection of physiological spasms. We might well say that all 'psychology' is 'social psychology' on the grounds that man is a social animal. But such a solution would not help us because within the whole subject of the study of human conduct there must be some division of labour. Sharp lines of demarcation cannot be drawn, but it is not difficult to make a rough distinction between what is quite obviously a matter of 'social psychology', because it explicitly concerns the interaction of persons, and what is clearly more 'general'. There are three sorts of topic which explicitly deal with inter-personal relation: (1) The way different cultures mould the characters of their participants, (2) psychological facts which are involved in social facts (e.g. class consciousness, or public opinion) and (3) the observation of small groups. In each case we are studying the way in which individuals are affected by other individuals, (1) in the training they receive for the roles they will have to play, (2) in their participation in the social structure, and (3) in personal face-to-face intercourse. In a sense we are not studying what is common to human beings as such, but rather the ways in which they differ according to their social environment. This means that 'general psychology' will on the whole be concerned with the general principles governing all human conduct, so far as these can be found out. It seems that sense perception and its rules are the same for all mankind. We assume that the laws of learning are the same for all mankind. We assume that all men have certain basic needs and have the same kinds of emotional disturbances when they are not satisfied. We assume that we can apply the same dispositional words such as habit or intelligence, and trait-names such as aggressive or greedy, to anyone and that the problem of assessing these latter is the same everywhere. One might say that 'general psychology' is concerned with form and 'social psychology' with content.

Of course there will be overlaps, or rather the same general topic will often appear in both disciplines. For example, the analysis of intelligence and its measurement is a subject for 'general psychology'; a consideration of the way in which an I.Q. may be raised by transferring a child to a more encouraging social *milieu* is a matter which obviously interests the social psychologist.

Again, there may be transfers of territory. For example, if the 'Oedipus Complex' proved to be universal, then the 'general psychologist' might claim it; if it turns out, as seems to be the case, that it is engendered by a certain social structure, but not by others, it becomes a 'social psychological' matter.

In attempting to separate the field of 'social psychology' from that of 'general psychology' we must not lose sight of the relations between them. 'Social Psychology' is based upon 'general psychology' in the sense that it applies general psychological principles in different social contexts. At the same time a study of different social contexts modifies our notion of what is 'general'. In the first place much that we used to consider 'general' to all mankind may turn out to be a cultural product, and in the second place the study of interpersonal relations may reveal general characteristics of human nature.

We may, then, distinguish what is the subject matter of Social Psychology by saying that it always carries a specific reference to interpersonal processes, either in the form of general cultural pressure, or in the form of the co-ordinate psychological activity that constitutes social phenomena, or in the form of direct face-to-face interaction. Our task of discrimination, however, is not accomplished. Social Psychology lies midway between 'general psychology' and sociology and we have now to consider its relation to the latter.

Quite clearly the subject-matter of all the social sciences is psychological in at least two senses. In the first place societies large and small consist of individual human beings in relation to one another. Social institutions, the class structure, the distribution of power, the binding customs and traditions are ultimately based upon the needs, desires and intentions of men and women. In the second place the social framework itself is a mental construct. It is not merely that the needs of men and women are basic to the institution of marriage, the very concept of marriage is an abstraction. The intentions of multitudes of men and women throughout the years are basic to the existence of a nation, but a nation only exists because appropriate numbers of people believe it exists. The same is true of all the ideas which form the subject matter of the social sciences:—the market, property, class, kingship and so on.

And yet these constructs do have a quasi-independent existence; they confront the new-comer as objective constituents of the environment to which he must adapt himself. Moreover, in their origin these constructs themselves are not intended in the sense in which the conduct from which they are abstracted involves intentions. Men and women have mated in order to satisfy their desires, they did not intend to establish monogamy and polygamy. Men have intended to reap where they have sown, they did not intend to establish the institution of landed property. If we call the actual intention which people have 'first-order data', then the socially accepted form in which these intentions are satisfied may be called: 'second-order data' and it is with them that sociology is concerned.

There is, however, an obvious modification we must make. When men become aware of 'second-order data' they may make them the object of their intentions. We cannot suppose that anyone had the notion of property before some form of exclusive use was acquiesced in, whether because each social unit was in fact quietly occupying some area, or because the occupiers were strong enough to resist intruders, or a mixture of both. But when land becomes scarce it may well be that friction forces the social participants to become conscious of their own custom as presenting them with a problem. Then they may, or some of them may, intend to establish a different system of property relation. It is quite on the cards that the new form of the institution of property has its own 'logic' and presents new, and quite unintended problems to future generations.

The point is that whereas in the earliest days of human social history 'second-order data' came into being through the unconscious acceptance of use and wont, as time goes on they become material for manipulation. They do not cease to be the subject matter of sociology because they are the objects of conscious intention. The emphasis for the sociologist is on their impersonal aspect.

The social psychologist is interested in the 'first-order data' which lie at the basis of 'second-order data'. The sociologist is interested in the 'second-order data' in their own right as quasi-independent entities.

PART I

THE STUDY OF GROUPS

CHAPTER I

GROUPS AND SITUATIONS

SOCIAL Psychology is concerned with the ways in which a person's conduct and dispositions are influenced by the conduct and dispositions of other people. It may be argued that a person would not be a human being at all but for his interaction with other people, and this question will be taken up in Chapter VIII. In this chapter we shall take as our unit the abstract human being with his independent self-hood, his capacities for doing the sort of thing that human beings can do: perceive with his various senses, reason, have standards of conduct, etc., and consider the sorts of social influences to which he is subjected.

It is important to recognize that his capacities themselves are what they are because of the personal contacts which he has had. His intelligence, for instance, is what it is partly because its use has been encouraged by the people by whom he has been brought up. Our starting-point here, then, is somewhat unreal, but so long as we are aware of the unreality no harm will be done. The problem of the order in which topics are taken is complicated by the very nature of the subject. Groups are made up of individuals; individuals are made by groups. It is silly to ask which came first. Doubtless a good case might be made for starting with the way in which the individual is moulded by his social interactions, but that would involve referring to 'groups', and this word stands for a number of different concepts which it is important to distinguish. On these grounds, as has been said, we are going to leave the detailed development of the individual to a later chapter, and differentiate the various kinds of social influence in this one.

The first thing which has to be emphasized is that all social influences make themselves felt in actual social situations. By a social situation is meant what might be called the 'inter-behaviour' of one human being with one or more other human beings. There are two limiting types of social situation. We can accept, as a limiting type at one end of the scale, a man 'by himself'. When he criticizes himself: 'I wonder why I said that,' or even says to himself : 'I should not do that if I were you,' there is a social situation in one person. At the other end of the scale we can envisage the case of several people, each independently taking a walk on the sands or over a moor in sight of one another. The limit here is, of course, the extent to which it can be said that the conduct of each is totally unaffected by the presence of the others. Between these limits, wherever there is adjustment made by a person to the presence, or immediately expected presence, of another person or of a collection of other persons, there is a social situation.

The class of social situations is enormously varied. It includes the mother talking to her child, the teacher and his pupils in the class room, the workers in a shop at any given time, and the crowd at a football match.

There are other characteristics to be noted. A. The situation may be relatively momentary or it may persist and develop. Examples of the former type would be a man raising his hat to a lady as he passes her in the street, or an urchin cocking a snook at the back view of his teacher. Examples of the latter type would be a conversation, a lesson period, a committee meeting or a period of work in a factory.

B. A situation may or may not involve the relation of leader and follower. This problem will be taken up later.

C. Again we may distinguish between a situation in which all members are on an equality and a situation in which some participants deem themselves to be superior or inferior to others in respect of some characteristics accepted by the society to which they belong as establishing an appropriate scale of evaluation. What such characteristics will be will vary from one situation to another, and a definition is by no means easy. In any group of four or five people there may be difference of height, weight, beauty, intelligence, strength and so on. The group might nevertheless be egalitarian in the sense with which we are here concerned if no gestures of deference were made with respect to such qualities, so that we should say: 'Height, weight, etc., makes no difference in their intercourse.' When we come to inegalitarian situations we come up against certain difficulties.

Let us first consider the comparatively easy case of a party at which the guests come from different social classes. Let us assume that everyone in the room is aware of this difference. Let us further assume that

influenced by class-affiliation. The resultant behaviour
f two sorts: either such as to mark the difference or
it up. Those who deem themselves superior may cold-
se they deem their inferiors, or they may be patronizing or
, while the 'inferiors' may withdraw among themselves or
e respectfully and deferentially to their 'superiors'. Alternatively
e superiors may be more effusive to the inferiors than they would be
to one another, while the inferiors may manifest an elaborate ease of
manner to show that they recognize no difference in status. Obvious
permutations and combinations of conduct are possible, all of them
determined by a felt difference in social class.

Now what is the difference between such a situation, which is common enough, and, say a group of freshmen at a university entertaining
a rowing blue, or the meeting of a dining club at which are present
several connoisseurs of wine, whose taste and knowledge is recognized
to surpass the taste and knowledge of the other members of the
party? In both these two cases respect is paid, in the former to rowing
prowess, in the latter to taste and discrimination. In both these
cases, too, the conduct might either be such as to mark the difference
or such as to minimize it: 'Of course I only got my place in the
boat by sheer luck' for instance, or 'I don't really think one man's
taste in wine is any better than another's. The whole thing's a ramp.
I just happened to. . . .' All the same there is a difference between the
class distinction situation and the other two, a difference in what we
might call 'typicality' or 'general social acceptance'. In the first case
we should say that class-difference was generally recognized in our
society, which means that it is a recurrent theme, manifesting itself
over a wide variety of situations, while in the other two cases we might
say that prowess in rowing or connoisseur-ship of wine only receives
recognition in a comparatively small number of situations and in the
eyes of comparatively few persons.

There are certain prestige differences which receive what we have
called 'general social acceptance' and there are others which receive
'restricted social acceptance'. What is meant by 'restricted social
acceptance' is that the prestige value in question enters into the assumptions of a comparatively small number of persons.

The phrase 'enters into the assumptions' requires explanation.
Consider the case mentioned above of the undergraduates entertaining
a rowing-blue, or consider the case of a group of speedway fans entertaining a celebrated speedway cyclist. They *might* be old friends, of

course, and the prestige-value might make no difference; the situation would then be egalitarian at any rate with respect to rowing or cycling skill. But we are assuming that this is not the case. What would be meant by saying that 'in the world of undergraduates interested in rowing, a rowing-blue is a man to look up to' or making the same sort of remark about 'the world of speedway fans'? Surely it would mean that among the assumptions which the members of the two groups make in their conversations are assumptions about the prestige-value of rowing-blues and skilled speedway cyclists. The sorts of things each member of these two groups will say will be partially determined by certain assumptions of knowledge, and approbation in the persons to whom he is talking and by expectations of certain responses rather than others. 'I had a drink with old X,' one of them might say, assuming that his partner knew who 'old X' was, and valued 'old X' for the same reason as the speaker. He would expect some such reply as: 'Lucky fellow' or words to the same import, and he would be startled and affronted by the bleak question: 'So what?' unless he could interpret it as sour grapes. The 'world of speedway fans' is thus marked out as a collection of persons who have certain interests and values which we might call 'speedway' interests and values, and who can safely make 'speedway' assumptions about knowledge and value when they are talking to other 'speedway' fans, and safely expect certain sorts of responses from them rather than others. As we should say: 'they speak the same language'. This means that the 'world of speedway fans' defines its situational inegalities, that is to say that within that 'world' the presence of a celebrated speedway rider will produce a situation of prestige-inequality. Within other 'worlds' the presence of a man who 'happens to be a celebrated speedway rider' might introduce no prestige-inequality whatever.

Other 'restricted social acceptances' can be treated in the same way. Other 'worlds' could be marked out in terms of the knowledge, interest, assumptions, conventions and expectations of their denizens. Each would 'define' certain prestige-inequalities in the appropriate social situations. The points to notice are: (1) prestige is not a quality like height or weight, but depends on the evaluation system of the collection of persons for whom this, that or the other characteristic has prestige (2) this evaluation-system *consists of* feelings of respect in persons for whom this that or the other characteristic has prestige, certain conversational assumptions and expectations, and what I have called 'deference-behaviour', direct or indirect, in situations in which the prestige-bearing persons are present. If a difference in, say, wealth aroused no feeling of respect, involved no conversational assumptions or expectations of a wealth-prestige order, and if the more wealthy received no deference-behaviour from the less-wealthy—then that would mean that the evaluation-system of the persons of whom this were true would not include wealth, and in such a 'world' wealth would have no prestige.

So much for 'restricted social acceptance' which has been distinguished from 'general social acceptance'. The question may now be asked: Is this distinction fundamental? The answer is: No. The 'general society' which 'defines' such prestige values as class is merely a more inclusive collection of persons. What we mean by 'general social acceptance' is that over a very wide range of human beings feelings of respect or disrespect with regard to such characteristics as 'birth', occupation or wealth may be inferred, certain conversational assumptions about such matters can be made with confidence, certain expectations of response are almost certain to be fulfilled, and certain classes of 'deference-conduct' are likely to be observed in social situations of class inequality. In fact what we mean when we speak of the 'society to which a man belongs', whether on a large or small scale, is in ultimate analysis, the system of assumptions, expectations, and coherent responses to which his own conduct has been trained to adapt itself in the social situations in which he is placed.

There is a difference between such systems which should be mentioned, though it is not of fundamental importance. A man is, as it were, born into certain systems—his national or tribal system, or his class system, for example, while he joins—either compulsorily or voluntarily—other and more restricted ones, such as a school system, or a factory system, or a 'speedway fan' system.

This discussion of social situations in which socially significant differences in status play a part has been prolonged in order to bring out the central and dominating position of the social situation itself. This is, in fact, the beginning and end of social psychology. The 'society', the 'group', the 'culture-pattern' are constructs, the social situation, in an important sense, really exists. Of course in some sense the 'social situation' is an abstraction because one picks out of the real existent complexity certain features (e.g. the co-operating performance, or the deferential gesturing) for special notice, much as in a piece of music one might call attention to a tune which recurs in different contexts. What is meant by saying that the social situation is the reality is simply that we can go and look at it, while the 'society', the 'group', the 'culture-pattern' cannot be inspected in the same sense. They are systems of dispositions, of probable behaviour, of likelihoods, which we make use of in interpreting and predicting what actually happens in social situations.

It might be objected that a 'group', if small enough, could be observed or photographed. So, in a sense, they could, but if you observed all the members in a room, or took a photograph of them sitting in rows, you would be photographing or observing all the members *in a social situation*. The notion of a group as a persistent entity with certain standards of value, a certain code of conduct, and a scheme of conventions is a tool of thought by means of which we co-ordinate the conduct we observe. It is a model which we make and not an observable thing. It may be said to stand in much the same relation to social intercourse that the notion of 'personality' or 'character' stand to individual conduct.

We must now turn to a consideration of these models, and we can start with the notions of 'personality' and 'character' which have just been introduced. What we have before us is a stream of conduct performed by the same physical organism. By 'conduct' we mean not only the *overt* behaviour, the movement of limbs and the utterance of speech, but also the *covert* behaviour which we infer in the case of other people and of which we have a private view in the case of ourselves. The overt behaviour of any given person is something we can watch for varying lengths of time, infer from distant communications such as letters and telephonic conversation, and hear about from the reports of other people, in which case we learn about the overt behaviour of A from the overt behaviour of B and C. The covert behaviour, feelings, perceivings, thinkings, we 'infer' in the main from overt signs— gestures, facial expression, speech, and so forth. The word 'infer' in this context is somewhat misleading. We do not usually see a gesture and then go through a process of inference: e.g. 'When I make that gesture it is a sign that I am feeling so-and-so, therefore this person must be feeling so-and-so'. What happens is more immediate than that. We see the angry look, we hear surprise in the exclamation, and we sense hostility in the smile.

In order to simplify matters, and indeed keep closer to our actual experience we can take 'observing a person's conduct' to include the overt elements which we observe and the covert elements which we impute, or in terms of which we interpret the overt ones. Now we observe a person's conduct (including hearing about it) for long or short periods at a time, but our observation is cumulative and we observe it in terms of a model which we call the person's 'personality' or 'character'. The glimpses we get begin and end, but the construct in terms of which we make our observation persists, and our observations themselves are in terms of it. How we come to see gesturing and speaking bodies in terms of persons it is by no means easy to say; the fact is that we do. One thing, however, seems pretty certain: we could not form such a frame of reference unless what is presented to us had some consistency about it. The object we observe is a recognizable human being and looks much the same from one observation to another, so that the appearances are apprehended as appearances of the same person.

In addition to this, and for our present purpose of great importance, there is a certain consistency of behaviour. The person does not merely behave like other human beings in a general way, he manifests certain regularities peculiar to himself. It is on a basis of these that we fill out our model of the person's 'personality' or 'character'. Again, however, we come to do it, we do this immediately. We apprehend a new acquaintance as a potentially fill-out-able person, and proceed at once, with or without sophisticated reflection, to note regularities and consistencies in his conduct. We immediately form an hypothesis about him, which guides our further observation and is modified when our expectations have been falsified. The more his actual conduct fits in with our expectation the more we say we 'understand' him. Conversely, when we say: 'I can't understand how so-and-so could do that,' it means that our model is inadequate, though we usually do not like to admit our mistake, and tend rather to blame the person in question for not fitting in with the model we have made of him. The expression: 'I cannot understand X' nearly always carries a note of disapproval.

'Personality' and 'character'—there is no point here in drawing a distinction between these two words—are models built out of observed continuities and attendant consistencies and regularities of conduct. Some are characteristic of human beings as such, some are characteristic of relatively small groups of human beings, and some are characteristic of one human being.[1] The model is, as it were, held together by the guiding forces of value and reason. Our model is, of course, very

[1] cf. Kluckhohn, C. and Murray, H. A. (ed.) *Personality.* Cape, 1949, p. 35.

like that which Professor Ryle[1] condemns as misleading to philosophers, and psychologists, and it may very well be that for their
purposes another kind of model is better. However that may be, we
do in fact view people in terms of the 'ghost in the machine', with
desires, values, and endowed with reason by means of which the
desires are satisfied and the values achieved.

The same factors—continuity, consistency and regularity of conduct
rendered intelligible as being directed towards the rational pursuit of
values—are the material out of which we construct our models of 'a
society', 'a group' and 'a culture-pattern'. A very simple illustration
will make the point clear. We are told that one of the features of the
Kwakiutl Society is the achievement of prestige by means of the
destruction of property. How is this discovered? Someone must have
observed at least one case of a Kwakiutl man burning his goods. But
that obviously is not enough. Suppose you come across a man,
coloured differently from yourself, engaged in destroying a large
bundle of mats or pouring upon a blazing fire oil which it has taken
months to accumulate. You start off with your 'personality model'
and assume that there is likely to be some 'meaning' in what he is
doing. Suppose, now, lit up by the conflagration our man turns round
to the assembled multitude, his chest braced to receive the impact of
their applause. And now suppose that nothing but pitying looks and
murmurs of contempt are his reward, and yet he still persists in boastful
posturing. You would probably, particularly if you had been brought
up in certain circles, say that he was a 'social deviate'. Supposing, on
the other hand, his conduct was rewarded with acclamation, and advantageous comparison was made with other burnings. Supposing
you saw a somewhat dejected character moving from the scene muttering that he will prepare a better and bigger holocaust, then you
would be inclined to find a place for the conduct not merely in the
'personality pattern' you are unwittingly constructing, but in the
'culture-pattern' you are endeavouring to piece together.

Just as we start with an abstract scheme of desires and values which
we fill out into the 'personality' or 'character' of our friends and
acquaintances, so we start out with an abstract scheme of desires and
values commonly held by many persons—it may be by millions—and
from the regularities of social conduct which we observe together with
the signs of approval and disapproval, we fill out our scheme into the
'culture' pattern or the 'way-of-life' of the collection of persons whom

[1] *The Concept of Mind.* Hutchinson, 1949.

we are studying. Just as we try to make our personality model meaningful by organizing observed regularities of conduct round desires and
values which we 'understand', because they bear some resemblance to
our own experience, so we try to make our social model intelligible by
organizing the socially accepted or socially condemned conduct round
desires and values with which we can sympathize.

Frequent burnings of property attended by approving audiences is
not all we see. The question: 'why?' is scarcely spoken. The glow of
pride on the face of the destroyer is a sign that he has achieved something he wants, the acclamation of the bystander at once gives us a clue
because wanting social approval is already part of our abstract scheme
of all social life. Now our questioning begins: why on earth should
social approval in such high measure be given to something which we
should regard as extremely silly? Our model is deficient until we can
link *that* up with something with which we are familiar—perhaps a
fashion set by some great man in the past. Part, indeed, of the work of
anthropologists consists of laying down principles for the effective
construction of models of this kind.

Whatever may turn out to be the best technique for improving our
constructs, the important fact remains—that they are *constructs*. This
carries with it the obvious implication that they may be faulty. They
may be defective in at least two ways. In the first place they may not
be coherent; there may be too many gaps and unintelligible items for
our liking. This can be cured by further knowledge, if further knowledge is forthcoming. A worse defect is almost the reverse: we may
be too satisfied with our model. Language and the contemplation of
our models themselves tempt us to think that a 'society' or a 'group'
or a 'culture pattern' or a 'way of life' can be observed as a whole, that
we can look at it, just as we can watch a man burning his house down.
The whole point of this discussion has been to attempt to show that
this is nonsense, and that what happens is exactly the opposite. We
take a bit here and a bit there, choosing our bits in accordance with such
principles as regularity and signs of approval and disapproval, and
we construct the 'way of life'.

Now we know perfectly well how often we are mistaken in our
personality constructs and how often we are wrong in our interpretation of social situations; how much more tentative should be our
constructs of culture-patterns. We ourselves have been drilled to adapt
ourselves to, to participate in, to be part of a system of assumptions and
expectancies and all our observations and interpretations are bound to

be influenced thereby. In order to forge tools for the interpretation of another system we must at least be aware of the peculiarities of our own perspective. Doubtless this difficulty can, in a measure, be overcome, but that it is by no means always overcome is witnessed by the culture-pattern constructs of all too many people who have woven them out of a minimum of observation and generous measure of prejudice. Such sources of defect, however, can be detected. A more dangerous source of defect is the inevitable selectivity of the observer. It may well be that the field anthropologists, living for a year or so with the tribes they are studying, can paint a picture which is recognizable to anyone following in their footsteps, because the numbers are relatively small and one may have good reason to suppose that everyone lives much the same sort of life. When one is dealing with a society of any size one cannot observe all its members and the chances are high that the samples one meets are not representative.[1]

This is undoubtedly one reason why descriptions of national character so often differ. Indeed, one has only to think of the wild notions of 'the French' constructed by visitors who only know Montmartre, and that but little, to see the danger. The matter gets more serious when the model is constructed of what we might call 'political' rather than 'domestic' elements. Disapproving adjectives like 'war-like', 'aggressive', 'tyrannous', or approving ones like 'democratic' or 'peace-loving', even if true of any member of the society are only likely to be true of comparatively few. It is obviously of importance to know the qualities of people whose decisions have far-reaching effects and when we speak of 'the Russians', the 'Japanese', the 'Americans' and so on, it is more often than not to these that we are really referring. Unfortunately, however, we run the risk of spreading what is true of the few over the many and thus get an entirely false picture of the majority of the population, who probably scarcely think in terms of political aggression or tyranny or democracy at all. If this were merely a defect in scientific hypothesis the methods of correcting it would be fairly simple: we should tell our scientists to do their job better. The real danger of defective models will appear when we consider the part played by these models in social life.

First, however, we must consider the way in which the social models define social boundaries. Supposing we were to view the world from a distance we can imagine (another model is being used) seeing central places at which decisions are made, setting in motion other decisions

[1] cf. Nadel, S. F. *The Foundation of Social Anthropology*. Cohen and West, 1951.

over an area on all sides of our centres. Let the decisions be what we call 'administrative' decisions and the range of the net-work of any set of such decisions would determine an administrative area. If we drew lines round such areas we should get a 'political map', and the areas would be 'states'. It is quite clear that a precise definition of any state in such terms would be very complicated because we should have to include in our major or inclusive areas, the smaller areas of what we call 'local government', and it is not necessary for us here to pursue the subject. The point is—and it is an important one—that states are not things, but administrative systems in which certain people have the 'right' to tell other people what to do, and the boundary between states comes when people on one side of the fence will not take orders from, or are not administered by, people on the other side.

Turning now to our more immediate problem, 'cultures', or 'ways-of-life', or 'societies' are similarly discriminated. We find areas within which there are certain regularities of conduct—overt and covert—sufficiently distinguishable from one another to make us give them special proper names. Almost always the areas marked out by cultural models will coincide with the areas marked out by the political-state models. Almost always one of the differentiating regularities will be language, but it may be, as in Switzerland, that the regularities of conduct among people speaking different languages transcend in significance the linguistic classification. It may be that the regularities we note have a long history behind them and transcend political boundaries, as in the case of Toynbee's[1] Civilizations. It may be that in spite of certain differences, the regularities of conduct of a group of persons may be worth attention even though some of them belong to one political area, and others to another. Such would be the case if, for instance, the aristocracies of two countries resembled one another in their way of life more than either of them resembled their co-nationals in *their* way of life.

The choice of regularities in thus marking out culture-areas, or 'societies' is theoretically an arbitrary matter. Practically, however, there is at least one guiding principle. We want to use our way of life models for interpretation and prediction. We want to be able to say : 'if this person belongs to that culture then he is likely to behave in such and such a way' or 'he does this because the X's, of whom he is one, do that kind of thing and it means so-and-so.' The regularities we shall select for this purpose must therefore be of a certain complexity and

---

[1] *A Study of History.* Royal Institute of International Affairs, 1934. Vol. I.

their value will, broadly speaking, be in direct proportion to the verifiable inferences we are able to draw from them. For this reason Toynbee's notion of a civilization may not be very useful because you cannot infer very much about a person if you only know that he participates in, say, Western Civilization.

Similarly a narrow behaviour-range is not likely to be of much use. To know that a person participates in the culture of film-fans does not tell us much more about him than that he is likely to talk about films, take in certain journals, and attend the cinema fairly frequently. Since, however, these models are constructs and not observable entities, there are no limits to our multiplying models save those set by the purposes for which we make them. It is as sensible for W. F. Whyte to write about the culture of corner-boys as for Ruth Benedict to write about the culture of the Zuni Indians, if the corner-boys have a way of life sufficiently distinctive to help us to understand the conduct of any one of them, or predict what we should have to do to gain their approval as 'one of them'.

Everyone, as we have seen, has to learn to do the accepted things and refrain from the unaccepted things so as to fit in with the system into which he is born. The method of training we shall consider later; here it is sufficient to say that it takes place in the social interchanges he has with his father and mother, his sisters and brothers, his uncles and aunts, his boy friends and girl friends, the neighbours, the school teachers and so forth. There is no mysterious inculcation, impregnation, or contagious infection wrought by 'society' or 'culture'. All the same, for purposes of exposition our models are extremely useful—provided we remember that they are models. We may then ask what system of assumption and expectation, what regularities of value-judgment will confront the infant, demanding his participation? Our answer will depend, as might be imagined, on the amount of detail we wish to take into consideration.

In the first place there will be what we might call the 'general culture' or the 'general inclusive society' into which he is born: the Mundugumor, the Arapesh, the English, the Japanese, the Brazilian or the Malay. Training will be necessary to ensure that the child grows up with the traits, values, dispositions and skills expected of a socially approved participant in the way-of-life denoted by these proper names.

But the child is not only a Zuni, a Chinaman or a Balinese, it has a sex, and it may belong to a social class with distinctive conduct. More detail is required in our models: the culture-pattern of a male (or female) of a certain social status.

Again he lives somewhere—in Bavaria, in Kent, in Kwangsu. Are there, we ask, cultural distinctions which mark out Bavarians from other Germans, Kentish men from other Englishmen, and inhabitants of Kwangsu from other Chinamen? So we go on until we come to his village or his street and the culture pattern of his home.

A useful method of dealing with all this is provided by Linton, who analyses culture in terms of a net-work of statuses, each with its appropriate behaviour and role. This scheme is discussed in a later chapter.[1]

Some cultural determinants—we use the expression with caution, because all we mean is: such regularities of conduct as fit the models we have constructed—some cultural determinants may be relevant to the explanation of a person's behaviour in a general way more or less all the time. There are other models which are only relevant to his behaviour in special circumstances. His membership of a dart team, for instance, will involve, in fact will *be*, behaviour specific to that particular interest. Somewhere between the general cultural model, and the small-scale group model, we can place such models as 'the lawyer', the 'doctor', the 'clergyman'.

The upshot is a set of models differentiating one general culture from another, and then each model turns out to include other models within it in accordance with the differentiation into what are sometimes called 'sub-cultures' within each 'society'. The importance of this intra-cultural differentiation can hardly be exaggerated. Insistence on it corrects the over-simplified models to which reference has already been made above. By way of example, consider one aspect of the problem of delinquency. We hear a great deal about lax discipline, bad companions, bad neighbourhoods and so forth—all in general terms. Such phrases are, in fact, tautologous. Lax discipline is discipline which has not prevented the delinquent from doing whatever he has done; he has done what he has done because he has not been prevented from doing it. Companions and neighbourhoods are 'bad' because they have 'bad' results, a boy has gone to the 'bad' because his companions have been such as not to prevent his going to the 'bad'. The pseudo-explanations evaporate on inspection. What we want to know is the actual culture in which he has been brought up, and the actual variety of it which is manifest there in the street in which he lives. We want to know what

[1] P. 153.

is fashionable, what is admired, what values he has acquired, if we are going to grasp the social influence to which he has been submitted, and if we want to subject him to counter-influences. All too often the amateur criminologist tries to interpret a working-class boy's behaviour with a model derived from middle-class conduct. No wonder his behaviour seems odd, and is put down to 'inherent naughtiness'.

What has been said may appear to contradict what has been said above as to the utility of small-scale models. This is not, however, the case. A distinction can be drawn between pervasive traits and intermittent conduct. For the understanding of the former one wants the richest picture of 'life down our street' one can possibly get, even though the picture applies to no other street. The model which we form of the 'Bowls Club' is not so illuminating because it is only concerned with a narrow range of fairly specific conduct.

Mention has been made of the part played by models in the social life of group members. We must now consider this in greater detail. So far we have used the concept of regularity or consistency of conduct as distinguishing one set of persons from another and thus identifying 'ways of life' and 'culture patterns', when we emphasize the conduct itself, and 'societies' and 'groups' when we emphasize the persons who carry out the conduct. This 'behaviouristic' or 'objective' approach, however, is not adequate. The Alorese, the English, the Iroquois and the French not only go through the motions which *in abstracto* we call their 'way of life', they *know* that they are Alorese, English, Iroquois or French. This means that they, too, have 'models' just as the sociologist or social-psychologist has. To put the matter in terms of overt behaviour, they use such expressions as: 'we Alorese', 'we English', 'our tribe', 'our country', and 'you French' 'you Iroquois', 'those Russians'.

'Germany', 'America', 'groups', 'societies', 'nations', 'states', 'countries', 'tribes', 'associations', etc., are part of the ideological world of human beings. Whatever we may say about the ultimate analysis of such 'things' into probabilities of behaviour, we must now complicate our story by introducing these conceptual entities as determinants of the behaviour they define. A child, born into what the social psychologist with his culture-pattern model will distinguish as a 'society', will almost certainly acquire his own, doubtless rather vaguer, model with which he will identify himself. This will be mediated by instructions from older persons, who in their turn have been instructed by persons who ... and it will be reinforced by the observations of similarities of behaviour about him, and sharpened by observation of differences. Thus the important 'we'—'they' distinction comes about. By saying that the child gradually *identifies* himself with the 'we' group we mean that his desires and ambitions are focused not only upon himself but also on what he deems to be the vicissitudes of the 'we'-group. To varying extents from person to person behaviour will be determined not only by 'what I want irrespective of my group' but also by 'what I want as a group-member'.[1]

In this description of the sort of way in which group-ideas function, we have had to bring out into prominence what is often only vague and latent. A member of the Rotarians, when behaving 'Rotarian-ishly', does not have to keep muttering: 'We Rotarians do this but not that,' all the time. To say he has a 'Rotarian-model' in his mind is to say that he understands such a question as 'Are you a Rotarian?' To say that he 'identifies himself' with 'We Rotarians' is to say that he will be pleased when he hears things that mean to him 'The Rotarians have done well', appropriately displeased when the reverse happens, prepared to forgo personal advantages if they conflict with the 'Rotarian-ishness' which he had acquired (and which *constitutes* effective membership) and proudly adept at the ritual which adorns the weekly lunch. He need not, as it were, take out his Rotarian model and contemplate it all the time, in fact he may scarcely ever do so. If cross-questioned, however, he has it ready to hand. The same may be said of all the groups with which men identify themselves, national and local associations, community, club and empire.

We are, of course, perfectly familiar with this phenomenon of 'we'-identification and 'they'-non-identification, but what is not so obvious is the constructional nature of the 'we' and the 'they'. Once this is realized we are prepared for varieties in the content and clarity of the models we use. It is obvious that the 'England'-model is likely to be richer in content in the case of an administrator than in the case of a man who has never moved away from some remote corner of the country. Education, communication and mobility all play their part in changing people's ideas of 'England' and making them more alike. The medieval serf can hardly have had the same model as his lord, if, indeed 'England' meant anything to him at all. One of the aims of the educational developments among illiterate peoples, of which the U.S.S.R. is so justly proud, is undoubtedly to implant in the minds of such remote tribesmen the model of the Union of Soviet Socialist Re-

[1] cf. Sherif, M. and Cantril, H. *The Psychology of Ego-Involvements*. Wiles, 1947.

publics and to induce them to identify themselves with it. This development of similar models is going on all the time as education within an area becomes more uniform, and communications bring people with the same identification into closer contact with one another.

So much for the clarity and elaboration of our models. More important is the qualities they embody. The models with which we identify ourselves will, of course, have 'good' qualities, because that is what identification involves. Characteristics which the impartial observer will include in his model, but which identifiers admit to be 'bad' ones, will tend to be ignored or said to be 'Un-English' or 'Un-American' by the latter. The models with which we identify ourselves are 'ideal' in both senses of the word.

When it comes to the 'out-groups', we distinguish sharply between 'friends' and 'enemies', the latter having 'bad' qualities. Furthermore the 'enemy' models function as intimately in the lives of those who have them as the ones with which they identify themselves. There is good reason to suppose that we attribute to the enemy groups not only 'bad' qualities for which we have evidence, but disapproved-of qualities in ourselves. This is called 'projection'. Thus the 'enemy' group is believed to be aggressive, mean or sexually perverse on very little objective evidence, but because the believer himself, who has unwittingly constructed the image for his own purposes, projects his own aggressiveness, meanness, and unsatisfied sexual desires upon it. It can easily be seen that these constructs can be shaped and reinforced by propaganda, judiciously directed to capture potential projection. It can also be seen that these 'out-group' models will change from time to time. At one time the 'French', at another the 'German' and at another the 'Russians' will be hostile models. Another, and equally potent, model is the 'under-dog' type, frequently found in contrasting conjunction with the 'wicked' type, who feature as oppressive. 'The Workers', 'the Jews', the 'Negroes' are further examples, the last two functioning either as 'wicked' or as 'good-oppressed'; the 'Workers' are always 'good'.

In passing we may note that these fixations of 'out-groups' as friendly and hostile are mediated by means of *language*. Without such a method of creative intercourse, which at once provides a medium of communication and a device for giving such communication a certain degree of permanence, it is difficult to see how groups could persist in coherent identifying unity.

The importance of language as a social product has been stressed by M. M. Lewis. 'Without communication,' he says, 'there can be no community.'[1] In any group activity it provides a means of recalling past experience, a means whereby the *whole group* becomes aware of the immediate present environment, a means of collectively planning, and carrying out a project, and at the same time it helps to arouse and maintain group feeling. All this is perfectly true, and Lewis goes further to remark: 'If, as Plato says, individual thinking is internal conversation, then it is equally true that group thinking is external conversation.'[2] Having gone so far, why not, Lewis asks, think of such essential intercommunication in terms of a 'group mind', for is not 'mind' behaviour mediated by symbols? That, of course, is a matter of convenience. What is indubitable is that without language no group collaboration of any complexity could ever come into being, and this surely means that language was, as it were, 'invented' for this purpose. The 'private' use of language for thought is a secondary development from the 'public' and 'primary' function of language as a method of communication.

A final type of group must be mentioned. When we say that a man is an American, a Samoan, a male middle-class Frenchman or a Comanche Warrior we are saying something about the kinds of conduct that will be expected of him in appropriate situations as defined by the models we make of the culture-pattern named by these expressions. The range of variety named by any one of them is enormous. Let us take by contrast some of the things we mean when we say that a man is a barrister or a gunner. His membership of these two classes will entail a more precise prediction of the sorts of things he will do. Some of the social situations in which the barrister and the gunner will participate will be highly structural or formalized. As a barrister he has to fit in with the procedure that *is* a Court of Law in Session and the gunner has, on occasions, to carry out his part of a drill. Some roles involve the performance of specific actions on certain occasions, others do not.

Looking at the matter from the situational point of view we can distinguish between the 'structured' situation and the 'unstructured one'. The distinction can best be imagined as a scale with the purely 'informal' party, or conversation at one end and the strictly formalized ritual at the other. The distinction is important for three reasons. (1) The knowledge of the formalities obviously influences the actions of participants. (2) The formal situation itself acts inhibitively, making certain conduct inappropriate. This, of course, says nothing because it is what we mean by a 'formal' situation. The interesting thing is that

---

[1] *Language and Society.* Nelson, 1947, p. 68.   [2] Ibid., p. 100.

the very framework of the formal situation often inhibits more than we would expect. This is instanced by the contrast between what a participant may intend before the situation and what he actually does in the situation.

A committee meeting is a formal situation. The members of the Committee may intend to raise issues, speak for or against proposals but in the event the situation may so develop in accordance with the formal rules of procedure that much gets unsaid. This is partly due to the very presence of a number of people confronting each member, which means that he is addressing persons there before him, apprehended as having hostile or friendly attitudes, axes to grind, anxious to 'make their mark' for fear of being ignored and therefore ready to pounce upon the slightest flaw, sticklers for propriety and so on. But this is not all. The agenda may not provide opportunity, the opportunity may be missed, the motion which you want to oppose may be worded in a way which makes your intended opposition irrelevant or some other formal barrier may block your path. The skilful committee-man is he who can adapt his intention to the formalities, the skilful chairman is often he who can manipulate the formalities so as to prevent decisions with which he is not in agreement.

(3) There seems to be a general formalizing tendency which operates as a harmonizing, and, indeed, a consolidating agent. A group of friends may meet for discussion on several occasions in the same room. There will probably be a tendency for them to sit in the same seats every time, they may take turns in opening the discussion or reading a paper, and it is on the cards that one of them—maybe the host—will act as an 'informal' chairman. The oftener this happens, the more formalized the proceedings become. Roles are generated, and an idea or model of the 'group' is formed in the minds of each. Bit by bit innovations are resisted, each identifies himself with the 'group', a stranger is an interloper, and the members become bound by their own creations. All this is in the interest of harmony because they cannot all talk at once or sit in the same chair, and it is in the interest of consolidation because the more ordered the situation the easier to make a model for identification. The example given may seem a little fanciful, but it will be noticed that any class of students, who meet regularly, tend to disperse themselves in a regular way about the room, any collection of persons who meet regularly for recreation tend to develop their conventions, and even a group of two tend to form regular mutually adjustive habits.

Conclusion. The social situation, relatively formal or relatively informal, is the reality which Social Psychology studies. These situations and the conduct that constitutes them are not haphazard. There are recurrent patterns of assumptions and expectations in their participants, recurrent expressions of approval and disapproval. These regularities enable us to abstract models in terms of which the actual conduct can be interpreted and, within the limits of individual variety, in a measure predicted. These are called 'culture patterns' or 'ways of life', and, if we want to refer to the performers, 'societies', 'nations', or 'groups', or 'tribes'. One feature which helps to consolidate groups (i.e. reinforces and modifies the regularities of conduct) is the acquisition on the part of the participants of the idea of the groups to which they belong, and the idea of their membership.

The child, then, grows up, not merely drilled to go through certain motions on appropriate occasions, but in a world of models which he has been taught to construct. With some he 'identifies' himself, others are friendly, and others hostile. These are real constituents of his universe and the very notion that they are models constructed by himself seems absurd, because he does it unwittingly. So used are we to handling model-words, such as clan, group, culture, nation and the like that constant reference to their nature as constructs would be wearisome. In what follows such words will be used from time to time without cumbrous parentheses; this, it is hoped, will not be misleading if we remember that social situations are the beginning and end of our subject.

CHAPTER II

FURTHER DISCUSSION OF GROUP AND SITUATIONS

IN this chapter we propose to consider certain group influences in greater detail.

Mass-society. In a small-scale inclusive society, such as a primitive tribe, the way of life is much the same from one family to another, the model with which the members identify themselves is rich and common to them all, and each one can see the point of what he does in the light of his role in the society considered as a whole. He has duties to some and claims on others, often determined by the scheme of kinship into which he has been born. He knows personally those who will befriend him and he knows those whom he must befriend. On the whole his life is spent in social situations with people he knows, likes, dislikes, hates, envies, loves or admires, and by whom he is, in turn known, liked, admired, or hated.

Such intercourse in social life, which may be called 'personal', contrasts with much of the intercourse which we have in a modern industrial society. Communications by road, rail, telephone, wireless, and telegram have made possible a highly complex administration of society and its commercial and industrial activities. The massing of human beings in high concentration has thrown into personal contact people who do not know one another personally. Education, the Press, the wireless, transport, mass-production, and better wages have all tended towards uniformity and the abolition of local differences. In 'mass society' there is, says Kimball Young,[1] 'a stress on rationality, specialization of role or function, impersonality and impermanence of contact, and self-assertiveness; these indicate the loss of the warm intimacy and emotion of unity and solidarity that we find in the primary group and in the older secondary associations that drew their social support from the primary contacts of their members.' To put the matter rather exaggeratedly, we may be said in 'mass society' to *have* our friends but not to *live our lives among them.* Unless we live in a

[1] *Handbook of Social Psychology.* Kegan Paul, 1946, p. 408.

village, which most of us do not, we spend a great part of our time in social contact with specialized roles rather than with persons, and we ourselves are either numbers or abstract customers. The young lady at the post office, the young man at the labour exchange, the woman at the food office, the ticket-collector, the bank-clerk are all met as efficient or inefficient specialists whom we know as such and in no other way, and who have no interest in us whatever. It is very different from the old friend who keeps the village shop and walks round to cast a critical eye on our runner beans after closing time.

The difference between 'personal' and 'impersonal' contact is clear enough, and few will deny the attraction of the former. Such, indeed, are the attractions of the more personal relationships, in which each participant is of some significance as a person to his *vis-à-vis*, that it looks as though such relationships were required to satisfy deep seated needs. 'Mass-society,' says Kimball Young,[1] 'fosters a sense of personal insecurity, loneliness and incompleteness,' and from this, he suggests, springs a demand for 'social-cultural conditions which will restore at least some of the needed emotional warmth, integration, and sense of security'. This demand is partially satisfied in 'crowd-contacts as at sporting events, political rallies, prize fights, and motion-picture houses.' While Paul Reiwald suggests that the very conception of the social-man itself offers a welcome identification-model to the depleted personality: 'He tries to bolster up his "individualité vacillant" by means of the mass itself, which takes on the role of the individual. It is precisely this phenomenon that induces the masses to exaggerate the differences which distinguish a nation, a party or a group from the others. The collectivity has to replace what the individual has lost. He gains as a collective being what he loses as an individual.'[2]

One feature, then, of what is called 'Mass-society' is that it does not satisfy man's desire for personal significance, so that he feels unimportant, lonely, and incomplete. Another source of dissatisfaction is that ambition is no longer contained within accepted bounds of the possible.[3] All the factors we have mentioned: education, communication and so on, have helped to undermine traditional codes, and the 'masses' in the popular sense of the word, are now demanding a higher standard of life. In a society in which a traditional standard of life is accepted as in the nature of things, the very fact that it is accepted and

[1] ibid., p. 408.
[2] Reiwald, P. *De l'Esprit des Masses.* Delachaux et Niestle, 1949, p. 353.
[3] Cf. Sprott, W. J. H., and Stewart, A. H. *Living in Crowds.* Bureau of Current Affairs Bulletin, No. 81, 1949.

attainable makes for a sense of satisfaction, or at any rate lessens the likelihood of dissatisfaction. We are not concerned here with the question: is it right that people should be satisfied with a share of the community's wealth which we may deem to be 'unfair'? We are only stating what we believe to be a plausible (and a verifiable) hypothesis. If this hypothesis is accepted, then the removal of traditional limits is likely in the first instance to produce a discontented scrambling, and a heightened sensitivity about one's self.

Thus both the impersonality of so many social contacts in modern large-scale society and the removal of the traditional frame-work in which everyone had a station to which he was called, contribute to the same result: a sense of personal insecurity. This disease of our time has been the subject of a considerable literature out of which we can only pick a few examples. Broadly speaking three solutions are proposed.

(1) There are those, who recommend decentralization. If men feel lost in large societies, let them find themselves in smaller ones. Such advice is likely to be countered by the sociologists, who might argue that the unintended results of decentralization would be a lowering of material standards, a result which certain moralists might welcome.

(2) Fromm[1] recognizes the discontents of modern society but attributes them to its faulty system of infant education. Our sense of insecurity does not spring, as it were, directly from the fact that we do not know personally the girl in the post office, the man in the labour exchange or the neighbour next door, but rather from the authoritarian upbringing we receive which leaves us in need of support instead of enabling us to stand on our own feet. We need the sense of personal worth acutely because an undermining sense of our own unworthiness has been implanted in us. That is why we have to identify ourselves with the big battalions, seek the warm embrace of the crowd, and look for a leader to whom we can devote ourselves in nostalgic dependence. The remedy implied is an alternative system of discipline which will enable us to enjoy freedom rather than fearing it.

Karen Horney gives a somewhat different account of the sources of our troubles, but for her, too, it would seem, the sense of isolation is derived from our way of life. She distinguishes three major causes:[2] (*a*) 'Modern culture is economically based on the principle of individual competition' and 'competitiveness and the potential hostility that accompanies it, pervades all human relationships' in our culture.

---

[1] *The Fear of Freedom.* Kegan Paul, 1942.
[2] *Neurotic Personality of Our Time.* Kegan Paul, 1937, p. 284 f.

(*b*) 'The potential tension between individuals results in a constant generation of fear' and (*c*) 'Under the pressure of the existing ideology, even the most normal person is constrained to feel that he amounts to something when successful, and is worthless if he is defeated. Needless to say this presents a shaky basis for self-esteem.'

'All these factors,' concludes Horney, 'result psychologically in the individual feeling that he is isolated,' and the result is a neurotic demand for response in others which surpasses all that is rationally possible.

K. Popper[1] derives our fear of freedom in the open society from our remote past. An atavistic longing for the comforting support of the primitive group is the cause of our malaise, and anything that bears some resemblance to its regulated unindividualistic way of life makes an appeal to the savage in our breast. The 'closed society', ordered and regimented, is secretly preferred by part of us to the 'open society' in which we are burdened by having to make our own decisions.

(3) The Marxists naturally accuse the defective nature of capitalist society at this juncture of social history. Competition and hostility are inherent in the capitalist régime and can be removed only by a change of order. People are dissatisfied partly because they realize the tricks that have been played on them, and partly because in what is deemed to be a dying culture there is no inspiration to be found. The implication is that under communism class hostility and the competitiveness of capitalism would be abolished, and that the ideal of a community, however large, working for the interests of the many and not for the profits of the few would become so actualized that identification with it would provide everyone with a sense of purpose in his life.

A word should, perhaps, be added about such expressions as 'Mass-society' and 'the Masses'. Both are what we have called 'model-words'. The former is a label attached to the model we construct of certain aspects of modern large-scale industrial societies. Such societies, while differing in their way of life in certain respects, have the features in common which we have been discussing. The actual way in which these features will manifest themselves will depend upon other cultural features peculiar to the society in question. 'The Masses' is an expression used to denote large numbers of people who have emerged from a condition of quiet social insignificance into a new political and social importance. This causes pain to some people and therefore the expression tends to have a pejorative ring about it. Both expressions must be clearly distinguished from what it meant by the word: 'Crowd.'

[1] *Open and Closed Societies and their Enemies.* Kegan Paul, 1945.

Social Class. Among the models used by Sociologists and Psychologists the one labelled: 'Social Class' has received considerable attention. Social class is of interest to the social psychologists because to say that a person belongs to such-and-such a class is to say something about how he will feel, how he will behave, whom he will treat as an equal, and whom he will treat as inferior or superior to himself. Any basis of classification—income, occupation, or intelligence—which does not result in grouping people together in such a way that the resultant categories display distinguishing regularities of conduct is of no value to the Social Psychologist in his study of social class.

From this it follows that there are broadly speaking four lines of approach: description, the questionnaire method, detailed observation and a combination of any of these.

A. DESCRIPTION: This consists, as the word implies, of the description of the habits, standards and traits of members of different social classes. A threefold grouping into upper, middle and lower, or a fourfold one which includes 'lower-middle' or 'new middle' or a sixfold grouping into upper-upper, lower-upper, upper-middle, lower-middle, upper-lower, lower-lower is assumed, and impressionistic accounts of any one category are provided. A vast literature may be tapped for information of this kind, and among the source books the works of certain novelists rank very high. Mere description may not be the only purpose of a writer. They may wish to depict the conduct of a class in transition. Such, for instance, is the purpose of Lewis and Maude in their book on *The English Middle Classes*.[1]

B. THE QUESTIONNAIRE METHOD: One piece of behaviour which has been taken as critical of social class is self-assessment: the free answer to the question, 'to what class do you belong?' or the choice of answer out of alternative possibilities such as: 'If you were asked to use one of these four names for your social class, which would you say you belonged in; the middle class, lower class, working class or upper class?' The alternative 'Don't know' is also added on the schedule. This formulation has been taken from the 'Interview schedule' used by R. Centers[2] in his enquiry. He took as his starting point the proposition that 'a man's class is a part of his ego, a feeling on his part of belongingness to something; an identification with something larger than himself'.[3] He also held the view that class-identification is determined by

---

[1] Phoenix Ho. 1949.
[2] R. Centers. *The Psychology of Social Classes.* Princeton University Press, 1949.
[3] ibid., p. 27.

'the status and role of the individual in relation to the means of production and exchange of goods and services' and that his status and role
also determines certain attitudes and values.

To test the theory, therefore, one obviously has to ask people having
different statuses and roles to what class they affiliate, and then see
whether the status-role grouping fits the class-affiliation grouping, and
also whether views held on certain issues are appropriately divided
among the two groupings. This is what Centers did. He compiled
a quota sample of males over twenty-one covering the United States,
and using as criteria: region, urban-rural, size of town, age, standard of
living. Altogether 1,100 interviews were obtained, and among the
questions asked was the one we have just reproduced.

The wording of the question is a delicate matter. In 1939 Gallop[1]
found that 88 per cent. of his replies to a similar question plumped for
the middle class, and only 6 per cent. in the upper or lower classes,
while in 1940 the magazine *Fortune*[2] found that 79 per cent. identified
with the middle class. Cantril,[3] too, found much the same: 87 per cent.
claimed middle-class membership. These results were surprising because they did not fit in with expectations based upon the data concerning income and occupation. Was it, perhaps, that in the social
situation of the interview, levels of aspiration came to the fore a little
too insistently? Or was it, as Centers thinks, that the wrong labels were
used? It appears that the expression 'lower class' is disliked and therefore avoided. If the expression 'working class' is included different
results are obtained, and, indeed that category was chosen by 51 per
cent. and 52 per cent. respectively of the respondents in two polls taken
by the American Institute of Public Opinion in 1946 and 1947.[4] Centers, then, seems justified in his nomenclature. Three per cent. voted
themselves upper class, 43 per cent. middle class, 51 per cent. working
class and 1 per cent. lower class, while 1 per cent, 'did not know' and
1 per cent. were tiresome enough to say that they 'Don't believe in
classes'.

The sample had also been classified into seven Urban and three
Rural 'role and status' categories: large business, professional, small
business, white collar, skilled manual workers, semi-skilled manual
workers and unskilled manual workers for the urban group, and farm

[1] Gallop, G. and Rae, S. F. *The Pulse of Democracy.* N.Y. Simm and Schuster, 1940.
[2] *The People of the United States—A Self Portrait.* Fortune, 1940.
[3] *J. Abn. and Soc. Psychology*, 1943, p. 474.
[4] O. Klineberg. *Tensions Affecting International Understanding.* Soc. Sc. Research Council. N.Y., 1950, p. 71.

owner and manager, farm tenants, and farm labourers for the Rural group. Another question asked was: 'Which of those in this list (of eleven occupations) would you say belonged in the . . . . class (naming the class chosen by the respondent).' From the results of this question it appeared that on the whole there was uniformity in class ascription, most of the people who said they were, for example, middle class agreed in allocating the same people in the list to the middle class, and the same for the other three classes. In the main the self-ascriptions were what one would expect on other grounds. The number of people considering themselves upper class decreases as one passes from the 13 per cent. among the large business group, the 4 per cent. of the professionals to the 1 per cent. of the semi-skilled manual worker. The number of large business men voting themselves working class is 7 per cent. as compared with 71 per cent. skilled manual workers, 83 per cent. semi-skilled and 75 per cent. unskilled.

It is claimed therefore that self-assessment varies with economic role and status. What about the other part of the hypothesis—the theory that there will be corresponding variation in 'attitudes, values, and interest'? This was tested by means of six questions of such a kind that the answer may be taken to indicate a 'conservative' or a 'radical' attitude—e.g. 'Do you think that working people are usually fairly and squarely treated by their employers, or that employers sometimes take advantage of them?' A system of marking was devised and the answers actually given were compared with the status and class memberships of the respondents. The kind of result obtained was that more of the business, professional and white collar-workers who identified themselves with the middle class were conservative in their opinion than was the case with those of the same category who identified themselves with the working class. Again, there were more people who were radical or indeterminate among the manual workers, than among the business, professional and white-collar group, but if a manual worker identified himself as middle class, he would be more likely to be conservative in his attitude than if he identified himself as working class.

Another example of the question method is the research now being conducted by John Hall and Caradog Jones into the prestige of occupations.[1]

C. OBSERVATION : Of course description implies preliminary observation, but what we have in mind here is rather more systematic.

[1] *British Journal of Sociology*—I, 1950, p. 31.

As an example we may take Warner's and Lunt's[1] study of 'Yankee City', a town of some 17,000 inhabitants in New England. Centers as has been said, takes as the basis of his study self-ascription and the socio-economic factors associated with it. He distinguishes between 'status' and 'class', defining the latter in terms of subjective identification, with the result that in his terminology ' it may be entirely possible for people of different status to belong to the same class'.[2] Warner and Lunt are concerned with the kind of phenomena that Centers calls 'status' and define their use of the term 'class' accordingly as referring to 'two or more orders of people who are believed to be, and are accordingly ranked by the members of the community, in socially superior and inferior positions.'[3] In their first volume they divide the community of 'Yankee City' into six classes: two uppers, two middles, and two lowers.

In the 'Status System of Yankee City' they proceeded to a closer analysis, coming down to the social situations in which class differences display themselves. This led to a systematic positional system of great complexity which is worth a brief description because the method employed might be used elsewhere. In 'Yankee City' there are some hundreds of *Associations*, some thousands of *families*, some thousands of *cliques, economic organizations* (stores, factories, offices), *churches, schools, political parties,* i.e. seven methods of grouping. Now you have six classes and you can take any one of the groups under these seven headings and consider their membership. An *association*, for instance, may have only 'upper-upper' members, or it may have upper-upper, lower-upper, and upper-middle members, or it may have lower-middle and upper-lower members or only lower-lower members. These are only examples and many other combinations are found. When the *associations* have been classified according to their class membership, a 'positional' chart is constructed. The types of *association* according to membership are numbered—e.g. Type 1 is only upper-upper, Type 12 is upper-middle, lower-middle and upper-lower. Now for the positions. Consider Type 12. A man who is upper-middle class is in a position of superiority when he attends a meeting of any Type 12 *association* of which he is a member. Now consider Type 7. This type consists of *associations* whose members are either lower-upper or upper-middle. These *associations* are therefore, by definition open to our

---

[1] Warner, W. L. and Lunt, P. S. *The Social Life of a Modern Community.* Yale Univ. Press, 1941. *The Status System of a Modern Community.* Yale Univ. Press, 1942.
[2] Centers, op. cit., p. 228.   [3] *Social Life of a Modern Community,* p. 82.

upper-middle-class man, but his position is different. Here he is in an inferior position, and—this is the point—his conduct will be different when he is in session with any Type 7 association to which he belongs from what it is likely to be when in company of a Type 12 association.

Exactly the same method was employed on the other six methods of grouping. In *families*, for example, there are obviously families all of whose members are upper-upper, and others who are all lower-lower, but there seem to be plenty of cases in which members of the same family belong to different social classes. For instance in Type 7 you have some of them lower-upper and some of them upper-middle, while in Type 17 you have upper-middle members and lower-lowers with no intermediate ranks represented. Picture a *family* reunion and you will see that the social situation is very different in a Type 17 *family* from what it would be in a Type 7 one, and both different again from, say, Type 10 where all the members are upper-middle. We need not dwell on the *cliques* and *economic organizations* which are treated in the same way, and we need only mention that there are three *Church* types (1 all classes, 2 lower-upper to lower-lower, 3 upper-middle to lower-lower), two *school* types, and one *political* type including all ranks.

The seven positional systems represent (1) positions of participants in social situations which occur in the seven contexts, and (2) the various shapes of social situation which may emerge. We are reminded that, 'a man may be a member of two or more associations and several cliques', but 'an individual usually belongs to but one church and school, and ordinarily, by reason of his occupation, is a member of but one economic organization'.[1] Thus he may occupy various positions in the association and clique contexts, and only one in the others, while he may change the type of his family by rising or falling in the social scale. This, however, is not all. The total positional system of any person is, as it were, cumulative, his position in one context affecting his conduct in another positional situation. Furthermore, since it is with other 'Yankee Citizens' that he has most of his social contacts, *their* variable positional status comes into the picture, so that the whole community of individuals may be viewed as an inter-related, inter-connected and interdependent system of membership.[2] In order to present the 'general positional system' the authors composed a chart in which all *types* of group in terms of class combinations are represented with a rubric indicating which of the seven contexts have instances of each type; thus group Type 4 consisting of upper-upper and upper-middles is represented only in *cliques* and *families* while groups consisting of lower-upper and upper-middles are found among the *associations, cliques, families* and *economic groups*.

An example will indicate the use to which this analysis is put.[1] Mrs. Breckonridge (UU) gave a political tea, the Starrs (LU) were there so were the Frenches (UM). We have, therefore, a face-to-face group of Type 3. The positions in each chart, and in the generalized scheme are numbered on a perfectly straightforward scheme and the numbers here for Type 3 happen to be: UU, position 3, LU, position 13 and UM position 26. At the tea, the conduct is appropriate to the positions. Those in position 3, who often went in position 1 as upper-upper equals in situations only consisting of upper-uppers, now are in a situation which demands 'semi-formal, polite behaviour', while the purpose of the party to promote political solidarity, makes it 'imperative to mark "natural feelings"'. The Starrs (position 13) 'act superior than' the upper-middles in position 26. Mrs. French (position 26), finding that she cannot, try as she may, compete with the ladies talking to Mrs. Starr (LU) and Miss Alton (UU) because they all belong to the House and Home Club (Type 2. UU and LU only) and therefore 'have something to talk about', moves across the room to another UM lady who belongs to a UM clique. Still, Mrs. French did try to muscle in, as she had tried over and over again to join the House and Home Club, but always without success. 'Mrs. Breckonridge declared that the Frenches were "pushers and climbers and always scheming to get into your house".'

By means of the positional system everyone can be 'placed', situations and their development can be interpreted, their backgrounds can be analysed, and the whole society allocated numerically to various positional possibilities. It may appear to some that enormous labour and cumbrous elaboration have forged a gigantic weapon to crack a very small nut. It is true that situations, such as Mrs. Breckonridge's party, are familiar enough and that the casual observer, sensitive to class-differences, is well aware of what is happening without this elaborate formulation, but it is up to the social psychologist to produce such formulations and one of the merits of the 'Yankee City' investigation is to show how complicated these formulations must be. Another merit is that the authors keep the social situation itself well in view.

Methods of Investigating face-to-face Groups. Warner and

---

[1] *Status System of a Modern Community* p. 37.

Lunt, when they describe a social situation, often supply a diagram constructed out of the symbols defined in their positional charts, to represent the actual contacts—conversation and listenings—that take place. This method of representing social relationships symbolically has been developed independently by two 'schools' of social psychologists: the 'Topologists' and the 'Sociometrists'.

Field Dynamics and Topology'. Kurt Lewin, influenced by the Gestalt theory to which he himself made contributions, developed a systematic technique for handling social situations. The central concept in his scheme is the 'field'. The 'field' can be analysed into 'subjective' and 'objective' elements, these two words being used commonsensically and without any further analysis. Picture a child in a room with a piece of chocolate. There are obvious 'objective' elements of which we have mentioned three: the child, the room with its boundaries, and the piece of chocolate. Now add the 'subjective' element: the child wants the chocolate. At once the 'field' springs into dynamic life. The piece of chocolate is said to have 'positive valence' for the child and exercises an attractive force. Change the scene by introducing a threat of punishment, and a 'negative valence' is added which alters the dynamic character of the 'field'. What happens will depend on the distribution of forces in the 'field'.[1] Furthermore, the 'field' may include persons who are not physically there.

Now we come to the notation which Lewin has devised for representing the forces operating in the field.[2]

$f_{P,g}$ means a force acting in a person P in the direction towards g.
f_{P-g} means a force acting in a person P in the direction away from g.
$rf_{P,g}$ is a restraining force against P's moving towards g.
$cf^*_{P,g}$ means a resultant force which has the direction towards g.
$|f_{P,g}|$ indicates the strength of the force $f^*_{P,g}$.

Now a 'social field' can be treated in the same way, either in terms of persons or in terms of groups or in terms of a person and a group. The technique of analysis, with its graphic representation and symbolic formulation, can be applied to relatively long-term or short-term social phenomena; i.e. to social changes which operate over months or to social situations lasting for a matter of minutes or hours.

In an article,[3] posthumously published in 1947, he gives instances

[1] Lewin, K. *A Dynamic Theory of Personality.* McGraw-Hill, 1935.
[2] Lewin, K. 'The conceptual representation and the measurement of psychological forces.' Contributions to *Psychological Theory*, Vol. I, No. 4. Duke Univ. Press, 1938.
[3] Lewin, K. 'Frontiers in Group Dynamics.' *Human Relations*, 1947, p. 5–41.

of his method and its application to group psychology. In the first place it is asserted that what happens in a social field depends upon the distribution of forces throughout the field. All of these, however, often cannot be known and certain forces have to be selected so that one really operates with an abstract field of forces called the 'phase space', by means of which we analyse certain aspects of the complex whole.

Social change may be considered in relation to social processes in quasi-stationary equilibrium. Any level of equilibrium may be analysed as the resultant of forces in opposite directions. A level of production is what it is because the forces making for more meet at a certain level forces making for less. If in factory A the forces making for more are represented by $f_{A,g}$ and those making for less by $f_{A,s}$ then $f_{A,g} + f_{A,s} = O$ and if the resultant of the forces $f_{A,g} + f_{A,s}$ is represented by f^*_A then $f^*_{A,x} = O$. What, however, of the strength of the forces? Take the case of a level of discrimination against the Negroes in town A. It may remain the same at time 1 as it was at time 2, but the strength of the component forces might have increased; i.e. $|f_{A,s}|^2 = |f_{A,g}|^2 > |f_{A,s}|^1 = |f_{A,g}|^1$. This would mean that group tension had increased. Furthermore field forces may vary in their 'gradients', i.e. in having a few strong forces constituting a 'steep gradient' or a summation of smaller ones constituting a relatively 'flat gradient'. 'Given the same amount of change in the strength of the resultant force, the amount of change of the level of the social process will be smaller, the steeper the gradient,' and '*ceteris paribus* individual difference of conduct in a group will be smaller the steeper the gradient of the resultant force field in the neighbourhood of the group level'.[1]

Now let us consider three of Lewin's examples. The first we shall meet again, it is the experimental study of Lewin and Lippitt and White on the influence on a group of boys of different types of leadership.[2] Here we are only concerned with the aggressiveness associated with Autocratic and Democratic Leadership. There were three levels. In some cases Autocracy resulted in high aggression, in some cases in apathy and in the Democratic régime the aggressive level was between the two, in fact at twenty-three aggressive acts in a fifty minutes meeting. This is represented by $f^*L,^Dx = O$ for $L^D = 23$. Now in the Aggressive Autocrat group the level was high; it stood at forty. The forces making for aggression were increased by, say m, so that, if,

---

[1] ibid., p. 18.
[2] Lewin, K., Lippitt, R. and White, R. K. 'Patterns of aggressive behaviour in experimentally created "Social Climates".' *J. Soc. Psych.*, 1939, 10, 271–299.

'Gr' stands for 'group' and 'g' for aggression $|f_{AAGr,g}| > |f_{DGr,g}|$. The forces making for peace (the 'we-feeling') are reduced by, say n, so that $|f_{AAGr,s}| < |f_{GDr,s}|$. The Apathetic group 'P' on the other hand, showed very little aggression. This may well be due to heavy forces operating against aggression, in fact restraining the 'P' group, so that we have $rf_{\overline{P,g}}$, an unstable condition as was found when the autocratic régime was changed for a *laissez-faire* régime. The state represented by $rf_{\overline{P,}}$ (i.e. a force against P proceeding to g) is one which presents a problem to all dictators. The principle that a change brought about by adding forces in its direction leads to an increase in tension has important practical implication. It means that a more fruitful method is to *reduce* the forces opposing the direction in which you want the change to be made.

The second example is taken from industry. A worker is changed from one sewing machine to a different sewing job and her output drops. Before transfer her output at level L^1 was the resultant of forces making for and against output. She is now subjected to the restraining force of lack of skill in her new job. Supposing the forces operating in the field remain the same as before, they are now countered by the restraining force which stabilizes output at L^2 level so that $|rf_{\overline{L^2,g}}|$ (after the change) $= |f^*L^2,g|$ (before the change). A state of tension might be expected. In fact it turned out that this analysis of the L^2 level was wrong. Her output fell to L^2 partly because she lost heart, so that actually at time 2 after the change $|f^*L^2,g| < |f^*L^2,g|$ before the change.

Finally there is the problem of another influence making for stability. Supposing you want to change well established habits. You may try to do this either by increasing the forces operating in the direction you want, or by reducing forces operating against you. You may, however, find that this does not work out as simply as you hoped. Something else is at work—a resistance in the individuals you are trying to influence. 'An individual P,' says Lewin,[1] 'may differ in his personal level of conduct (L^P) from the level which represents group standards (L^{Gr}) by a certain amount n ($|L^{Gr} - L^P| = n$). But this difference of conduct is met at a certain point by ridicule and ostracism so that conformity has its own "positive valence", corresponding to a central force field with the force fP, L keeping the individual in line with the standards of the group.' When this force is operating one has, as it were, two 'phase spaces'—to use Lewin's terminology—one, the general forces in the

[1] ibid., p. 33.

field, and the other the intrinsic value of group standards to the members. In order, therefore, to make your change, the group standard valence has to be 'unfrozen', changed, and 'frozen' again at the desired level. Now this is a new way of saying something we know already, but there is contributory evidence of a less obvious kind. It seems, from experiments on habit changing in a group that the changes are more stable if they are introduced by group discussion than if a lecturing or individual instruction are used. One group of mothers in a mid-western town was induced to listen to a lecture on the merits of fresh milk, another discussed the matter and decided collectively to drink more milk. After four weeks 50 per cent. of the second group were consuming more milk, while only 9.25 per cent. of the former had succumbed to enticement. The same thing happened in the State Hospital of Iowa in connection with feeding orange-juice to babies; here the method of group discussion was superior to individual instruction. Bavelas,[1] too, working with sewing machine operators found that group decision was effective in stepping-up output. The same principle is doubtless at work in the group-discussions reported from the U.S.S.R.

This account of Lewin's 'topological' or 'vector' analysis of group situations is intended to give some indication of his conceptual framework, and his methods of notation, which are accompanied by graphic representations with long or short arrows indicating the forces in the 'phase-space'. In assessing its value the two aspects of his theory should, perhaps, be kept apart. Lewin insists that we must not waste our time worrying about the 'reality' of group-dynamics and field forces. They are 'intervening variables' of a kind which every science interposes between one observed datum and another. He would, presumably, deprecate the tone of voice in which we have discussed 'models' in the preceding chapters. We may concede his point. As tools our 'models' are as necessary as his 'field-forces', and there is no doubt that his conceptual frame-work is extremely valuable. It puts life into social processes and social situations, and his advice to those who are trying to bring about a change that they 'should not think in terms of the "goal to be reached" but rather in terms of a change "from the present level to the desired one" '[2] is useful. Process and change are the very essence of group and situational conduct. What is more questionable is the value of the notation. The examples that have been given are only

[1] N. Maier. *Psychology in Industry.* Houghton Miffling, 1946, p. 264.
[2] 'Frontiers in Group Dynamics.' *Human Relations,* I, p. 32.

a fraction of the whole scheme. They may be criticized as introducing a fictitious precision into an imprecise field of discussion, and, at any rate to the unskilled, each symbol is only meaningful when explained in ordinary language. For example when we read that 'forces against inter-group aggression might be: friendship between members; the presence of an adult leader; the dignified character of the setting' we understand what he is talking about. It does not add much to have that symbolized by $|f_{DGr,s}|$. The real defect is that from the symbols one can infer nothing that cannot be inferred from verbal descriptions.

Sociometry. We have all heard of the dark saying that 'a man is known by his friends', and we have all witnessed the spectacle of a community which appeared at first homogeneous, dissolving into its component friendships, alliances, and antagonisms. Such are the phenomena which J. L. Moreno and his followers aim at reducing to order by the techniques known as *Sociometry*. The key-work of this approach to the delineation of face-to-face groups is Moreno's *Who shall survive?*[1] 'The basis of sociometric classification,' we are told,[2] 'is not a psyche which is bound up within an individual organism, but an individual organism moving around in space in relation to things or other subjects also moving around him in space.' This reminds us of Lewin's approach, and indeed the two are similar in some respects but whereas we are invited by the Topologists to conceive of the whole field as charged with vector forces, the Sociometrists depict the scene in terms of links between person and person, in terms—to use their language—of *tele:* 'A feeling which is projected into distance; the simplest unit of feeling transmitted from one individual to another,'[3] which may be 'positive' or 'negative'. This vision of a group as pervaded—indeed, constituted—by strands of like and dislike is backed by a somewhat fanciful hypothesis of a 'monistic origin of life from a common unit' out of which existing networks of 'tele' have been differentiated. The 'social atoms'—as Moreno calls them—with which Sociometry deals are of two kinds: (1) Individuals as centres from which liking and disliking reach out to other individuals, and towards which liking and disliking are directed by other individuals all in respect to a certain criterion (living together, working together,

---

[1] Washington, Nervous and Mental Disease Pub., Co., 1934.
[2] *Who shall survive?* p. 377.
[3] ibid., p. 432.

etc.), (2) Work communities or home communities presented as a criss-crossing of likes and dislikes between the participants.

The problem of harmonious grouping first presented itself to Moreno during World War I when he had an opportunity of observing the difficulties involved in the settlement of Italian refugees in Austria. In America he was able to clarify the ideas which had been engendered in his mind by this episode. He pursued his enquiries in kindergartens, in schools, and in the State Training Schools for Girls, Hudson, N.Y His method of investigation is twofold: observation of groups to see who is friendly with whom, and where rejections lie, and 'testing' or asking the members of groups who they would like to sit next them in class, or who they would like to live with them in the cottage home of the Training School. He rightly emphasized the importance of the *context*. Again the actual social situation comes to the fore. It is no use, he says, asking in general: whom do you like/dislike? You must particularize the situation.

There are three possible relations: like, dislike, or indifference and each of these three attitudes may meet with any one of them from the other person. Thus A may want to live in the same house as B, but B may reject A as a companion, or be indifferent, or, of course, reciprocate. By means of suitable conventions the relation between A and B can be depicted in a 'sociogram'. In Moreno's own convention a red line from A towards B represents 'positive tele' and it may be met by a black line from B to A or a dotted line or a red line signifying rejection, indifference and reciprocation respectively. The materials for the portrayal of atoms are ready to hand. Either you take, say A, as a centre and draw the appropriate line to B, C, D ... and back from B, C, D ... to A, or you take a community and draw the appropriate lines, signifying positive or negative tele or indifference between its members. When the latter is done certain characteristic patterns are found. There are mutual pairs, chains and triangles, when A wants B, B wants C and C wants A. There are stars, wanted by many, and, alas, isolates who reach out their unreciprocated teles to the void.

By this means four things can be investigated. Firstly, the 'emotional expansion' of the individual, his predicament as isolate or leader, and the tensions to which he is submitted. Secondly, the 'morale' of the home in terms of (*a*) how far the friendships are between its inhabitants and how far the inhabitants seek their friends elsewhere, and (*b*) how it is structured, i.e. how many isolates there are, how much antagonism there is, what exclusive pairs, or triangles it contains. Thirdly, if one

takes, as in the case of the Hudson School, the whole population irrespective of its division into homes we can trace more general 'networks' (a technical term here) of relationship along which rumour,
plots and fashions spread. Fourthly one can compare groups of different
ages to see whether there are any characteristic differences.

In the course of these investigations the following points emerged.
(1) People differ in their spontaneity, in their ability to adapt them
selves to varied human relationships. This, it was found, could be cor-
rected by getting the subjects to act out a situation in which either they
were called upon to 'throw themselves into a state of emotion towards
X. The emotion may be either anger, fear, sympathy or dominance'[1]
or else they were left free to 'choose the situation and the roles which
they wanted to act and the partner whom they wanted to act opposite
in a certain role'.[2] The theory is that in our highly differentiated society
we specialize in certain roles, and thus lose our emotional flexibility.
The 'spontaneity training', from which the so-called 'Socio-drama'[3] has
been developed, can be used by the observer as a source of information
about the subject, and by the subject as a means of enlarging and
differentiating 'the spontaneous base of his heritage, his spontaneability'.

(2) The study of the structure of groups revealed their resistance to
change and, in some cases, the need of it. It was found possible by
reshuffling to improve the social atmosphere in the houses of the
Training School, and the morale and character of the home gave a clue
to the allocation of newcomers. These were carefully 'tested'. They
were given a chance to meet the 'house-mothers' and a 'girl who represents the general tone of the cottage'. On a basis of the likes and dislikes expressed on all sides, together with an assessment of the 'home'
in relation to the needs of the newcomer the assignment (and, if need
be, the reassignment) was made. It was found that such a method has
far better results than haphazard allocation. Light has also been thrown
on the 'racial' problem. It seems that the Negro girls and the white girls
both preferred some degree of segregation, but more interesting is the
concept of 'saturation'. In New York City public schools the amount
of friction between whites and Negroes was found to be in inverse
proportion to the number of the latter present. There seems, indeed,
to be saturation limit below which harmony may reign.

[1] ibid., p. 177.   [2] ibid., p. 321.

[3] Moreno, J. L. 'The Concept of Sociodrama; a new approach to the problem of intercultural relations.' *Sociometry*, 6, 1943, p. 434.

Moreno, J. L. 'Sociodrama, a method for the analysis of Social conflicts.' *Psychodrama
Monograph*, No. 1, 1944.

(3) The broader net-work systems of psychological currents have suggested a general social principle. Two processes are at work: 'One process, the process of differentiation, draws the groups apart; the other process, the process of transmissions draws the groups together. This alternating rhythm can be called the *law of social gravitation*.'[1]

(4) Finally it was found that when infants of twenty to twenty-eight weeks are placed in proximity to one another they begin to notice, and react towards one another, which they do not do before that age. From about forty to forty-two weeks onward 'one or another infant commands disproportionate attention'. As they grow older and up to the age of seven to nine years they form more and more social contacts, but these relationships are instantaneous and too inconstant and undifferentiated to produce co-operative action. At this early age boys and girls choose one another with a certain frequency. Between eight and thirteen more stable relations are established: pairs, chains, and triangles appear and the number of isolates diminishes. Indeed, there is a positive 'desire to have a function in association with individuals of the same level of differentiation',[2] often in opposition to adults. Intersexual choices are fewer until, at thirteen to fifteen, they start increasing again, while racial differentiation only starts at about the fifth grade. Such findings fit with Piaget's observation in Switzerland,[3] and the occasional disparity between chronological age and the social conduct usual at that age gives rise to the concept of 'social age' which has been used by the Gluecks[4] in their investigation into delinquency.

The sociometric technique has obvious value, not only in therapy and in the planned organization of small communities which aim at combating delinquency. It could be used in industry and—though the problems of investigation are more formidable—to make larger-scale movements of population more efficient. An attempt has been made by Loomis[5] to analyse the structure of a New Mexican village by sociometric methods.

---

[1] *Who shall survive?* p. 266.   [2] ibid., p.59.
[3] esp. *The Moral Judgment of the Child.* Kegan Paul, 1932.
[4] *After Conduct of Discharged Offender.* Cambridge, 1945. Cf. Murphy, Murphy and Newcomb. *Experimental Social Psychology*, p. 515 f.
[5] Loomis, C. P. 'Informal grouping in a Spanish-American village.' *Sociometry*, 4, 1941.

CHAPTER III

SYSTEMATIC STUDY OF GROUPS

IN the last chapter two general methods of studying groups have been discussed. In this chapter some examples of experimental and systematic observations will be given. An invaluable source-book for information on this subject is Murphy, Murphy and Newcomb's *Experimental Social Psychology*[1] from which much of the material has been taken.

Children are naturally among the most watched of creatures. They are of professional interest to the parent and the educationalist and they, of all instances of humanity, are most accessible. The study of them for the purposes of social psychology is by no means easy. Impressionistic observation, valuable as it no doubt is, must be supplemented by more careful methods when any hypothesis has to be tested. In 1929 D. S. Thomas and A. M. Loomis[2] worked out a technique of systematic codification of children's conduct, providing record forms for classified types of behaviour. Armed with these the investigator records how many times, e.g. one child has physical contact with another, and what kind of contact it was: accident, assistance, passivity, resistance, etc.

M. B. Parten[3] made use of a similar method of recording in her studies of social participation and leadership among nursery-school children. The results of the observation from day to day were correlated so as to see whether there was consistency in conduct, while the records of assistant observers were correlated to ensure consistency of recording.

T. M. Newcomb[4] concentrated on certain types of response. This

---

[1] Harper and Brothers, N.Y., 2nd ed., 1937.
[2] Thomas, D. S., *et al.* 'Some new techniques for studying social behaviour.' *Child Dev. Monog.*, No. 1, 1929.
[3] Parten, M. B. 'Social Participation among pre-school children.' *J. Abn. and Soc. Psych.*, 1932, 27, p. 243.
Parten, M. B. 'Leadership among pre-school children.' *J. Abn. and Soc. Psych.*, 1933, 27, 430.
[4] Newcomb, T. M. 'The consistency of certain extrovert-introvert behaviour pattern in 51 problem boys.' *Teach. Coll. Contrib. Educ.*, 1929, No. 382.

has obvious advantages over the mass-recording of social participation. The latter might, of course, be used to compare social participation at various ages, or between children differing in intellectual ability, but the task itself is a formidable one. Newcomb had his boys at a camp and the kind of behaviour he wanted noted was: 'Did X cry for help when hurt and in trouble? Did he take the initiative in organizing games?' The scoring sheet provided a device for grading the answer. The results showed less consistency than casual observation seemed to indicate and the method is clearly one which has a value in providing a check on the rash judgments we are inclined to make.

C. R. Sewall's[1] investigation into jealousy and its expression aimed at a specific type of response, and revealed that among her children jealousy of younger siblings was a function of the standard of home-adjustment, though in this and similar investigations, the material studied was not studied *as a group;* the conduct of each child towards its younger siblings was studied separately.

In the Child Development Institute Teachers College, Columbia, a number of fifteen-minute records of pre-kindergarten group life have been made which illustrate friendship and conflict in real life such as this: Alice says something about a puppy. Kenneth says, ' I'm not a puppy, you are.' Alice: 'You're a puppy.' Kenneth: 'No, I'm a conductor on a train.' Alice: 'You are a puppy.' Kenneth: 'I'll give you a sock. I'll give you a kick in the forehead.'[2]

This kind of detailed reporting of conversation and action as they occurred was used by Susan Isaacs in her study of the *Social Development of Young Children.*[3]

The next most available material is found, of course, in schools and boys' clubs. It was in schools that some of the earliest social 'experiments' were made by Mayer[4] in 1903 and by Schmidt[5] in 1904. Both of them wanted to find out whether there was any difference between the work of school children when they worked alone as compared with their performances in the class-room. Was there what F. H. Allport later called 'Social Facilitation'? On the whole there was. These studies

[1] Sewall, C. R. 'Some Causes of Jealousy in Young Children.' *Smith Coll. Studies of Soc. Work,* 1930.

[2] Murphy, Murphy and Newcomb. *Experimental Social Psychology,* pp. 533f., cf. pp. 605 f.

[3] Routledge, 1933.

[4] Mayer, A. 'Über Einzel—und Gesamtleistung der Schulkinder.' *Arch. f. d. ges. Psychol.,* 1903, 1, p. 276.

[5] Schmidt, F. 'Experimentelle Untersuchungen über die Heraufgaben des Schulkindes.' *Arch. f. d. ges. Psychol.,* 1904, 3, p.33.

were followed up by Moede[1] in 1920. He found that boys bore greater amounts of pain, and pressed a dynamometer harder when in the presence of their schoolmates than when alone. This was particularly the case when rivalry was present. In performing such tasks as 'cancellation tests', on the other hand speed was improved but accuracy diminished in the case of the best subjects, but there was an all-round improvement in the case of the poorer ones. This bore out the findings of Triplett[2] in 1898 that at any rate some people are over-stimulated by competition and that their work suffers in consequence.

The same problem—the influence of a group situation—was investigated by F. H. Allport.[3] The presence of others improved simple motor tasks and increased the number of word associations, but when it came to arguments, those produced in the group situation were more numerous but of poorer quality than those produced by people working alone. This means that working in a group may be profitable for some tasks but not for all. The general upshot of Allport's work confirms the results announced by Moede.

Now in these cases the contrast is between working alone and working in the presence of other people. This distinction of situation is, however, not as easy to draw as we might think. Another factor—rivalry—which is known to make a difference may be present without the investigator knowing it. Whitemore,[4] making use of a rubberstamp printing task, tried to compare the competitive situation with the non-competitive one by telling the subjects not to compete. The most significant result of this investigation was that it revealed how difficult it was to avoid competition entirely. Gradually and almost imperceptibly it asserted itself, usually with deleterious results on the quality of the work done. Dashiell,[5] using multiplication problems, a mixed relation test and serial associations, made a more elaborate investigation in which he tried to compare the effects of working alone, working together in non-competition, competing, and working in the presence of an audience. From the

[1] Moede, W. *Experimentelle Massenpsychologie,* 1920.

[2] Triplett, N. 'The Dynamogenic factors in pace-making and competition.' *Am. J. Psychol.,* 1898, 9, p. 507.

[3] Allport, F. H. *Social Psychology,* 1924.

[4] Whitemore, I. C. 'Influence of competition on performance.' *J. Abn. and Soc. Psychol.,* 1924, 19, 236. 'The Competition Consciousness.' ibid., 1925, 20, p. 17.

[5] Dashiell, J. F. 'An Experimental Analysis of Some Group Effects.' *J. Abn. and Soc. Psychol.,* 1930, 25, p. 190. cf. shortened version. *Readings in Social Psychology.* Holt and Co., N.Y., 1947, p. 297.

results of the experiment no clear generalization can be drawn. The effect of an audience seemed powerful, increasing the speed at which the subjects did their sums, worked out their 'mixed relation' and reeled off serial associations, while the accuracy of many of them was impaired. According to Dashiell the effect of working in the presence of others without competition is meagre, but this is not borne out by all his tables; sometimes it seems to have impaired speed and sometimes to have improved accuracy. Rivalry, too, is uncertain in its effect. A further part of the experiment showed that the 'alone' situations produced different results when the subjects worked in different rooms at the same time, as compared with what happened when they came by themselves at their own convenience. Distressing though the fact may be to those who seek simplicity, we cannot help coming to the conclusion, supported by Dashiell himself, that other factors beside the ones he tried to isolate were playing a part in each of the social situations he examined.

The part played by the presence of an audience has also been explored. Gates,[1] using a steadiness test, colour-naming, analogies, and saying as many nouns as you can in a minute found that the audience had but little effect on performance, though the poorer workers slightly improved. This result conflicts with Dashiell's findings and with those of other experimenters, but here, again, the special nature of the audience and the tasks used are bound to have an effect on the results, making comparison extremely difficult. Rather more drastic measures were taken by Laird[2] to investigate the effects of an audience. Fraternity members covered a group of neophytes with insults as they performed tests of motor speed and steadiness. The results were, as might be expected, ambiguous. Steadiness was impaired by trembling indignation, but there were cases in which the subjects tapped the faster.

In the preceding type of experiments the subjects have been working on their own tasks, either by themselves, together, competing or before an audience. Another type of experiment aims at investigating collective and group judgment. What is meant here by 'collective' judgment is illustrated by the investigation of Knight,[3] who compared

---

[1] Gates, G. S. 'The effect of an Audience upon Performance.' *J. Abn. and Soc. Psychol.*, 1924, 18, p. 334.

[2] Laird, D. A. 'Changes in Motor Control and Individual Variation under the Influence of Razzing.' *J. Exper. Psychol.*, 1923, 6, 236.

[3] Knight, H. C. 'Comparison of the reliability of group and individual judgment.' Master's Essay in Columbia University Library, 1921. See Murphy, Murphy and Newcomb. *Experimental Social Psychology*, p. 710.

the individual guesses about the I.Q. of children whose photographs were shown them, the effectiveness of fifteen advertisements and the temperature of the room with pooled judgments. On the whole pooled judgments were 'better' than a great many individual ones. Gordon[1] compared the results of individual estimation of weights, and also of the beauty of oriental rugs, with the same records grouped into sets of five or ten. Such investigations have really very little to do with social psychology, because they are not concerned with social inter-action.

What might be called 'group judgments', on the other hand are a different matter. Bechterev and Lange[2] studied the results of discussion in improving or modifying judgments. The subjects were shown pictures for fifteen seconds and required to write down as much as they could remember. Then there was a discussion in which very naturally the total number of details remembered increased, though several more mistakes were made. In another experiment the results of discussion on moral judgment was examined. One issue was: 'Should a boy be beaten for stealing apples?' and the kind of effect that discussion had is illustrated by the fact that before discussion three of the twenty-four subjects said that if the boy had been hungry he ought not to be pun-ished, while after the discussion this point was made by eighteen. Changes of view were registered and also an increase in the range of topics to be noticed.

A more detailed investigation was conducted by Shaw.[3] The material used was composed of difficult problems such as that posed by transporting missionaries and cannibals across a river with inadequate resources. These were tackled by individuals, and by groups of four, and records were kept of the proposals and rejections made by each member. It was found that the groups did better than the individuals and that their better performances could be put down to the rejection of incorrect moves—usually by someone other than the proposers of them. Much the same result was found by Watson,[4] who compared group and individual performances on ten different tasks, including

[1] Gordon, K. A. 'Study of Aesthetic Judgments.' *J. Exp. Psychol.*, 1923, 6, p. 36.
'Group judgments in the field of lifted weights.' *J. Exp. Psychol.*, 1924, 7, p. 398.
'Further Observations in group judgments of lifted weights.' 1936. *J. Psychol.*, 1, p. 105.
[2] Bechterev, W. and Lange, M. 'Die Ergebnisse des Experiments auf dem Gebiete der Kollectiven Reflexologie.' *Zsch. f. angew. Psychol.*, 1924, 4, p. 224.
[3] Shaw, M. E. 'A comparison of individuals and small groups in the rational solution of Complex Problems.' *Am. J. of Psychol.*, 1932, 44, p. 491. Cf. digest in *Readings in Social Psychology*, p. 304.
[4] Watson, G. B. 'Do groups think more efficiently than individuals?' *J. Abn. and Soc. Psychol.* 1928, 23, p. 328.

solving a cipher, reading comprehension, and sentence completion. As may be expected, the advantage of group discussion over individual work varied greatly with the task.

The advantages of group-discussion are due, as has been indicated, to the increase in the number of new ideas put forward, and to the criticism of false moves. It is in these ways that two or three heads may be better than one. Discussing the question: should Judges of Appeal read the details of cases in the privacy of their chambers, or should they hear each case unfolded before them as they sit together? Sir Raymond Evershed, M.R. observes: 'The three Appeal Judges learn the case together: each, by hearing the questions of his colleagues, has the benefit of understanding the working of two minds in addition to his own.'[1]

The difficulty of studying groups at work is obvious, and accounts for the fact that investigators have concentrated on small groups working on quite definite problems. J. L. Carr[2] has devised a method of studying committee work not so much from the point of view of the solution as the changing incidence of the initiators. A chart has to be made in the form of a time-sheet and symbols devised with which the observer can quickly register such events as: who makes a suggestion, who opposes it, who speaks most and so on. This kind of charting is required for the investigation of such problems as the working of a joint-consultative committee. South,[3] for instance, found that small groups were on the whole better for material which lends itself to immediate formulation of opinion, such as the matching of photographs against the names of emotions, while larger ones are better when many hypotheses are needed. His results also point to the advantage of groups composed of the same sex. The importance of the nature of the task for the superiority of group discussion over individual reflection has been discussed by R. L. Thorndike[4] and R. W. Husband.[5] There is general agreement that a group is better when a wide variety of responses is needed to meet the situation.

Such generalizations, however, do not carry us very far. The fact

[1] Evershed, Sir R., M.R. *The Court of Appeal in England.* Athlin Press, 1950, p. 26.

[2] Carr, J. L. 'Experimental Sociology: a preliminary note on theory and method.' *Soc. Forces*, 1929, 8, p. 63.

[3] South, E. B. 'Some Psychological Aspects of Committee Work.' *J. Applied Psychol.*, 1927, 11, p. 348.

[4] Thorndike, R. L. 'On What Type of Task will a Group do well?' *J. Abn. Soc. Psychol.*, 1938, 33, 409.

[5] Husband, R. W. 'Co-operation versus Solitary Problem Solution.' *J. Soc. Psychol.*, 1940, 11, 405.

is that a 'Committee'—or, rather, a group so labelled, may come together for a variety of purposes of which the intellectual solution of a
problem is only one. In some cases of urgency, when action is called
for, the prestige and/or obvious pre-eminence of a single person may
not only carry the day but it may well be that the 'leader's' decision is
better than any that could have been hammered out by the committee
in discussion. Again a 'Committee' may be a statutory body existing
for the purpose of making decisions within a defined area of competence. In such cases procedural factors play their part, remote objections
not concerned with immediate issues may divert the discussion from its
immediate considerations, while, as we all know to our cost, the suggestions that are made from time to time are prompted by the desire
to be noticed rather than by the desire to follow the light of reason:
Finally the function of a 'committee' may be not only to arrive at a
decision, but to commit the members to united action. This is the
function emphasized by Lewin[1] and his followers, and has been
referred to above (p. 33).

So far we have considered the systematic observation of groups as
they affect individual members doing tasks by themselves, and as fields
of co-operation in the solution of problems. A final type of experiment
must be mentioned, devised to study the effect of a group in modifying
individual judgments, though this topic has already come to the fore in
some of the experiments mentioned above. What we have now in
mind is illustrated by an enquiry undertaken by H. T. Moore.[2] He
presented each of ninety-five subjects with paired ethical propositions,
and paired musical stimuli. Judgments of preference were made, and,
two days later, remade so as to gauge what we might call 'uninfluenced'
change of mind. Then the same thing was done two and a half months
later, but this time, on the second occasion of judging, the subjects were
told what the majority decision was before they made their choices and
in the ethical judgments a larger number of reversals were made than
was the case in the first part of the experiment. An even greater rever-
sal of judgment came about when, in a third trial, the opinions of
'experts' were mentioned. These results were confirmed by C. H.
Marple[3] who tested the effect of 'majority' and 'expert' judgment in
bringing about a change in the opinion of some hundreds of persons of

---

[1] Lewin, K. 'Group Decision and Social Change.' *Readings in Social Psychology*, p. 330.
[2] Moore, H. T. 'The Comparative influence of majority and expert opinion.' *Am. J. of Psychol.*, 1921, 32, p. 16.
[3] Marple, C. H. 'The Comparative Susceptibility of Three Age Levels to the Sug-
gestion of Group versus Expert Opinion.' *J. Social. Psychol.*, 1933, 4, p. 176.

different ages on no less than seventy-five controversial issues. At the same time P. R. Farnsworth[1] found no tendency to social conformity in his study of attitudes. It is clear, that, as usual, the effect of knowing that such-and-such is the 'majority' opinion or the 'expert' opinion will vary with the subject matter, and we are not surprised to find that Moore reports much less effect in the case of musical judgments than in the case of ethical ones.

Somewhat similar is the curious experiment of H. Clark[2] who uncorked a bottle of water in front of 168 students, and asked them when they smelt it. Slowly, the 'odour' spread itself, reaching the sixth row back after some 85 to 155 minutes. It looks as though it were not merely a matter of individual responses to the experimenter's suggestion, but also a general tendency on the part of those who smelt to want to do the thing expected by the group as a whole.

In Allport's experiments his 'group tasks' were the estimation of weights and the judgment of the pleasantness and unpleasantness of odours. When these judgments were made in public they tended to be less extreme than when made in private.

Allport has also invented a simple method of registering graphically the degree of conformity to a rule.[3] If you take any rule which aims at producing a uniform pattern of action, such as stopping at a crossing when the traffic lights are red, or clocking-in at a factory at or before a certain time, you can count the number of people obeying the rule and mark this upon a graph, the vertical lines of which refer to numbers of people, while the horizontal ones refer to degrees of conformity, with extreme conformity at the left-hand end. Then you count those who do not quite conform, e.g. those motorists who go very slow but do not stop, or the worker who arrives a little late, and mark their number on the graph. So you go on through progressive degrees of iniquity until all the relevant population or sample have been catered for. If the rule is completely effective the result should be a straight line because the population will all conform. In fact, of course, the shape obtained by this method is like the letter J the wrong way round. The shape of the curve, its uprightness or spread-outness indicates the effectiveness of the rule.

[1] Farnsworth, P. R. 'Further Dates on the Obtaining of Scale Values.' *J. Psych.*, 1945, 19, p. 69.

[2] Clark, H. 'The Crowd.' *Psychol. Monog.*, 1916, 21, p. 26.

[3] 'The J-Curve Hypothesis of Conforming Behaviour.' *Journal of Social Psychology*, 1934, v. 114. Cf. *Readings in Social Psychology*, p. 55.

Another set of experiments on perceptual judgment are those of Sherif[1] on the 'formation of group standards or norms'. Much has been built round these experiments and it may help the reader to see the point of them if we start from a more theoretical position. Every stimulus to perception and every topic introduced to our minds for consideration is, as it were, received by us, not in naked isolation, but in what Sherif calls a 'frame of reference'. We see things as 'near' or 'far', 'large' or 'small' according to scales of reference which have been established in us by experience. We judge incomes to be 'large' or 'small' in relation to a 'frame of reference', partly determined by our social position. The price of an article is so many shillings; it is 'cheap' or 'dear' in terms of our 'frame of reference'. Political propositions are what they are; they are judged 'right' or 'wrong', 'misguided' or 'red', in terms of our 'frame of reference'. Indeed 'personality' and 'moral codes' are nothing but such 'frames of reference', of which the reflective mind makes 'models'. Now 'frames of reference' and presentations to be received by them may differ in firmness and clarity. This is obvious in the case of perception, and one can easily see from common experience that some people on certain points are, as we should say 'unshakable', while others wobble. The less structured a presentation, the less uniformly will it be apprehended and the more 'subjective factors' will come in. This is the rationale of projective technique for bringing out individual differences, such as the Rorschach and the Thematic Apperception tests. Again, the vaguer the stimulus and the less firm the frame of reference when it comes to political or ethical issues, the more open we are to social pressure.[2] This has been formulated in the following terms by Krech and Crutchfield:[3] 'A suggestion concerning an ambiguous situation will be more readily accepted than one concerning a clearly structured situation,' while 'a suggestion that fits in with other systems of beliefs and frames of reference will be more readily accepted than one that does not.' These principles no doubt account for the divergency in the results of experiments on the influence of 'group' and 'expert' opinion.

Now 'frames of reference' are set up imperceptibly in us during the course of our social interactions, that is to say: it is our 'nature' to

---

[1] Sherif, M. 'A study of some social factors in perception.' 1935. *Arch. Psychol.*, No. 187. cf. Sherif, M. *Outline o Social Psychology.* Harper and Brothers, N.Y., 1948, pp. 162 f. and *Readings in Social Psychology*, p. 77.

[2] cf. Luchins, A. S. 'On agreement with another's judgment.' *J. Abn. and Soc. Psychol.*, 1944, 39, p. 97.

[3] *Theory and Problems of Social Psychology.* McGraw-Hill, 1948, p. 358.

acquire such schemata, and our social interactions are very largely responsible for their content. Sherif's experiments are an excursion into this field of enquiry, an attempt to give an example of these forces at work. The material used was the phenomenon of 'autokinetic movement'. If you are in a room so dark that you cannot find your 'whereabouts', as we significantly say, you are deprived of the normal 'frame of reference'—the walls, ceiling and so on. Supposing then a tiny spot of light is presented to you in the darkness, what will happen? If you can see it in relation to a fixed object, of course you just see a stationary light, but if it is too dark for that, then the light appears to move. Now Sherif found that a person, when placed in this situation several times, at first estimated the movement variously, but gradually came to a uniform estimation, and, presumably, from now on *saw* the light moving about the same distance every time. In Sherif's language, a 'frame of reference' had been subjectively established. Now suppose you get two people with different frames of reference, or 'norms', i.e. each seeing the light move a different distance from that seen by his fellow subject, what will happen if they give their estimates out loud? After some three sessions the 'norms' converge and the participants acquire another frame of reference different from the one acquired previously by each; and *this* frame of reference persists when the subjects are re-tested individually. Furthermore most of the subjects were unaware of the influence of the group and declared that they had decided on their judgment before anyone else spoke.

Of course a group of people in a dark room suffering from an illusion is remote from everyday life, but the concept of 'frames of reference' shaped and moulded by other people is a useful one. As has been said above we all develop them without noticing it, and in so far as we are not subjected to disorientation our frames of reference remain much the same. With an upheaval, however, we may find our old frames of reference—particularly moral ones—in conflict with new ones and there is likely to be a strong suasion in us to conform, a suasion which we may, of course, resist. Or else, it may be, we are faced, together with other people, with what may be called an 'unstructured' situation. This happens, for example, in war. Sherif[1] has collected instances of people in prison camps and in isolated places, where 'group frames of reference' with regard to stealing or 'winning' were different from those which were characteristic of them in normal

[1] *Outlines of Social Psychology*, p. 178.

life. D. Clemmer is quoted by Sherif[1] as finding that when men enter prison they are 'confused and uncertain about the social world they have left' and they feel 'swallowed up' and lost in the new community. If they accept the 'frame of reference' which the other prisoners have established and handed down they are less disoriented than if they don't. All this has brought us back again to a subject we have already discussed: the structuring tendency of groups (p. 18).

Before leaving the point we may call attention to the 'naturalness' of the process, and therefore to its needfulness. Perhaps one way of formulating such malaise as so many people claim to experience and observe nowadays is to say that such people are lacking, and believe others to be lacking, an adequate set of frames of reference.

The groups brought together for therapeutic purposes have on the whole been used to provide situations in which the individual members find opportunities for self-expression, self-knowledge and self-revelation.[2] They have seldom been used for the purpose of analysing the group as such.

An attempt in this direction is being made by W. R. Bion, who has contributed a series of articles to *Human Relations*[3] in which he describes his 'experience in groups' and makes some tentative suggestions as to the conceptual tools which may be found helpful in the understanding of group behaviour in the small face-to-face group and in the larger society.

Groups for Bion are of different kinds. There is the 'sophisticated' or 'work' group with its specific tasks, its powers of adult co-operation, and its techniques of organization, administration and the like which are elaborated to provide an efficient frame-work for action. They feel comfortable when the normal apparatus is present. There are, however, groups in which more basic and emotional factors are operative, and a group which meets consciously as a 'work' group may become suffused with these other factors, so that the different groups are not groups of different people, but rather different types of group manifestation. It is these emotionally-bonded types of group structure that are of special interest and importance. For the understanding of these groups Bion introduces the concept of 'group mentality', which is 'the unanimous expression of the will of the group, contributed to by the individual in ways of which he is unaware, influencing him disagreeably

---

[1] Op. cit., p. 403.

[2] The application of social psychology to psycho-therapy is discussed in Chapter XI.

[3] Vol. I, 1948, pp. 314–320; 487–496, Vol. II, 1949, pp. 13–22; 295–304, Vol. III, 1950, pp. 3–14; 395–402.

whenever he thinks or behaves in a manner at variance with the basic assumption'.[1] These 'basic assumptions' are (1) 'fight or flight', a group preservation theme which assures the importance of the group and unimportance of the individual member, and responds with hostility to any hint of disruption or attack; (2) the group may break into pairs and when this happens it looks as though the basic assumption is that the members of the pair are sexually attracted to one another; (3) the basic assumption may be dependency upon a leader for help. In groups under the dominance of these 'basic assumptions' the role of the member is unconsciously determined and what he does or says is interpreted (or ignored) in terms of the prevailing assumption. Therefore if any one of them says something 'out of key', his 'group-component' senses the disparity and he cannot continue. The adult 'work' group fears the emotional undercurrents which may spring from the unconscious depths and therefore tries to cling to its formal frame-work; on the other hand when a group is in the grip of a basic emotional concord, it fears the disruptive technique of 'work'-group activity with its stress on intellect and reason. The individual in the 'basic assumption' groups is uneasy because he is trying to preserve his adult integrity, and all the time contributing to the 'group mentality' and swayed by its influence. Thus, though it may be true that 'the group is essential to the fulfilment of a man's mental life',[2] there are deep layers—possibly, indeed of a phylogenetic order—which have to be understood before that fulfilment can be mature. In a group, for example, which is dominated by the unanimous assumption of dependency, a leader is necessary, and it appears to be the case that if the therapist refuses the role for which he is obviously cast by the group, they turn to the most pathological 'case' among them and exalt him. This fact alone suggests the wide field of social phenomena to which Bion's analysis of therapeutic groups can be applied. Indeed he has pointed out how a priesthood so often tries to preserve the dependent group with its need for religious consolation by resenting the spontaneous choice of a leader, as though they were unconsciously aware of the dangers.[3] Bion's investigations are, as has been indicated, still in progress and no definity is claimed for them, but the subject is of such importance that some reference to his views has to be made.

In conclusion let us consider one or two more general studies of groups. The close-up systematic observation of groups in action has its limitation, as will have been gathered from the examples given

---

[1] *Human Relations*, II, p. 16.   [2] ibid., I, p. 493.   [3] *Human Relations*, III, p. 399.

above. One cannot help wondering whether Riddle's[1] study of a series of poker games does not go beyond the limits inevitable to experimental procedure. The players, as a photograph (reproduced in Murphy, Murphy and Newcomb's *Experimental Social Psychology*, p. 704) shows, were trussed up with measuring apparatus, the conduct of each was recorded in detail, and they had to fill up forms answering such questions as 'Did you try to bluff anyone during the game?' Among the data handled by Riddle were the correlations between a player's hand, his desire to win, and his bet, and it was discovered by manipulating the correlation coefficients that the highest correlation was between the desire to win and the amount staked. It was further revealed that 'successful and unsuccessful efforts at bluffing are at the very heart of the situation',[2] which can scarcely be called startling, and that in these games at any rate, bluffing was directed against the successful and aggressive players rather than against the weak ones.

No one would for a second deny that social psychological factors are operating in a game of poker. The trouble is that one hesitates to extend to any other situation the findings recorded in these. In this connection we must protest against the prejudice in favour of rigorous experimentation. Naturally if the type of situation is appropriate, the more rigorous the technique the better, but there is a risk of the ideal being the enemy of the good. There is a risk, that is to say, that less rigorous methods, which are often the best one can apply, should be condemned or ignored.

A good example of informal but careful observation of group life is provided by studies which have been made of gang society.

The pioneer in this field was F. M. Thrasher.[3] He participated in the sociological investigation of Chicago organized by Robert E. Park and Ernest W. Burgess, during which he studied no less than 1,313 gangs in Chicago. They operated in the poorer districts and the ages of their members ranged from six years old to late adolescence, so that he included 'criminal gangs', as ordinarily understood, in his survey. They were almost all of them engaged in dubious activities for some part of the time, but that, as Thrasher points out, is because 'the exploits of the gang tend to follow patterns in its own social world.'[4]

As a social phenomenon, ' it is characterized by the following types

---

[1] Riddle, E. M. 'Aggressive behaviour in a small social group.' *Arch. Psychol.*, 1925, No. 78.

[2] Murphy, Murphy and Newcomb. *Experimental Social Psychology*, p. 705.

[3] Thrasher, F. M. *The Gang.* Univ. of Chicago Press. 2nd. ed., 1937.

[4] Op. cit., p. 256.

of behaviour: meeting face-to-face, milling, movement through space as a unit, conflict (against other gangs) and planning. The result of this collective behaviour is the development of tradition, unreflective internal structure, *esprit de corps*, solidarity, morale, group awareness, and attachment to a local territory.'[1] They go through a sort of evolution from a diffuse and loosely organized group into a solidified and, possibly even a 'conventionalized' gang with formal activities like organized athletics and dancing. Some of them, of course, are secret, and some explicitly criminal, but they all provide the new experience, the excitement, the romance, and the collective entertainment which their members cannot get elsewhere. The leader emerges out of the gang rather than the gang being formed round the leader, and therefore different qualities—strength, daring, sophistication and intelligence are found in varying proportions among the leaders as one passes from one group to another. Within the group there may be a variety of roles: the 'brain', the 'comic' the 'bluffer', the 'goat'—anything but the 'sissy'. Thrasher expresses the view, which is after all very reasonable, that in attacking the problem of undesirable gangs it is unsatisfactory to take individual members away from his gang unless you can provide him with one which *he* prefers. Far better, if it can be done, to transfer the gang as a whole into something which fulfils the same function as it did before without being a social menace.

A more detailed account of gang life is to be found in W. F. Whyte's study of *Street Corner Society*.[2] The setting was the slums of Chicago and the members had a sense of being looked down on by the larger society. They therefore gravitated together and, their ethos being one in which physical toughness was accorded high value, the leader, Doc, achieved his position by licking his predecessor. The priest-kings of Nemi look down in ghostly recognition. 'Each member of the corner gang', says Whyte[3] 'has his own position in the gang structure,' and these positions are sociometrically displayed. Solidarity is established and is evidenced by remarkable acts of self-sacrifice. Interestingly enough a kind of exogamic principle seems to have been felt: 'It is only with an outsider, with someone who is not related to him or to a friend, that the corner boy feels free to have sexual relations.'[4] Even prowess is affected if it is likely to bring a member 'out of his place'. Frank, who was not important, was good at bowling, but, 'accustomed to filling an inferior position, Frank was unable to star even in his favourite sport

[1] ibid., p. 87. [2] University of Chicago Press, 1943. [3] op. cit., p. 262.
[4] ibid., p. 28.

when he was competing against members of his own group.'[1] The group disintegrated when Doc entered politics. This brought him into relation with the outside world in which he was at a disadvantage because of his poverty. He gave up the struggle, his followers felt themselves 'let down', and the gang broke up.

The formation of 'in-group' cliques are described by Ernie Pyle[2] and Bill Mauldin in[3] their vivid description of life in the American Army. They both tell a familiar story of exclusiveness, private joking, the spontaneous development of loyalties, and the discomforts of the misfit and the outsider.

All groups, as we have seen, tend towards structuration which is evidenced by (or, more correctly, *is*) a role system, an ethos, a certain formalization of action-patterns, and the generation of the idea or model of the group in the minds of its constituents. They differ, however, in the degree of organization they achieve. French[4] compared the conduct of members of boys clubs and athletic teams with that of *ad hoc* groups of college students when faced with difficult problems and dangers. He found that the organized groups displayed 'definitely *more social freedom*, "we feeling", interdependence, equality of participation in the group activity, motivation, frustration, and aggression against other members of the group'. The last part of this not very happily worded report is significant. In danger the organized group *might* be less effective.

Conclusion. Everyone is influenced by social patterns at varying distance from him. There is the general social pattern into which he is born, whose influence is mediated by his family, playmates, acquaintances, and—in a wide sense—his neighbours. Then, nearer at hand, are the more specific patterns of social life which bring in the peculiarities of his class, his county, his city, his village, his street. As we come down nearer to what actually happens, we come to his family, his gang, his school, his dart-club, his work-mates and so on. Krech and Crutchfield[5] make a distinction of terminology to mark the kind of conceptual distinction to which we are referring. They speak of 'Psychological Groups' as cases when: (1) 'All the members must exist as a group in the psychological field of each individual, i.e. be perceived and reacted

---

[1] ibid., p. 19.   [2] *Here Is Your War*. World Publishing Co., N.Y., 1945.
[3] *Up Front*. Holt, 1945. Quoted by Sherif. *Outline of Soc. Psych.*, 103.
[4] French, S. R. P. Organized and unorganized groups under fear and frustration in *Studies in topological and vector psychology*. Univ. of Iowa Press, 1944.
[5] *Theories and problems of Social Psychology*. MacGraw-Hill, p. 363.

to as a group; (2) the various members must be in dynamic interaction with one another.' This they contrast with 'Social Organizations'. These are 'specific groupings of actual people, which are characterized by the possession of the following: (1) cultural products (such as buildings, robes, prayers, magic formulas, songs); (2) a collective name or symbol; (3) distinctive action patterns; (4) a common belief system; and (5) enforcing agents and technique. The distinction is a good one because it brings into consideration the informal and transitory groupings which are real enough in their effect upon behaviour but not organized or long-lived enough to develop into 'social organization'. At the same time the field of social psychology does not lend itself to tidy pigeon-holing, and we must emphasize, as Krech and Crutchfield themselves do, that the same group—or rather the same label—may be found under both headings. A family is certainly a 'social organization', as defined here, and every household is, from day-to-day, a 'psychological group'.

Leaving aside the large-scale 'social organizations' and concentrating upon the 'psychological groups' and smaller 'social organizations' which permit of face-to-face relationships, we may ask what function they perform in the lives of their members. To begin with we may make a distinction between *extrinsic* and *intrinsic* motives, solely for our present purpose. By 'extrinsic' motives we mean aims which are directed beyond the actual enjoyment of participation, while by intrinsic motives we mean those desires, whether conscious or unconscious, which are satisfied in participation itself. It is these latter which interest us here.

The 'function' of a group from the extrinsic point of view may be related to the part co-operation plays in the satisfaction of needs or acquired desires, such as the desire for sexual intercourse, for home-making, for economic security, for athletic pursuits of various kinds, for political action and so on. Clearly some groups exist solely for such purposes, while others—the ones we are discussing—doubtless would not come into being save for such motivations, but seem to provide *intrinsic* satisfaction as well. 'All groups,' remark Krech and Crutchfield[1] 'seem to meet the dominant needs of some of their members and the belongingness needs of most of their members.' Whether we trace these latter needs to the dependence of the infant on other people in childhood, or whether we choose to disguise our ignorance by saying that there is an 'instinct' which makes man look for company, prac-

[1] ibid., p. 383.

tically everyone seems to thrive in groups which make his actions 'meaningful' and to feel lonely and uncomfortable if he has no 'place' to fill. Of course such satisfactions and discontents need not be consciously related to their source, and many people are perfectly happy pursuing what, if they reflected upon it, they would deem to be their function in the world, without being conspicuous 'joiners'—indeed, the very reverse. They may relate themselves to a wider society. There are others who pursue their interests with gusto and who would be both bewildered and exasperated if anyone ventured to ask what their function was and in what group.

Anyone who attempts to estimate what is conducive to good living should weigh two opposing hypotheses. On the one hand it may be said that man 'by nature' seeks group participation, that those who are unhappy are often so because they are naked and alone, and that those who claim to be happy living their own lives by themselves are not 'really happy' at all. On the other hand it may be that group life, save for insecure adolescents, is only needed by those who have not outgrown the dependence of infancy. On this view it is those who can stand alone who have grown up, while those who love to get into huddles are not 'really happy' but only assuaging their sense of being unloved. Between these extremes it is difficult to choose; as usual in such conflicts of value the concept of being 'not-really-happy' is a source of much misgiving.

Whatever view we take on this issue, the fact seems to be that participation in group activity does give zest to the lives of enormous numbers of persons. It provides them with a sense of security and worth; it provides them with frames of reference, by which to orientate their conduct and their views. As Ralph Linton[1] says: 'The average individual is unhappy and unsure of himself unless he feels that a number of other individuals share his particular ideas or habits and are his friends.' Again 'there is the need for companionship and for the reassurance and emotional security which comes from belonging to a social unit whose members share the same ideas and patterns of behaviour'.[2] Furthermore, besides providing security, companionship, and a stable perspective, a group frequently provides an objective for devoted labour. If there is one thing about which ethical writers seem to be agreed it is that contentment can only be achieved if action is directed towards an end outside the person acting. Service to the

[1] *The Study of Man.* D. Appleton. Century Co., 1936, p. 216.
[2] ibid., p. 218.

group may be such an end. Finally we may note that membership of a tightly consolidated group relieves one of independent choice. One takes on the frame of reference of the group and this saves one from having to correct one's own frames of reference with every change in the situation.

In view of all this, what wonder that groups are conceived as having an instinct of preservation of their own? Such is the 'ego-involvement', as the Americans elegantly call it, such the advantages, that all the 'good' members have a vested interest in keeping it alive. For all, it satisfies the need to belong, for the dominant it provides a field of action such that their entire personality may be wrapped up in the single group.[1]

This accounts for many of the characteristics of groups which we have noticed in this chapter. New members are suspect partly because they may change the pattern of life to which everyone has got used, and partly because they present a new stimulus for which the frames-of-reference are unprepared. New ideas tend to be shunned for the same reason, and so far as possible adapted to the old system of belief.

In order to avoid possible conflict, and also to reinforce their bonds, groups with a narrow extrinsic purpose tend to expand and develop accessory activities, often of a 'social' nature. But harmony and endurance cannot be ensured without resistance to disruptive forces. Of course if the extrinsic function ceases to exist and the intrinsic function is provided by other groups, then after a more or less lingering illness the group will die. But that is by no means the only threat. It may be, as we have seen in the case of the Corner Street Boys, that a particular leader is an essential feature of a group, and if he leaves the group may evaporate. Far worse, however, is the threat of internal tension, and when this develops something has to be done to save the structure from being torn asunder. The disruptive element may be extruded; the familiar technique of 'scape-goating' may be used; some method of arbitration may be established for the composition of differences; or else the intra group hostilities may be externalized on to a common foe.

Among primitive peoples most of these devices will be found and to them we must add the institutionalization of potentially disruptive tendencies which may take the form of mock fights, the canalization of aggression into the prestige-giving role of the warrior, and the development of accepted techniques of magic and counter-magic.

[1] cf. Krech, D. and Crutchfield, R. S. op. cit., p. 385.

Group morale with its attendant manifestations of loyalty and self-sacrifice is intelligible enough once one accepts the value of the group for individual satisfactions. A man will defend the life of his group not only because he fears the ostracizing accusation of cowardice but because in some sense its life is identified with his own.

CHAPTER IV

CROWDS

TWO types of social situations have been the subject of considerable discussion and speculation because of the dramatic nature of the one and the topical importance of the other. They are situations which come under the heading of 'crowd', and those in which the 'follower-leader' relationship is emphasized. In this chapter we shall deal with 'crowd-psychology' and in the next with the problem of leadership.

Crowds. The word 'crowd' is, unfortunately, ambiguous. 'A crowd', writes Kimball Young[1], 'is a gathering of a considerable number of persons around a centre or point of common attention.' That, no doubt, is simple enough, but there our difficulties begin. Riots, lynchings and panic flights swirl before the eyes of our imagination only to be replaced by visions of a demure audience listening in rapt attention to a celebrated musician or an orderly but enthusiastic mass-meeting addressed by a political speaker. The common basis of such diverse phenomena is, perhaps, the emotional element. The general concept of an 'audience' covers a wide variety of situations, but when an audience is charged with a common emotion we are likely to think of it as being more like a 'crowd' than would be the case if it were composed of people engaged in critical or intellectual contemplation of what is going on. Of course there are borderline cases in which emotional polarization and intellectual interest are both at work, but the greater the common emotional disturbance the more crowd-like the situation. Such a situation, however, is very unlike a seething mob, so that we must draw a distinction to start with between the 'institutionalized crowd' and the 'informal crowd', with the proviso that the former may on occasion—as when a fire breaks out in a theatre—turn into the latter.

The Informal Crowd. By way of simplifying our task it will be convenient to start with what we have called the 'informal'

[1] *Handbook of Social Psychology.* Kegan Paul. English Edition, 1946, p. 387.

crowd, first, because the crowd-like feature of the audience when they manifest themselves can best be understood as special instances of crowd behaviour in general. It is agreed by all writers that when a person is a member of a crowd he is liable to behave differently from the way in which he would behave if he were by himself. The most celebrated writer on the subject, Le Bon, was so impressed by the transformation that he wrote of the '*évanouissement de la personnalité consciente*'.

Such language tempts us to think of a crowd as something totally different from its components, into which, indeed, they are absorbed. An intelligible reaction against such a view is that of Allport and most American social-psychologists who prefer to say that 'The individual in the crowd behaves just as he would behave alone, *only more so*'.[1] Such a point of view is certainly more acceptable than one which hints at a super-personal entity, but, in view of the description of crowd action and the theoretical explanation which seem most appropriate, Allport's statement cannot be taken as the final word unless the words in italics are interpreted in a very odd way.

The changes in the individual in extreme cases may be listed as follows (1) heightened emotionality; (2) heightened suggestibility with its correlates of decreased self-criticism and intellectual alertness; (3) diminished sense of responsibility and disinhibition of normal social controls; (4) a sense of power and anonymity. In so far as a crowd is made up of people charged with the same emotion, and undergoing the processes mentioned above it will act 'as one', though really it is a system of individuals in reinforcement relationships to one another.

Let us take the characteristics of the crowd-individual in turn. The most significant is the first, heightened emotionality. Before considering the factors responsible for the *heightening*, a point of fundamental importance must first be made. On becoming a member of a crowd, a man does not suddenly shed all his dispositions and become, as Le Bon put it, 'an automaton'. Very far from it. His whole system of dispositions which we call his 'personality' is involved. A man devoid of fear would not panic and a man incapable of aggression would not participate in mass-murder. The initial stimulus to emotion must therefore be one which is calculated to elicit a response from a large number of people. Danger, frustration, the spectacle or image of cruelty, or the cognizance of people in trouble have the effect they do have because we are prone to respond to them. This is obvious enough, but subtler issues are involved. Anyone may feel frightened if a fire

[1] Allport, F. H. *Social Psychology*, 1924, p. 295.

breaks out in a theatre, but certain preliminary conditions are required for a great deal of crowd action. The great instances of mob violence— the taking of the Bastille, scenes in the Russian revolution, lynching in the Southern States of America—can only be understood if we take the general state of affairs into consideration. This is brought out by Theodor Geiger[1] who expresses himself as follows. 'Although the "mass" is dispersed, it acts at a distance. The essential point is that individuals as they leave their homes are already at that very moment in the state of mind which characterizes the collective attitude. In other words their state of mind does not result from the excitation of an agitator, nor is it born in the tumult of action.' Geiger phrases his account in terms of 'supra-individual collectivities' and much that he says is expressed in terminology with doubtful implications, but how- ever we put it we must certainly insist that what is ordinarily called 'states of unrest' are conditions in which large numbers of people are specially liable to be thrown into an emotional state, and to be prompted to action by stimuli which otherwise would not affect them. Their threshold is lowered with respect to certain responses and, as Barham once observed: 'When the little heart is big, a little sets it off.'

Crowd action, then, may be a release of social tension, but that is not all. We are all of us from time to time—and some more than others—the victims of internal tension. Pent-up aggressiveness and the desire to feel the security of social contact are likely to seize upon any opportunity for expression and crowd action often gives them their chance. Charles Bird[2] draws attention to the 'geography' of the crowd, its compactness near the centre and the thin fringe at the periphery. 'Individuals near the centre have elbowed and pushed their way into favoured positions. They are people who enjoy or covet social con- tacts, who seek or crave excitement, who are given to action and not to reflection, and who may be expected to profit from the activities spon- sored by the leader.' To the last words we would add: 'Whether they are aware of such profit or not.'

Finally, we must add that the general cultural habits of the crowd members will operate to make a crowd in one culture different from a crowd in another. This may well account for the mixture of aggres- siveness and obedience which Hitler was able to instil into his audience, and for the institutionalized crowd-like frenzies described by anthro-

[1] *Die Masse und ihre Aktion.* Enkl. Stuttgart, 1926, p. 80. Quoted Reiwald *De L'Esprit des Masses,* p. 154.
[2] *Social Psychology,* Appleton Century, 1940, p. 349.

pologists.[1] At any rate the extent to which the members of a crowd are culturally 'conditioned' to give expression to their emotions or to hide them will certainly have its effect on the character of the crowd, perhaps making it less lively because it is not 'done' to display emotion, or making it more lively because the occasion sanctions a letting-off of steam.

The responses of each member of a crowd are multi-determined. He may respond purely to an overwhelmingly frightening situation, in which case his response is still to a certain extent determined by his acquired habits of conduct in the face of danger. He may, however, be in a restless state which he shares with many other people, and also in a state of conflict peculiar to himself. It is partly because of this multi-determined response to the stimulus that crowd emotion is unexpectedly excessive. Many writers have drawn attention to this, among them Tarde,[2] who writes of the unbridled extremes of emotional outburst: 'Between execration and adoration, between horror and enthusiasm, between cries of "Vive" and cries of "A Mort" there is for a crowd no mean.' It is because crowd action is often so disproportionate to the situation or so excessively unlike the cooler responses of rational men that some writers have sought to explain it by reference to an up-surge of mysterious underlying forces. Le Bon for instance, explains the unity of a crowd by reference to an unconscious racial soul, and Jung[3] who describes crowds as 'blind beasts', and sees them as moved by the irruption of forces from the collective unconscious.

Such fanciful sources of energy need not be called in to account for the excesses of crowd-behaviour. Multi-determination will carry us a long way, and there is a further factor which heightens the emotion of each, and that is the inter-stimulation of each by everyone else in sight or hearing. 'Each man [in a crowd],' says MacDougall[4] 'perceives on every hand the symptoms of fear, the blanched distorted faces, the dilated pupils, the high-pitched trembling voices, and the screams of terror of his fellows, and with each such perception his own impulses and his own emotion rise to a higher pitch of intensity.' This, according to him is due to the 'direct' induction of emotion by way of the 'primitive sympathetic response'. The principle of the primitive sympathetic

---

[1] cf. Hardy, Georges—'La Foule dans les sociétés dites primitives' in Reiwald, op. cit., p. 222.

[2] *L'Opinion et la Foule Paris.* Alcan, 1901, p. 36.

[3] *Psychologische Betrachtungen, eine Auslese aus den Schriften von C. G. Jung*, Jolan, Jacobi. Rascher, Zürich, 1945, p. 179. Quoted by Reiwald, P., op. cit., p. 117.

[4] *The Group Mind.* Cambridge, 1920, p. 25.

response is that 'in man and in the gregarious animals generally, each instinct, with its characteristic primary emotion and specific impulse, is capable of being excited in one individual by the expression of the same emotion in another, in virtue of a special congenital adaptation of the instinct on its cognitive or perceptual side.' The same view was held by Espinas[1] who asserted that 'it is a universal law operating throughout the whole field of intelligent life, that the expression of an emotional state gives rise to a stirring of the same state in an observer.'

Such a view is no longer fashionable, and is condemned as methodologically weak. Allport[2] reminds us that we do not necessarily have the same emotion as the one whose expression we perceive, it may revolt us or make us laugh. When we do respond with fear to signs of fear it is because we have learnt to interpret such signs as signs of danger.

Another factor comes into play as we turn to our second feature of group experience: 'heightened suggestibility'. This is not the place to consider the theory of suggestibility, or to analyse all the phenomena that come under that heading. In most cases of the word 'suggestion' one is concerned with a social relationship; in this case with the uncritical doing of the same things as the other members of the crowd, and the uncritical acceptance of propositions and commands. The following factors would appear to be responsible for this: (1) the presence of a powerful drive, which tends to facilitate conduct, ideas and the acceptance of orders congruent with it; (2) if a leader is present, the acceptance of his leadership; (3) the social facilitation of the crowd itself. (2) and (3) need further examination. The leader's words are accepted partly because in the insecure position of childhood we have learnt to obey the voice of authority, partly because our attitude towards the leader may be one coloured by the devotion of a lover which gives the loved one a special position of authority, and partly because in a disoriented condition any hint of a stable frame of reference is welcomed.

The 'social facilitation' provided by the presence of others has already been discussed. 'A large number of people' say Miller and Dollard,[3] 'performing a response evoke it more strongly in any single individual.' Now Miller and Dollard have a theory as to why this should be so. Imitation, doing the same as someone else, has been found rewarding, and therefore *acquired* as a type of conduct. 'Many individuals in each crowd,' they say, 'have been separately punished or not rewarded for

[1] *Des Sociétés Animales,* 2nd Ed., Paris, 1878, p. 361.   [2] op. cit., p. 235.
[3] *Social Learning and Imitation.* Eng. Ed. Kegan Paul, 1945, p. 186.

doing acts with only one person or norm or model, whereas they have been frequently rewarded for acting as large groups of others act.' Thus both factors (2) and (3) are the result of social training of one form or another, and not due to any innate mechanism. Furthermore the 'inter-stimulation' of leader to crowd, and crowd to members, are circular processes. Obedience swells the importance of the leader, and his inflated prestige invites further submission, while the expression of terror and the flight of one excites his neighbour to the same response and his neighbour in his turn acts as a stimulus.

Thus, to return to heightened emotionality, the primary cause is the stimulus which has its effect either because it is exciting 'by nature' or because it affords relief to social and/or personal tension, and to this we now add the secondary effects of cumulative intra-group stimulation.

The third characteristic of the individual in the crowd is his diminished sense of responsibility and the disinhibition of normal social controls. This has already been accounted for. Responsibility requires intellectual alertness, and we have seen that this is in abeyance. However there is something more to be said. The crowd and the leader (if there is one) tend to take the place of our internalized social controls (our 'super-egos', as the Freudian would say). 'In a group,' says Freud,[1] 'the individual is brought under conditions which allow him to throw off the repressions of his unconscious instincts.' A permissive control has taken the place of the inhibitory one. This may be responsible for the sense of righteousness sometimes exhibited by crowds, to which E. D. Martin[2] has called attention.

Under appropriate circumstances crowd action, as we have seen, gives us opportunity to do things which social controls forbid, but which we nevertheless want to do. It is quite clear, however, that in cases, for instance, of extreme danger this factor is scarcely likely to apply, but forcing a Negro to eat his genitals before he is lynched is a very different matter.[3] This does not, of course, mean that all 'crowd action' is either timorous or vile. Under appropriate circumstances it may be noble, self-sacrificing and generous.

The last characteristic: the sense of power and anonymity are of the order of reinforcements. The presence of a multitude of people is encouraging if you are on their side, and among them—who will notice you?

---

[1] *Group Psychology and the Analysis of the Ego*, p. 9.
[2] *The Behaviour of Crowds*, 1920, p. 155.
[3] cf. Miller, N. E. and Dollard, J., op. cit., p. 205.

So much for the general characteristics of the crowd. We must now consider the more difficult question of the stimulus and the response. In the case of what we have called the 'naturally exciting' stimulus—the fire in the theatre, or the threat of disaster—the stimulus is simple enough, and to such situations we add the minor crowd-generating stimuli of a street accident, a fire or a fight in the alley. The latter assemblages are not of much interest because they do not provoke action; the onlookers are themselves not threatened and so the typical crowd manifestations do not develop. In the more formidable cases, however, we must remember that crowds are composed of people who have already developed certain standards of conduct, and therefore what will happen will in all cases be partly determined by the strength of such standards in relation to the situation. Le Bon[1] always painted the blackest portrait of the crowd because he feared revolutionary violence, and so he emphasizes the transmutation of men into something less worthy, but he does admit—rather, one feels, for literary purposes—that the miser may be changed into a spendthrift and the coward into a hero. The fact is that though transformation for the worse may occur in the most surprising ways and reveal the precarious nature of our self-control, this is not always the case.

Sighele,[2] for instance, gives two curious examples of strikes. In 1886 the miners of Decazeville murdered the chief engineer, but the actual murderer had a criminal background. In a strike in Rome a crowd of workmen were easily prevented from doing any damage by, it would appear, a single officer; the ringleaders turned out to have impeccable histories. These cases, admittedly, are cases of social tension, but although we may hear of men, whom we might have supposed incapable of cruel or cowardly behaviour, trampling upon women and children in their wild efforts to escape from the burning theatre, the sinking ship, or other places of danger, this by no means always happens. Shipwreck may be faced with calmer and self-sacrificing courage and Sherif[3] by way of example tells the story of the nobility displayed when an explosion wrecked the town of Halifax in 1917.

We have to take into account the nature of the disaster, or whatever may be the stimulus itself, the general stability of the people involved, and the immediate first move. LaPiere and Farnsworth in this connection give sensible advice: 'A few moments after smoke is evident

---

[1] 'Isolated [a man] may be a cultured individual; in a crowd he is a barbarian' (op. cit., p. 36), cf. *Senatores omnes boni viri, senatus romanus mala bestia.*
[2] *La Foule Criminelle.* Alcan, Paris, 1898, pp. 113 f.
[3] op. cit., p. 107.

in a theatre, a moment after it becomes apparent that something is wrong with the ship, or the instant after the first quake has passed or the first bomb has dropped is the "psychological moment" for the appearance of responses that may be imitated.'[1] Such is, indeed, the psychological moment for one kind of leadership; its function here, as in so many other kinds of situation, is to provide a 'frame of reference', a mode of response to the bewildered. *As such*, leadership is neither advantageous nor the reverse; the first to take flight, crying 'Fire' is as much a leader from the psychological point of view, as the calm courageous conductor who continues to conduct the orchestra as the ship goes down; 'Self-interested leadership' as LaPiere and Farnsworth say, 'results in general panic. Heroic leadership leads to heroic action, which may or may not be expedient.'[2]

In addition to these considerations we may also have to note the special circumstances in which the episode occurs. It seems, for instance, that 'After the tragic Iroquois Theatre fire in Chicago in 1903, theatre audiences [in America] were for many years so fire-conscious that it was dangerous for an actor to smoke as a part of his characterization.'[3] In such circumstances an audience is more prone to panic than if fires were comparatively rare. Kimball Young[4] gives an example of the flight of Italian soldiers at Adowa in 1896 when a small body of native troops suddenly appeared; the soldiers had been absorbing rumours about the ruthless cruelty of the Abyssinians. Again, when a regiment of Prussian cavalry were retreating from the battle of Trautenau in 1866 the commander sent an aide to the head of the column to bring it to a walk. In order to do this he had to gallop past the column. The troopers thought it meant that the situation was desperate and fled. One cannot but think that the soldiers were in a nervous state of mind.

The object of this discussion is to emphasize the fact that a crowd as such has neither this character nor that; crowd-action is a function of a number of variables. This is particularly true of 'panic' of which we have given several examples. Some psychologists follow MacDougall and Geiger in accounting for panic in terms of a heightened emotion of fear, pointing out that anyone may 'panic' when he is by himself, which is perfectly true. Freud,[5] on the other hand, relates panic to the loss of the leader in whom the followers have placed their confidence. This view is also held by Robert Michels,[6] whose contribution to

[1] *Social Psychology*. McGraw-Hill, 3rd. edit., 1949, p. 466.
[2] ibid., p. 468.   [3] ibid., p. 466.   [4] op. cit., p. 390.   [5] op. cit., p. 49.
[6] *Zur Soziologie des Parteiwesens*, p. 68.

sociology is his study of the functions of the *élite*. He writes: 'The best proof of the organic impotence of the masses is given by the fact that as soon as the struggle deprives them of their leader, they leave the field of battle in disordered flight, like an ant-heap overwhelmed by terror,' and he illustrates his contention by reference to the paralysis of the Danish Socialist party when their leader Pio was exiled in 1877.

This, too, is true enough—when there is a leader. But the loss of a personal leader is not essential to cases of panic. It may occur 'when some highly cherished, rather commonly accepted value is threatened and when no certain elimination of the threat is in sight'. Such is the verdict of Hadley Cantril on the extraordinary effects of the broadcast on 30 October, 1938, when Americans were told of an invasion from Mars.[1] 'Long before the broadcast had ended,' we are told, 'people all over the United States were praying, crying, fleeing frantically to escape death from the Martians.' In the home of one, Joseph Headley, 'that Hallowe'en Boo sure had our family on its knees before the program was half over. . . . Brother Joe as usual got more excited than he could show. Brother George wasn't home. Aunt Grace, a good Catholic, began to pray with Uncle Henry. Lily got sick in her stomach. I don't know what I did exactly but I know I prayed harder and more earnestly than ever before. . . . How soon we put our trust in God.' In the analysis of the cause of panic, Cantril and his colleagues emphasize the background of economic unrest as predisposing a great many people to be sensitive to disaster, and also the disorientation of those who had no frame of reference into which they could fit the news, or by means of which they could guide their conduct.

We have mentioned states of social tension as a factor predisposing people to a lowered emotional threshold, and now we must turn to crowd-action as a tension-releasing phenomenon. Allport[2] relates an episode in the course of a miners' strike in the Middle West. A troop of strikers captured forty or fifty strike-breakers and marched them through the streets intending merely to hold them up to ridicule. Before they had gone very far the angry cries of the strikers alarmed the ones in front and they suggested to the prisoners that they had better make a dash for it. The moment this happened a shot rang out and the strikers broke their ranks, rushed after their victims and beat them up unmercifully. Von Wiese[3] tells the story of a scene in Paris

---

[1] Cantril, H., Gaudet, H. and Hertzog, H. *The Invasion from Mars*. Princeton University Press, 1940. cf. *Readings from Social Psychology*, p. 169.
[2] op. cit., p. 310.   [3] Quoted by Reiwald, P., op. cit., p. 305.

in 1926 when there was a wave of xenophobia. A bus load of foreigners was stopped by the police near a fire and told to go by another route. The crowd thought that the travellers had come to the scene of disaster to gloat and before the police could prevent it a hail of stones fell on the unfortunate inhabitants of the bus. Again in 1939, a crowd in Liverpool at the time of the I.R.A. bombing outrages, set on an Irishman, while he was buying a balloon for his child, and would doubtless have killed him if the police had not intervened.

Finally, a story from MacDougall,[1] who was present at a gathering of natives of Borneo for the purpose of strengthening friendly relations between the tribes. All went smoothly until a small piece of wood fell on the head of one of the leading chiefs, drawing blood, 'in the space of a few minutes angry emotion swept over the whole assembly'.

In all these instances we have a latent unrest and some small episode which acts like a spark to tinder. A slightly different situation is depicted by Tchakotine.[2] On the 5th of March, 1917, crowds of people were milling about the streets of Petrograd. They were tired of the war, tired of privation, and as a last straw the price of bread had been raised. The police had disappeared, the soldiers were in their barracks, the trams had stopped and everyone from the offices and ships joined the seething mob through which rumour rushed like wild fire. At two o'clock in the afternoon someone ordered a party of about a hundred men who were trained in gas-warfare to march through the streets in their gas masks preceded by a band and red flags. The crowds were electrified by the spectacle and the word quickly went round: 'The revolutionary troops are here; they are going to attack the barracks.' The news reached the soldiers and out they came. Joy, relief and acclamation replaced bewilderment, anxiety, and fatigue.

This story provides an example of the aimlessness of crowds who merely assemble because of a common plight. It is because of this that people interested in crowd-action in revolutionary situations have stressed the need for leadership. 'It is the leaders who provide a movement with an objective and a programme, the masses give it weight,' says von Wiese. Michels, to whom we have already referred, constantly insists on the hopeless plight of the crowds without a leader, while Trotsky in his *History of the Russian Revolution* puts the leader in his place in relation to the led. There is, however, the other side of the story. The leader of the crowd is only accepted if in some sense he responds to their needs. 'We have been accused,' says Trotsky, 'of

---

[1] *The Group Mind*, p. 26.　　　　[2] Quoted by Reiwald, P., op. cit., p. 327.

creating the opinion of the masses. This is untrue, we only try to formulate it.'

In some cases vague unrest is relieved by what can be interpreted as the fulfilment of a widespread wish. In some cases a leader may just appear at the right moment, someone gets up and gives the crowd a voice and a direction. But all this may be prepared for. The function of minority groups is to prepare the potential members of crowds for action by propaganda and the spread of rumour, and to gauge their temper and their desires so that their weight can be used to secure the desired end. But it is not only in revolutionary situations that the minority group play a part. Miller and Dollard[1] describe the lynching of a Negro who was supposed to have murdered a white girl in McCord County. He had been arrested and put in gaol but the gaol was stormed, the Negro, Stevens, was seized and brought back to a spot near where the girl lived. The background is familiar—economic rivalry between Negroes and poor whites, sexual envy and so forth. The episode provided an admirable occasion for a release of tension, but what Miller and Dollard call a 'nuclear mob' gave the lead. It was they who managed to restrain the unwelcome ardour of the larger mob so as to ensure that Stevens would take a long time dying. He was tortured for ten hours on June 20, 1933.

We might leave the study of crowds on a less sombre note. So much is said, particularly by Continental writers, about the destruction of crowds, their brutality and their violence. We cannot quite accept MacDougall's[2] allegation that 'a crowd is more apt to be swayed by the more generous of the coarser emotions, impulses, and sentiments than by those of a meaner universally reprobated kind'; but we have drawn attention to acts of gallantry and we may here add acts of generosity. Neither must we forget the innocent 'celebration' crowd, who would seem to have no other motive than the enjoyment of watching a spectacle or catching a glimpse of an admired personage. Notoriously good-humoured they give the lie to Mirabeau's spiteful remark: '*Lorsque les hommes sont ressemblés il se produit de la pourriture comme pour des pommes.*'[3]

Audiences. We must now turn to a more formal situation. We have called the 'audience' an 'institutionalized crowd' because in the vast majority of situations which we should call 'audiences' there is an accepted pattern of conduct, a formal beginning and formal end.

[1] op. cit., Chapter XV. [2] op. cit., p. 39.   Quoted Reiwald, P., op. cit., p. 324.

'Audiences,' however, overlap with 'crowds' in the sense that both words denote similar phenomena. When a man mounts an eminence and addresses an angry or a frightened concourse of people, he gets an audience if they listen to him. When a man gets up in a thronged market place and warns the world at large of its imminent destruction, he, too, may get an audience, if only a melting one.

In so far as attention is polarized and a common emotion is established the audience develops crowd-like characteristics. Kimball Young[1] has suggested a classification of audiences into 'information-seeking', 'recreation-seeking' and 'conversional'. The first is obviously the least liable to develop crowd-like features, but even here there are degrees of polarization, or rapport. In the second type what is presented is designed to appeal to the emotions and the preliminary staging—the lowering of the lights, the playing of the orchestra—is designed to arouse a mood of expectancy. Here, more than with the information-seeking audience, the presence or absence of rapport and the concentration of attention on to the stage and away from the distracting variety in the audience itself are specially noticeable.

It is, however, the last type of audience which is of greater interest. Here people are gathered together, not for information, nor for pleasure, but to be persuaded, and persuaded in such a way that action will follow either immediately or at a later date. The crowd atmosphere which we have discussed above has to be created, in order that the heightened suggestibility can be manipulated. Here, too, we note the impetus of the general context and the mood in which the audience comes to the meeting. This is frequently, as is also the case with the other two types of audience, prepared by posters, rumour, press notices and the like. Even the timing may be considered. Hitler—and after all he was an authority on the subject—has given a great deal of admirable advice in that mine of social psychological information, *Mein Kampf.* He tells us there that: 'In the morning, and even throughout the day, the will of individuals seems to resist all attempts to subordinate it to the will of another. On the other hand in the evening it submits more readily to the dominating power of a stronger will.' In an American University town Wednesday night was said to be 'a bad night' at the theatre because so many young couples were there who seemed more concerned with each other than with the play.[2]

The *mise-en-scène* for a 'conversion audience' requires careful thought. The physical arrangement of the meeting, with flags, arc-

[1] op. cit., p. 400.   [2] ibid, p. 404.

lights, and ranks of uniformed party-members is important. The principal speaker stands upon a raised platform with every device employed to focus attention upon him. His appearance may be preceded by some form of repetitive and rhythmic action such as singing or clapping or raising hands at a given signal. This serves to increase the 'social facilitation' for further unison, by heightening suggestibility and reducing the distracting effect of individual difference in the audience. Even the emotion of boredom may be pressed into service. The audience, all agog to see the preacher, the Führer or the great Comrade, may profitably be subjected to a wearisome discourse just sufficient to keep their longing at a stretch, but not so much that they lose interest.

Hitler and others have provided recipes for successful demagogues. Reasoned argument is to be eschewed because it is to the heart rather than to the head that the speaker addresses his appeal. Repetition is recommended, though it is alleged that Mr. Ramsay Macdonald was inclined to over-do it. Imagery rather than abstract argumentation is advised, and all are agreed that the appeal must be couched in terms which are within the compass of the lowest intelligences present. This is no handicap because the higher intelligences under such circumstances are never very firmly seated.

Once rapport is established much may be done. Men may be induced to roll upon the floor, to bark like dogs, to quiver like aspenleaves, and to confess the sins they would like to have committed. The speaker himself is often in Geiger's words, 'a man possessed among the possessed'. He has at his disposal a set of emotive words: Liberty, The Workers, Democracy, Huns, Brotherhood, Any Reasonable Man, Bourgeois, Reds, Jews, Salvation, Blood, Sin, Repentance, to say nothing of The Destiny of Man. The appropriate selection is served up in a tureen of words, garnished with imagery. The speaker himself is in that situation the leader. We are about to discuss the problem of leadership in greater detail, but here it may be observed that this particular leadership-role requires, or at any rate is helped by, such qualities as conviction, vitality, showmanship, a lack of intellectual self-criticism (or a power to control it if it is there) and an adequate vocal apparatus.

CHAPTER V

LEADERSHIP

AMONG animals and birds a dominance-submission pattern or behaviour is often observed in which one animal or one bird is 'dominant' and another animal or bird, or a plurality of them is 'submissive' to the former. Dominance is manifested by successful aggressiveness, getting more food and exclusive access to females, while submission is manifested by crouching, avoidance, waiting for food and, in some cases, adopting a sexually receptive attitude by submissive males. Schjelderup-Ebbe[1] goes so far as to say that 'there are no two individual birds of any given species which, when living together, do not know which of the two has precedence and which is subordinate'. We are familiar with the stories about the pecking order of birds, which corresponds to so many of our own institutional procedures. Baboons fight for dominance, but Maslow[2] tells a story about two 'submissive' baboons who banded together, like the sons in the Freudian original sin, and defeated their master. Among the Hamadryad Baboons described by Zuckerman,[3] the older males lorded it over the females and younger males, and Chimpanzees have been shown to recognize difference in prestige.

Among human children the same difference in conduct is reported as occurring at a very early age by Charlotte Bühler,[4] who tells us that the older of two infants tends to dominate the younger, even though only separated by some three or more months. J. E. Anderson[5] studied the behaviour of fourteen children towards a toy, noting their methods of securing it and preparedness to release it. He, too, found certain differences which could be contrasted as dominant or submissive technique. Moreno,[6] in his Sociometric studies of the generation of groups, noted that infants seem to proceed from isolation (up to twenty to

---

[1] 'Social Life of Birds.' *Handbook Soc. Psychol.*, ed. Murchison, 1935, p. 949.
[2] Maslow, A. H. 'The Role of Dominance in the Social and Sexual Behaviour of Infra-Human Primates.' *J. Genet. Psychol.*, 1936, 49, p. 161.
[3] *The Social life of Monkeys and Apes.* Kegan Paul, 1932.
[4] *Handbook of Child Psychology* [ed. Murcheson, 1933].
[5] Young, K., op. cit., p. 224.   [6] *Who shall survive?* p. 23.

twenty-eight weeks of age) to a 'horizontal' arrangement (up to forty to forty-two weeks) in which they responded to their immediate neighbour. Then a 'vertical' differentiation takes place in which certain children get a disproportionate amount of attention.

McDougall has suggested that such conduct, appearing as it does in animals and young children can only be explained if we postulate two instincts: one of assertion the other of submission. Such an 'explanation' is no explanation at all; it merely means that the dominant are dominant 'by nature', and that the submissive are 'naturally' submissive. Before we accept so desperate a solution we should consider an alternative hypothesis. Seizing, grabbing, and the forcible removal of obstacles are indeed 'natural' ways of getting what one wants. Creatures who are physically larger, stronger, cleverer, and more vigorous than their competitors are likely to win. The weaker cringe or move off in the first place to avoid aggression, but if such conduct is rewarded by ultimate success, this method will become an habitual technique. Surely this is the most plausible account of the difference between dominant and submissive conduct, and renders the specific instinct hypothesis unnecessary.

In humans a more complex cultural training occurs. The vigorous and the less vigorous are no doubt physiologically different, but the more important factor is whether vigorous behaviour or fawning or pleading have been rewarded in infancy. If assertiveness is rewarded it will tend to develop as a personality trait, if it is unrewarded or even punished it will tend to be replaced by alternative and more efficacious techniques.

Dominance and submission, then, we may take as learnt methods of conduct, with the proviso that few people conduct themselves entirely in the one way or in the other. The question now arises: is 'dominance' the same as 'leadership'?

As a prophylactic against the emotional halo that hovers above the word 'leadership', let us consider as a first step the definition of leadership given by LaPiere and Farnsworth.[1] 'Leadership,' they say, 'is behaviour that affects the behaviour of other people more than their behaviour affects that of the leader.' This would seem to cover most, if not all, of the sorts of interacting conduct which tempt us to use the word. The leader is said to 'take the lead', making suggestions which are accepted, showing the way and so forth. Anyone who acts as a model to others is often called a 'leader'. A man whose opinions are

---

[1] op. cit., p. 257.

deferred to, or whose commands are likely to be carried out, is also often so-called. In all these cases what he does affects others more than what others do affects him. But such a definition would also cover instances of active aggression and compulsion. The officer who orders a party of prisoners to go to the gas-chamber certainly affects them more than they affect him, but there is no doubt whatever that he is 'dominating', rather than 'leading'.

The word 'leader', in fact, seems to imply acquiescence on the part of the 'followers' though there may be cases in which the acquiescence is at a minimum and yet we should speak of 'leadership'. We must insist that the goodness or badness of the direction in which the leader leads, the goodness or badness of the model he presents, the goodness or badness of his commands, have nothing to do with leadership as such. The astute organizer of a black market enterprise, the tough guy who engineers a successful coup by bashing an old woman on the head while his companion snatches her handbag, or the girl who introduces her friends to the delights of illicit love are all of them instances of leadership.

Another confusion should be noted. 'Leadership' is often confused with 'leading' when it occurs in such expressions as 'a leading scientist' or 'a leading artist'. In a sense the definition we have quoted might be strained to cover such cases, and of course a 'leading scientist' may be a 'leader' in a different sense, but it is convenient to distinguish, and to put aside, cases in which 'a leading ——' simply implies distinguished, or celebrated. One cannot help feeling that this confusion sometimes lurks in some of the studies that have been made of 'leadership' in schools, where the 'leaders' chosen for comparison with non-leaders *may* be merely successful or distinguished pupils who do not exercise leadership at all. At any rate the title of 'leader' must be backed by evidence of having 'led' in some sense or other.

The distinction between 'dominative behaviour' and what he calls 'integrative behaviour' drawn by H. H. Anderson[1] aims at much the same distinction as we have drawn between dominance and leadership. Anderson relates dominative behaviour to a rigid and inflexible personality structure which reveals internal tensions and provokes external ones. Integrative behaviour, on the other hand, springs from flexibility

---

[1] Anderson, H. H. 'Domination and Integration in the Social Behaviour of young children in an experimental Play Situation.' *Genet. Psychol. Monog.* 19, 1936, p. 341; 'An Examination of the Concepts of Domination and Integration in relation to Dominance and Ascendance.' *Psycholog. Review*, 1940, 47, p. 21, 1. 'Studies in Domination and Socially Integrative Behaviour.' *Am. J. Orthopsych.*, 1945, 15, p. 133.

and a preparedness to co-operate with, and pay attention to, other people. Interestingly enough—and this feature will reappear later—domination tends to call forth counter domination, while integrative conduct elicits a co-operative response. According to this theory the general characteristic of 'ascendency' is too coarse a concept because it fails to draw the important distinction between two fundamentally different ways of being 'ascendent'.

Another study by Pigors[1] makes the same kind of distinction under different names. 'Leadership is a process of mutual stimulation', while 'domination is a process of control in which by the assumption of superiority a person or group regulates the activities of others for purposes of his own choosing'. The only danger in such phrasing is that one should assume that the one is 'better' than the other.

Let us, then, agree that there is some sense in drawing a distinction between 'mere domination' and 'leadership'. We now have to consider the manifestation of the latter. This is by no means easy, and several attempts have been made to bring some order into the enormous variety of leader-follower situations.

We have drawn a distinction ourselves between actual face-to-face situations (which are all we actually 'have'), groups, and the general social background. We can consider leadership under these three headings, but before setting out upon this task we must insist that the leader of a group, and a leader in the general social background only operate in actual situations. The leader writes something or says something and the 'follower' reads it, or hears it, and transmits it to other people as the leader's opinion, command or plan. Always someone writes or speaks and someone reads or hears. Churchill, Hitler, Napoleon or Stalin operate in this way and in no other way. If they were persistently confronted by people who refused to listen to what they said in their offices or bedrooms, or wherever they utter their orders, or if their letters and minutes were destroyed unread, they could not lead. So far as that goes there is no mystery about 'leadership'.

We can, however, look at it from two points of view: on the one hand you have the immediate impact, and on the other hand you have the leader of the group—in the general social background viewed as a relatively persistent source of leadership. In the latter case he is the performer of a number of leadership acts directed towards the members of his group or the people who live in the society, and he is often explicitly thought of as 'the leader' or as an accepted figure of authority.

[1] *Leadership or Domination.* Mifflin, 1935.

With this distinction of perspective we have not reached the end of our tools of classification. We must employ a scale of 'formality', from the 'informal' leader at one end to the 'formal' or conventionally accepted leader at the other. This caters, among other things, for the distinction we commonly draw between the 'real' leader and the 'mere figure-head'.

Bringing these two differentiations together, we have the formal and informal execution of leading in a face-to-face situation; the formal and informal leader-group relationship; and the formal and informal leaders of the larger society. These categories are, of course, over-lapping. The leader in a society may speak to many of its members quasi-face-to-face over the wireless and the formal leader of a group will be placed from time-to-time in direct face-to-face relationship with its constituents. The purpose of the classification is to bring out in as orderly a way as may be the varieties and complexities of the leadership problem.

Formal face-to-face Leader-follower Relationship is present when any person formally recognized as 'leader' addresses anyone who recognizes him as such. The range of instances is enormous. The chairman of the Committee, the officer on parade, the officer who goes first into conflict, the patrol leader in action, the employer addressing his staff and so on. To these obvious cases we must add, to save our classification from becoming too unwieldy, parents admonishing or advising their children, older boys ordering younger ones about, the Chinese grandmother announcing her wishes to her daughter-in-law, a member of the working classes accepting a member of the upper classes as his model.

Now two points have to be made: (1) In so far as real compulsion is explicitly used in any of these cases, we are moving towards the realm of dominance and out of the region of 'leadership'. (2) In any situation in which one person gives orders to another which that other voluntarily obeys, or makes suggestions which he accepts, or serves as a model which he copies, or guides and directs the activity of other people with their consent, we have an instance of leadership. In some formal cases, as illustrated above, the leader exercises his influence at least in part by virtue of his office, though personal qualities may come in as well. In the other cases there is no actual office, but there is rather a cultural ascription of leadership. Children are supposed to obey their parents in our culture, the young are supposed to give way to the old, and there have existed cultures in which wives were expected to obey their husbands. In fact, of course, these cultural ascriptions do not always work. Parents in many situations 'follow' rather than 'lead' their children and older boys may follow the lead of a bright urchin younger than they are.

Informal face-to-face Leader-follower Relationship. In contrast to the situations in which followers follow because of the ascribed or acquired status of the leader we have cases in which there is no such formal status. The man who 'takes control' in a crisis, the person who happens to know the way, the expert who comes to the help of the unskilful, the child who says: let's play so-and-so and gets away with it, are examples. To these, following the lead of LaPiere and Farnsworth[1] we may add the shifting leadership in conversation and the prescribed changes of leadership in a game of cards, or snakes and ladders. It is odd to learn from Landis,[2] who spent a long time listening to conversations in Oxford Street and Regent Street, that an Englishman tends to adapt his conversation to the woman he is with, while in America the women adapt their conversation to the interests of the men. It only goes to show how variable leadership relations are from one culture to another.

Before leaving the social situation aspect of leadership we must notice an important point, and that is that a person who is leader in one situation is not necessarily leader in another. And not only that, but in several studies (e.g. that of Parten[3]) it has been noted that children who are most often followers are also most often leaders when compared with the average. Murphy, Murphy and Newcomb[4] draw attention to another combination of ways of behaving which at first sight would not be expected. They say that aggression often goes with sympathy. The explanation is that leading and following, and vigorous social behaviour, involve a certain degree of social maturity, a recognition of other people, and experience in dealing with them. This of course may lead to inflexible aggressive domination, as Anderson observes, but it is precisely the more lively and vigorous who make the most social contacts and who therefore have the best chance of achieving mature self-

[1] op. cit., p. 386.
[2] Landis, C. 'National Differences in Conversation.' *J. Ab. and Soc. Psych.*, 1927, 21, p. 354.
[3] Parten, M. B. 'Leadership among Pre-School Children.' *J. Ab. and Soc. Psychol.*, 1932, 27, p. 243.
[4] op. cit., p. 523.

confidence in which sympathy and co-operation find their place beside aggressive vigour and leadership.

Group Leader-follower Relationship. When we turn to the group as the unit and consider the relationship of the group to the leader, we have the same distinction between formal and informal leadership. In this case, however, the distinction is not so clear-cut because the informal leader of a group tends to become the formal leader in the eyes of its members. There are, however, numbers of cases in which there are, as it were, two leaders: the official one and the 'real' one. It is, indeed, arguable that in such cases, when the official leader does not in fact lead, we ought not to include him as a 'leader' at all, but this would often involve us in a paradoxical use of language and we must accept the contradictions of the formal leader who spends all his time following.

Instances of formal leadership of groups are easy enough to think of. The captain, the trade union official, the foreman, the teacher, the chairman of the county council, the scoutmaster and the youth club leader are all instances. These are names of official statuses and are 'followed' at least in part by virtue of their office. Krech and Crutchfield[1] have listed the following as functions which all leaders must perform to some extent for their groups. They must act as executives, planners, policy makers, experts, external group representatives, controllers of internal relationships, purveyors of rewards and punishments, arbitrators and mediators, exemplars and symbols.

By 'informal' leader of a group we mean anyone who leads a group not by virtue of his status, but rather by virtue of his personal qualifications alone. The leader of the Corner Boys, the leader of the schoolboy gang, the girl described by Moreno as being in a strategic sociometric relation towards others, being sought after by many who are themselves sought after, so that her influence can spread through a network of favourable dispositions, are examples. The main function of the informal leader is to consolidate the group. In part he may do it by his own personal attractions, in part by planning and devising long-term policies. In an experiment on leadership training, Bavelas and Lewin found that a group which had only been in existence for an hour and had been well organized were anxious to carry on with their own leaders in default of any adult to help them. Such a consolidation in a short time is by no means rare. According to a sociometric study by R. G.

[1] op. cit., p. 417.

Barker[1] the patterns of group relationships found at the first meeting of a group are sometimes very similar to those which exist after the group has been stabilized, and its members better acquainted with one another.

In the informal leadership of groups one has the phenomenon of shifting leadership during the life of the group. This does not necessarily mean the ousting of the leader, but rather the alternating prominence of his action with those of other members. In a study of families in a New York tenement district E. L. Koos[2] has described how the father, the mother, and the children change their position in the hierarchy in times of crisis, when the official 'head of the house' fails to do what the household expect of him.

Leader-followership in Societies. Observation shows that in the wider social background, too, there are official and informal leaders the latter being men of distinction and notoriety whose views and way of life have their effect.

Here, again, the distinction lies between the influence wielded by virtue of office, or some socially accepted qualification, such as class-prestige, and influence exerted by virtue of imputed personal qualities.

These remoter figures get much of their influence through the images built up in the minds of members of 'the public'. The portrait so constructed will vary from age to age and from culture to culture because the prestige-giving properties are not constant. Thus the 'magnificent' man, the 'rich' man, or the 'imperious' man will go down well at one time, but nowadays something more 'folksy' is preferred. The 'great man' should be 'just like ourselves, really', with a few foibles and reputable weaknesses. The military leader must share hardships and have a nice sense of 'mateyness', which does not go 'too far'. We do not require 'sin' of our own great men; we can find vicarious satisfaction in this respect from the legends of historical personages and the portraits we paint of our enemies. 'Simplicity' is what we like. Stalin is renowned for it and when J. D. Rockefeller wanted to redeem his reputation he employed Ivy Lee to construct the picture of a dear old gentleman, fond of the kiddies, and enjoying nothing so much as being quietly wheeled round his garden in a bath chair. A good broadcasting voice is also a help, particularly in times of trouble.

---

[1] Barker, R. G. 'The Social Interrelation of Strangers and Acquaintances.' *Sociometry*, 1942, 5, p. 169.
[2] *Families in Trouble*. King & Crown Press, N.Y., 1946.

In small groups there is a tendency for the informal leader to become the recognized official of a structured group because, as we have noted before, there is a tendency for all groups to perpetuate themselves and to become established as organized entities. In the general society the formal leader tends to become an informal leader in a variety of spheres. His views on reincarnation or diet are listened to with respect once his personal attributes, or those imputed to him, have made an impression which enables him to transcend the narrow competence of his office.

In the above discussion an attempt has been made to consider the problem of leadership from three points of view: the leader in action, the leader and the group, the leader on a national or even a world scale. Other classification of leaders according to the type of their leadership have been made.

Sir Martin Conway[1] distinguishes between the *crowd-compeller*, the *crowd-exponent* and the *crowd-representative*. Better known is Bartlett's[2] classification into the *Institutional* leader, who corresponds to our 'formal' leadership, the *dominant* leader, who appears in time of crisis, and the *persuasive* leader who makes use of promises rather than incitement. Bartlett's analysis of the 'institutional' leader is of particular interest. He calls attention to his remoteness and the barrier which he may erect between himself and the rest of the world. Behind these he can build his legend—often the legend of the 'good' man who knows so little about the wickedness of his subordinates. The chances of a sergeant are better than those of a lance-corporal when it comes to getting a good reputation.

Other classifications by Sanderson, Bogardus, Nape, and Munro will be found in Albig's *Public Opinion*.[3] They illustrate the variety of aspects from which leadership can be viewed, most of which we have considered here.

One fault from which many classifications suffer (e.g. Bartlett's) is a failure to distinguish between the 'type of leader', e.g. formal or informal and the 'technique of leadership', e.g. by domination or persuasion.

Two studies of leadership must be referred to in greater detail. H. D. Lasswell[4] has made an investigation into the different types of leader

[1] *The Crowd in Peace and War.*
[2] Bartlett, Sir F. C. 'The Social Psychology of Leadership.' *J. Nat. Inst. of Ind. Psych.*, 1926, 3, p. 188.
[3] McGraw-Hill, 1939, p. 96.
[4] *Types of Political Personalities.* Publication of the Am. Sociological Society, 1928, 22, p. 164.

who appear in the political arena in America. There are the political boss, the agitator, the administrator and so on, and Kimball Young,[1] quoting from Lasswell and others, has given thumb-nail sketches of these and other types. We need not pay special attention to them, but two points stand out, and they are: the variety of political typology, and the way in which a political régime may almost be said to choose its leaders. In America, for instance, the political régime is such that the shrewd, self-seeking, vigorous political boss has a place, and therefore a niche is provided for people with appropriate qualities, and thus a reward is offered for the possession of them. Under the English system there is no place for such a character. We have here an example of the complex interaction between characteristics valued by the community, the régimes such a community establishes, and the selective action of the régimes on the characters for which it provides opportunities. Lasswell in his *Psychopathology and Politics* gives case histories showing the personality development of his subjects and the way in which political activity provides them with an appropriate outlet. According to Lasswell the formula is as follows: a man acquires certain motives in his private life, he then displaces his motives on to political issues, and rationalizes them in such a way as to translate his operation from the plane of private to the plane of public acts.

The second study is concerned with the effects of 'authoritarian' and 'democratic' leadership. It is the celebrated experimental study of leadership under controlled conditions carried out by Lewin and his colleagues.[2] In 1939 and 1940 two experiments were prepared to see whether there was any characteristic difference in atmosphere and conduct when a club of children of ten or eleven years old was submitted to an alternation of authoritarian, democratic, and *laissez-faire* leadership. In the major experiment four boys' clubs were used, and the leaders were coached in the 'authoritarian' role, which entailed giving orders and no explanations, the 'democratic' role which involved discussion and group decision, and the *laissez-faire* role which was almost entirely passive. Each group had a dose of each régime. The findings are, as might be expected, extremely complex, but certain differences stand out between the responses to democratic and *laissez-faire* control

---

[1] op. cit., p. 234.
[2] Lewin, K., Lippett, R. and White, R. K. 'Pattern of Aggressive Behaviour in Experimentally Created "Social Climates".' *J. Soc. Psychol.,* 1939, 10, p. 271. Lippett, R. 'An Experimental Study of Authoritarian and Democratic Group Atmosphere.' 'Studies of Topological and Vector Psychology.' *Univ. of Iowa Studies in Child Welfare.* No. 16, 1940, cf. Lippett, R. and White, R. K., digest in *Readings in Social Psychology,* p. 315.

and those to authoritarian control. In the democratic atmosphere there was more 'ego-involvement', more talk about 'we', 'us' and 'ours', as compared with what happened under autocracy. The children left to themselves naturally spent a great deal of their time playing, and co-ordinated action was difficult for them, on the whole they did not care for it. Under autocracy there were two alternative reactions. Either the children were cowed into apathy or they responded with aggressiveness. The interesting thing was that the apathetic group showed marked aggression when the change-over occurred to a demo-cratic or *laissez-faire* order. The changes from one régime to another provided evidence for the hypothesis that the conduct of the group is a function of its structure, and not of its components. Under democratic leadership the aggression was almost always low, under autocracy it was either much higher or much lower, and this was the case whenever any given régime was established in any of the clubs.

Of course it must be borne in mind that the general background of the children was the American way of life. Whether the results would have been the same with children brought up under different cultural conditions is a matter of doubt. Furthermore some of the boys pre-ferred the autocratic to the democratic order. This was particularly the case of the son of an army officer who placed a high value on strict discipline. We are reminded of Peak's[1] study of Nazi membership in the course of which he observes: 'Persons reared in the authoritative family, which is common in Germany, typically find greatest security and satisfaction where they are dominated by superior authority on the one hand and where they can, on the other, "lord it over" someone else of lower status.' This means that when generalizing the results of any social psychological experiments, regard must be paid to the back-ground of the subjects; they do not shed it as they enter the laboratory.

Qualities of Leadership. It must be obvious from all that has gone before that an enormous variety of leader-follower contexts can be envisaged. The efficient administrator, the person who says: 'I know the way,' the man who first shouts: '*A bas les* ...,' the boy who says: 'let's ...,' the idol of the forces, and the beloved parson are all leaders in their several ways, and all may well be followers. What wonder then that we find Murphy, Murphy and Newcomb saying: 'An effective, accepted leader in one group may find

[1] Peak, H. 'Observation on the Characteristics and Distribution of German Nazis'. *Pyschol. Monog.*, 1945, 59, 276.

himself a non-leader or even an isolate in another; and few are they whose intra-psychic conflict is so great that they are inaccessible to all forms of social approach.'[1] Even a moron may have his moments. 'It is meaningless,' say LaPiere and Farnsworth, 'to say of a man that he is a leader. A leader in what? Leadership presupposes some sort of skill if only the ability to talk louder and faster than others. But there is no single kind of skill that will give an individual leadership in all kinds of circumstances and over all kinds of people.'[2] 'It follows,' adds Sherif, 'that the leader role is determined not by absolute traits and capacities but by the demands of the situation at hand.'[3]

And yet a considerable number of people have spent a considerable amount of time trying to pin down the qualities of leadership. As a subject for research it has a certain simple charm, but unless the results are related closely to the situation in which they are obtained, they are quite worthless. Terman set the experimental ball rolling in 1904.[4] He took small groups and watched which members were chosen as leaders. The same kind of thing was done by Partridge[5] with a troop of Boy Scouts. Terman found his leader less selfish, more daring, less emotional, better looking, of larger size, and in other ways conspicuous, while Partridge found that leadership among his group went with intelligence, athletic prowess, dependability and appearance. Fleming[6] found that the inter-correlation of traits of seventy-one girl leaders revealed a combination of four traits highly correlated with leadership: fairness, originality, liveliness, and a pleasant voice. Keith Sward[7] wrote a Ph.D. Thesis for the University of Minnesota in 1929 in which he describes how the intelligence scores of 114 college leaders were higher than those of 114 students who were not leaders. We are, however, warned by L. S. Hollingsworth[8] that the intellectual gap between leader and led must not be large. Superior intellects will appeal to those who can appreciate them, but not to the inferior. There is difference of opinion about the advantages of extraversion. Bellingrath[9] found but little difference in extraversion as between

---

[1] op. cit., p. 313.   [2] op. cit., p. 261.   [3] Sherif, M., op. cit., p. 101.

[4] Terman, L. M. 'A Preliminary Study of the Psychology and Pedagogy of Leadership. *Ped. Sem.*, 1904, 16, p. 413.

[5] Partridge, G. D. 'Leadership among Adolescent Boys.' Teachers College Contribution to *Education* 1934. No. 608.

[6] Fleming, E. G. A. 'A Factor Analysis of the Personality of High School Leaders.' *J. of Applied Psychol.*, 1935, p. 595.

[7] Quoted. Young, K., op. cit., p. 229.

[8] *Gifted Children: their nature and nurture.* MacMillan, N.Y., 1926.

[9] 'Qualities Associated with Leadership in Extra-Curriculum Activities in the High School.' Teachers' College Contribution to *Education*, 1930. No. 399.

leaders and non-leaders, while Caldwell and Wellman[1] found that leaders in the junior high school were more extrovert than the non-leaders. As to physique, common experience shows that the puny are not necessarily at a disadvantage in all contexts. However, E. B. Gowin[2] discovered that the people in executive positions that he measured were taller and heavier than the average of the group they controlled. He also found that small-town preachers weighed on the average 17 lb. less and were $1\frac{8}{10}$ inches shorter than bishops.

Happily we need proceed no further because Charles Bird has examined about twenty enquiries into leadership qualities and extracted from them no less than seventy-nine traits; only four (fairness, self-confidence, enthusiasm, and sympathy) are common to four lists, while a sense of humour and extraversion get mentioned five times and initiative six times. All the traits are socially approved ones, which would seem to indicate that the investigators kept good middle-class company.[3]

Surely all this lack of agreement is explained by the fact that the qualities of the leader are selected by the needs of the led; it is therefore quite ridiculous to expect to find that the qualities of a junior schoolboy leader are the same as those required by a group of strikers. Of course such considerations must not be pushed to extremes. A small, shy, deaf man will not be so likely to find himself in a leadership role as one less small, less shy, and with all his faculties. Again, in a class society, boys and girls brought up to give commands to and receive obedience from others will have a degree of self-confidence which will enable them to take the lead on certain occasions more readily than people who have not had such advantages.

It might be possible to define a set of social situations and then assess the relative advantage of certain groups of characteristics with respect to leadership in them. Indeed, this has been done in brief by Kimball Young for military leadership,[4] and it is the basis of any effective selection of officers whether for the army or for industry. You can, of course, invent ideal groups and the ideal and devoted leaders who will lead them gently but firmly along a route of which you approve. The danger is that you will end up with the vision of a starry-eyed clean-living athlete, who is retarded at the adolescent phase of his develop-

[1] Caldwell, O. W. and Wellman, B. W. 'Characteristics of School Leaders.' *J. Educ. Research*, 1926, 14, p. 1.
[2] *Executive and His Control of Men*. Macmillan, N.Y. 1915.
[3] Bird, C., op. cit., p. 379 [cf. Albig. *Public Opinion*, p. 102 for another list].
[4] op. cit., p. 344.

ment, and who is by no means everybody's cup of tea. If you want to lead people in one direction rather than another you must pay attention to *their* tastes rather than your own. It is no use looking for the 'born leader'; he is happily never brought to birth. Furthermore it is no use looking for your leader in the nursery because 'we do not have records as yet which would give any basis for saying that children who are leaders in the nursery could be leaders in high school or college, or even for that matter in kindergarten the following year'.[1]

In conclusion we must consider some general features of leadership; the choice of the leader, the relation of led to leader, and the problem of training.

From what has been said it will appear that the selection of the leader and the relation of led to leader are closely related, but we can profitably emphasize first one and then the other side of the relationship.

Leaders may be self-chosen, elected, appointed or reach their position by a conventional system of seniority. It will be observed that no distinction is being drawn here between various types of leaders; some methods of selection apply more to informal, others more to formal kinds, and in the sense in which we are using the expression, leaders who are elected and appointed may be 'self-chosen'. This expression is intended to refer to the leadership motivation of the leader himself, which made him put himself forward. These motives are obviously very varied. In a co-operating group, the leader may put himself forward because he knows something which the whole group wants to know and which it is necessary for them to know if their project is to be successful. More interesting is the leader who puts himself forward more persistently, because any such will be men who find in leadership a compensation for inferiorities which rile them. They will be of the more domineering kind and will tend to resent criticism and avoid discussion. Their insecurity displays itself in a sensitivity about their position and the marks of deference that go with it.

Of the other methods of selection mentioned above, little need be said, save to draw attention to cases where selection by appointment is accompanied by some kind of formal examination. Such examples of formal leadership are of interest because the appointing body only has before it candidates already selected by examination and the type of

[1] Murphy, Murphy and Newcomb. op. cit., 523.

examination—usually a written one—may eliminate candidates who would in point of fact be good leaders in the posts for which they would like to apply. Are there, it may be asked, other methods?

During the Second World War a technique was elaborated for the effective selection of officers by placing candidates in test situations. Leadership in general was thought of as 'the measure and degree of an individual's capacity to influence—and be influenced by—a group in the implementation of a common task'.[1] This means that leadership is regarded as a general capacity to participate in group-activity and that, provided there is no neurotic bar to such participation, anyone may be a leader in an appropriate group-situation. For their own purposes, the War Office Selection Board (WOSB) analysed 'group effectiveness' into three aspects: (*a*) ability in the purely functional aspect of the job; (*b*) group-cohesiveness or ability to bind the group in the direction of the common task, and (*c*) stability or ability to stand up to frustration. Any effective leader must have some capacity in all these directions, but situations will clearly differ in the degrees to which they demand high level power of planning, organization and execution, or the inspiration of group-solidarity, or stability in the face of stress.

In order to estimate the candidate's abilities a battery of tests were devised which included 'leaderless group tasks' in which groups of eight men were told to carry on a discussion or carry out a task of some difficulty so that the 'group-cohesion' man, who brings everyone into the field, can be differentiated from the 'group-disrupter' who is all out for personal prestige, and the 'group-dependent' and 'isolate' who are the hangers on, the 'passengers', or those who simply will not play at all.

This situational technique with appropriate modification was subsequently adopted by the Civil Service Selection Board (CSSB), but in that context 'group-effectivism' was not such an important matter, or, at any rate, had to display itself in a different kind of situation (e.g. in committees).[2]

Closely associated with problems of leader-selection by means of practical tests, is the problem of leadership training. It will be seen in a few moments that there are many people who relish the follower-role,

[1] Harris, H. *The Group Approach to Leadership-Testing.* Kegan Paul, 1949, p. 19. cf. Vernon, P. and Parry, J. B. *Personnel Selection in the British Forces.* Univ. of London Press, 1949.
[2] cf. Wilson, N. A. B. The Work of the Civil Service Selection Board. *Occupational Psychology,* 1948, 22, p. 204.

not necessarily in all situations, but in some. It is obvious that certain co-operative tasks require guidance and co-ordination. We have seen already that dictatorial methods arouse resentment. From this it follows that it is important for the army, for industry and for many other occupations to secure and train people who will perform the operation of leading effectively. G. L. Freeman[1] and his colleagues have devised real life situations for the purpose of training leaders. Bavelas,[2] in an experimental study of the training of personnel to supervise children found that the results of the trained supervisor in terms of participation in group activities and enthusiasm was markedly better when compared with the controlled groups under untrained supervisors. As may be expected of a follower of Lewin, the contrasted methods of leadership were authoritarian, which was to be eliminated, and democratic which was to be taught. Bavelas makes the point—and it is one which follows from the Lewin, Lippett and White experiment—that the training itself must be done democratically if the trainees are to become democratic. Bradford and Lippett[3] insist on the acting out of roles as being the most effective method of training.

From the point of view of the followers the leader may fulfil a variety of functions. He may simply know the way. Of greater importance are the cases where the leader is the objective of emotional fixation. The yearning of potential followers after a leader, and the adulation they are prepared to accord him has been frequently noted. Le Bon,[4] for instance, writes: 'Men gathered in a crowd lose all their force of will and turn instinctively to the person who possesses the quality they lack.' Their choice, according to him, is not a good one. 'The leaders are more frequently often men of action, than thinkers.... They are especially recruited from the ranks of those morbidly nervous, excitable, half-deranged persons who are bordering on madness.'[5] Michels,[6] too, as we have already mentioned (p. 64), notes the importance of the leader. 'The need of the masses, even organized masses, to be directed by leaders, accompanied by a vivid hero-worship, is unlimited.'

All this is undoubtedly due to the fact that the leader answers the prayers of his followers. He acts as an ideal of all they would like to be,

---

[1] Freeman, G. L. *et al.* 'The Stress Interview.' *J. of Ab. and Soc. Psychol.*, 1942, 37, p. 427.
[2] Bavelas, A. *Morale and the training of Leaders.* In *Civilian Morale* (ed. Watson). Houghton, 1942.
[3] Bradford, L. P. and Lippett, R. *Supervisory Training for Group Leadership.* Cambridge Publ. Research Centre. Grp. Dynamics, 1945.
[4] Le Bon. op. cit., p. 135.   [5] ibid., p. 134.   [6] op. cit., p. 77.

though very fortunately we do not all want to be the same kind of thing. The basis of the leader's attraction is the personality structure of the followers, and the degree of inflation which the leader undergoes is a measure of the unstable gases which he has generated within them. If the follower wants a father-substitute, if he wants security and protection, if he wants to avoid responsibility—the leader will be so tricked out in his imagination as to supply the need. Of course any given leader may fail, and be reduced to the plight of the man who was stopped by the police in Paris in 1848 during some commotion, and protested: 'Let me go. I must follow that crowd over there. I am their leader.' Or worse may happen. The attitude towards the father is ambivalent, and an unsatisfactory leader may become the objective of detestation. When the 'right' person is found there is established a complex system of relations forming a two-fold pattern. 'With the leader there is a person-to-person identification, marked by obedience and veneration. With one's fellows there is identification in mutual love and sympathy.'[1] Though one cannot accept Freud's[2] account of group solidarity as a satisfactory explanation for all loyalties, his theory that it is based upon an aim-inhibited love-relationship to the leader, combined with a renunciation of privileged access by all the followers, who are thus identified with one another and see to it that no one jumps a claim, covers a very large number of cases. This is particularly noticeable when 'fairness' is considered an essential quality for leadership, and when favouritism and 'teacher's pettery' are held in detestation.

Leadership, then, is essentially a two-way affair. Sometimes the use the leader makes of his opportunities is stressed and we have a 'great man' theory of historical events. Sometimes the fact that he could not have any opportunity at all, unless his general policy was in accord with the aims, and ambitions of his followers, is emphasized and we have a 'mass-movement' theory of history. Neither view is right in isolation, the intentions and the ability of the leader, and the climate of opinion in which he operates must always be taken in conjunction with one another.

---

[1] Young. K. op. cit. p. 253.
[2] *Group Psychology and the Analysis of the Ego.* International Psychoanalytic Library, No. 6, 1922.

CHAPTER VI

PUBLIC OPINION

EVERY child born into a community is confronted by gestures and vocalizations of approval and disapproval made by the people about him. At first, of course, the world is apprehended in terms of his own needs and desires and signs of approval and disapproval are only significant when directed towards his own conduct. Gradually, however, he becomes aware of approval and disapproval directed towards certain sorts of conduct, certain sorts of people, and certain sorts of symbols. The tones of approval and disapproval with sounds or certain key words: 'good', 'bad', 'right', 'wrong' have already gained significance in his intimate relationship with those who look after him. As time goes on these tones and these words are linked with such words as 'God', 'Church', 'Communism', 'Free Trade', 'Nationalization' and so forth. In G. H. Mead's[1] formulation, he 'takes' the attitude of the 'others' into himself, and develops a more or less coherent system of attitudes towards a variety of topics.

The consistency of his attitudes, such as it is, derives from three sources which interact with one another: the general tendency towards integration and meaningfulness, such needs as are satisfied by holding the particular attitude he comes to hold, and the relative consistency of the attitudes which he hears expressed about him, to which he in turn makes his contribution.

We can therefore view the general topic of *attitudes* from two angles. We can attend to the attitudes of particular people and groups of people or we can consider the general atmosphere of attitudes which we call 'public opinion'. In this chapter and the next we shall take them in the opposite order; 'public opinion' first, and then 'attitude research'.

It is difficult to put into exact terms what is meant by 'public opinion'. The trouble lies with the word 'public', which is used in many different senses, and which we want to use to refer to an essentially shapeless construct. We might, of course, define 'public opinion' on any particular issue at any particular time in terms of the people

[1] See p. 126.

who actually have an 'opinion' on that issue at that time. We should, indeed, be landed with a multitude of 'publics', which is what we are after, but one fundamental feature would be absent, and that is the coherence of certain sorts of opinion held by the same people over a long or short period of time. We must start, rather, with the groups of people who form the 'publics' first. Everyone will recognize the fact that as he passes from one company to another he may find himself in totally different atmospheres. Things that are approved by one set of people are disapproved by the next, and issues which agitate one set are unknown to, or indifferent to, another. It is not, however, easy to define the groups. In the first place there is the general society which is usually what is referred to by the word 'public', when it appears in the newspaper, or when it is 'polled' by the Institute of Public Opinion. There are certain issues about which every member of the nation may be expected to have an 'opinion'. 'There exist,' says Dicey,[1] 'at any given time a body of beliefs, convictions, sentiments, accepted principles and firmly rooted prejudices, which taken together make up the public opinion of a particular era, or what we may call the reigning or predominant current of opinion.' The issues are numerous; political, religious, moral, scientific and so on, and any model we make of the 'public' in this large sense must be somewhat vague because not every person has an 'opinion' on all the topics about which there may be said to be a 'public opinion'. All we mean is that as members of the 'general public' people may be expected to have views on a number of issues.

The views may be homogeneous, or they may be divided. This second possibility introduces us to the notion we may call 'sectional public opinion'; that is to say the various publics, within the large one, which are united by holding one view about an issue which divides the great public. Thus we may think of Conservative circles, left-wing circles, religious circles, atheistical circles, business circles and working class circles.

A third break-down of the general public is into groups united by some common characteristic and having special interests of their own which may be too parochial to be included in the purview of the extended public or may be special aspects of wider issue. Religious bodies such as the Roman Catholics, the Baptists and the Plymouth Brethren would be included, so would the professions, such as doctors, lawyers, estate agents and personnel managers. In this category of 'group pub-

[1] *Law and Opinion in England*, 1926, ed., p. 19.

lics', as we may call them, we can include the more specific publics constituted by a village, a town, a factory, a school, a university and so on.

We can therefore, at the risk of gross over-simplification, think of a man as being a member of the 'general public', and as such taking a line about various topics of 'public' interest. We can think of him as belonging to conservative circles, business circles, or religious circles, and thus sharing many of the views of these sectional publics, and, moreover, belonging to more than one of them. Lastly we may think of him as a constituent of one or more groups which have special interests about which he will be likely to have an 'opinion' in accord with or contrary to the 'predominant current'.

The smaller groups, too, may be homogeneous upon certain issues and divided upon others. The village may be unanimous in their disapproval of the parson, but divided on the subject of the village hall. The inhabitants of a town may be united in their feeling of civic pride, and countenance no criticism, but there may be two views about extending its boundaries. Doctors may agree on matters of professional etiquette and disagree about the National Health Scheme. So we might go on, but enough has been said to indicate the kind of analysis to which the construct 'Public Opinion' can be subjected.

We have, however, not done with analysis. The issues about which 'opinion' is held vary in what we might call 'depth'. We can distinguish between 'topical' issues, issues which persist over a period of time, and issues which are so fundamental, in the etymologically correct sense of the word, that they have ceased to be 'issues'.

Before expanding this classification something must be said about the word 'opinion', which has so far been written with inverted commas. The word is really too intellectual a one for our purpose and reminds us too much of the contrast drawn between 'knowledge' and 'mere opinion'. Dicey, with his collection of words: 'body of beliefs, convictions, sentiments, accepted principles or firmly rooted prejudices' gives us more what we want. The single word that best fits is, perhaps, 'attitude'.

'An attitude,' writes G. W. Allport[1], 'is a mental and neural state of readiness, organized through experience, exerting a direction or dynamic influence upon the individual's response to all objects and situations with which it is related.' Kimball Young[2] defines it 'as a learned

---

[1] 'Attitudes' in *A Handbook of Social Psychology*, ed. Murchison. Clark Univ. Press, 1935, p. 810.
[2] op. cit. Kegan Paul, 1946, p. 122.

and more or less generalized and affective tendency or predisposition to respond in a rather persistent and characteristic manner, usually positively or negatively (for or against) in reference to some situation, idea, value, material object or class of such objects, a person or group of persons.'

When we talk about the 'opinion' of a public we are not really thinking of their 'opinion' in the intellectual sense, as one might be interested in the opinion of a biologist on the Lysenko issue; we are thinking about the 'line' they take for or against some matter of dispute. Of course the distinction between what we mean by 'attitude' and what we mean by 'opinion' cannot be closely pressed, but the more emotionally charged, the more people *mind* about a matter, the more we would use the word 'attitude', the less they mind, the more they are 'purely' intellectual, the more we would use the word 'opinion'. When considering the 'line' taken by the 'public', it is the emotional content in which we are interested and so we would prefer to speak of 'attitude' rather than of 'opinion'.

An attitude, then, is a predisposition to respond, and we go back to our rough classification of topics about which publics of various kinds are ready to exclaim, agree, disagree, condemn or approve. Some, we said, are topical. That is obvious enough. It may be an event of national importance, like a pit disaster, which elicits a unanimous cry of: 'How dreadful!' It may be a matter about which we hear conflicting views. But the wonder may not last even as long as seven days.

This is different from the class of issues which, in various specific forms, last for a considerable period. Such are the issues which divide political parties, and long-drawn-out topics, like the propriety of marrying one's deceased wife's sister, or the advisability of disestablishing the Church of England.

A similar distinction can obviously be drawn when we think of small-scale publics. The village is scandalized at the birth of an unexpected illegitimate baby, and forget it in a week, while they return to their perennial brooding dislike of the local R.D.C.

We added a third category, and here join issue with one of the best known writers on the subject. In his book—*Public Opinion*, William Albig[1] defines opinion as 'an expression about a controversial point'. This would exclude 'public opinion being shocked at' such and such an episode—an expression very frequently and intelligibly used—unless there were obviously two ways of looking at it. It may be that Albig is

[1] McGraw-Hill, 1939, p. 5.

influenced by the intellectual flavour of the word 'opinion' which has already been noted. At any rate we want to include unanimous expression of shockedness as well as divided views.

There is, however, another issue. What are we to say about such fundamental matters as the universal condemnation of slavery, the universal approval aroused by expressions containing the word 'freedom', the universal agreement about compulsory education? Are these attitudes to be included in 'public opinion'? One good argument against their inclusion is that they are not often the subject of discussion, and it is in terms of discussion that 'public opinion' exists. If everyone happened to hold exactly the same view upon a topic and never mentioned it at all so that no one knew that anyone else had ever thought about it, there could be no sense in saying there is a public opinion about it. That is perfectly true, but the issues which have just been mentioned are not quite in that extreme category. No one seriously discusses the revival of the slave trade, or abolishing compulsory education and yet it is 'common knowledge' that slavery is wrong and compulsory education right. There are two arguments in favour of including these basic assumptions in Public Opinion and they are: (1) all changes and shifts of opinion occur in terms of them in the sense that they provide a mental 'set' or 'frame-work of reference' in terms of which attitudes operate. (2) There is a gradual shift from the controversial level to the assumption level. Dicey[1] was scandalized at the notion that old age pensioners should be allowed to vote; would any but philosophers think twice about the matter now? At one time compulsory education was a 'live issue', but to say that it is 'dead' is not to say that no one has a view about it; we all, or nearly all, agree.

On these grounds we include in our construction of the contents of Public Opinion, accepted standards and policies as a basis upon which the structure of Public Opinion at any moment is built. But that picture is too static. 'Public Opinion,' said Cooley,[2] 'should be regarded as an organic process and not as a state of agreement about some question of the day.' If we want an image we might think of the sea with its eddies and currents. Deep below the surface slowly moving changes are taking place, on the surface itself we have an ever changing scene with here and there a wave foaming and disappearing and a continuous surge and swell as of conflicting forces.

[1] op. cit., p. xxxiv.
[2] Cooley, R. H. *Social Process*, 1918, p. 378.

We must therefore cater for two opposing aspects of public opinion: its stability and its change.

By *stability* is meant that as we move from one region of the extended public to another we find the same sorts of things being said in appropriate circles for a fairly long time. As we move from conservative circles to left-wing ones, from the manor to the 'local', from the company of intellectuals to the company of football fans, we can calculate more or less on the sorts of things we can say and the sorts of things our 'social sense' will bid us repress. Such stability can be accounted for by the tendency to conform which we have acquired in childhood, and by the satisfaction almost everyone feels in having a point of view, which means that once it is acquired it is only abandoned with reluctance. We do not expect uniformity, of course; there are plenty of eccentrics or 'deviates', and it is a good thing there are because they are partly responsible for change, but on the whole the rewards of conformity are such that change tends to be resisted. This holds for all publics, great and small.

Change, however, certainly occurs, as we have already noticed, and nowadays opinion-attitudes change fairly rapidly. Things unsayable in our youth are now taken for granted; the ox that is ever ready to sit upon our tongues shifts his seat further and further to the left.

Furthermore it is not only the contents of opinion-attitudes that change; there are changes in range and significance. With modern methods of communication—newspapers and radio—and with improved education more people have heard of more of the same things so that the general public has increased in scope and size. By change of 'significance' is meant change in the location of important opinion. From the point of view of national affairs—what is going to happen—not all opinions are equally significant. When the workers were unorganized their attitudes, perhaps of grumbling acceptance of their fate, were not as important as they are now. When power was in the hands of the landowners, *their* opinions were obviously more important than were those of their tenants. At the present moment, in 1952, almost everyone is against war, but what we all really want to know is the attitudes of the small governing circles in America and in the Kremlin.

We can have no close-up view of how these changes come about. To get it we should have to listen-in to millions and millions of conversations, because that is where public attitudes, which are mere dispositions, come to reality. We can, however, get some idea of the chief factors which are responsible for change. 'A change of belief arises, in the main,' wrote Dicey, 'from the occurrence of circumstances which incline the majority of the world to hear with favour theories which, at one time, men of commonsense divided or distrusted as paradoxes.'[1] Among these 'circumstances' four stand out.

(1) *News.* You cannot have an opinion-attitude about nothing. Change in attitude may therefore occur when people are told something new which concerns them, something which, to use the expression of Sherif and Cantril, impinges on their 'ego-involvement'. This is where the importance of newspapers and the radio as formative influences comes in. Newspapers have been aptly described as the 'principal agenda-making body for everyday conversation',[2] and therefore, the way they present the news, whether they 'splash it' or hide it, the emotive language they use in presenting it, and the slant they give, are all far more important than editorial comment.

Changes of attitudes are often registered by the barometers of opinion published by the Institute of Public Opinion and other similar bodies. Cantril[3] has worked out such a barometer with respect to the attitude of America towards the Second World War between the declaration in 1939 and the entry of America in 1941.

The significance of emotive words is well known and we have watched the spectacle of rebels turning into provisional governments and governmental forces turning into 'reds'. Sargant,[4] in America, made a curious study of 'emotional stereotypes' used in the *Chicago Tribune* and the *New York Times*: what one paper calls 'Government Witch hunting', the other calls 'Senate investigation'; 'the dole' has as its alternative, 'Hire relief'. In this connection many people will remember how the perfectly sensible attempt by the Minister of Information to find out the attitude of the public in war time was almost ruined when an adversary referred to 'Cooper's snoopers'.

An entertaining series of changes in news presentation has been collected from the *Moniteur* of France in March 1815 when Napoleon left Elba.

9 March: 'The monster has escaped from the place of his banishment.'

10 March: 'The Corsican ogre has landed at Cape Juan.'

---

[1] op. cit., p. 23.   [2] PEP. *Report on the Press*, 1938, p. 33.
[3] Cantril, H. *Public Opinion* in *Readings in Social Psychology*, p. 591.
[4] *Sociometry*, 1939, 2, 69. cf. *Readings in Social Psychology*, p. 558.

11 March: 'The tiger has shown himself at Gap. Troops are advancing on all sides to arrest his progress. He will conclude his miserable adventure by becoming a wanderer among the mountains.'

12 March: 'The monster has actually advanced as far as Grenoble.'

13 March: 'The tyrant is now at Lyon. Terror seized all at his appearance.'

18 March: 'The usurper has ventured to approach within 60 hours' march of the capital.'

19 March: 'Bonaparte is advancing by forced marches, but it is impossible that he reach Paris.'

20 March: 'Napoleon will arrive under the walls of Paris to-morrow.'

21 March: 'The Emperor Napoleon is at Fontainebleau.'

22 March: 'Yesterday evening His Majesty the Emperor made his public entry and arrived at the Tuileries. Nothing can exceed the universal joy.'

(2) 'News', however, is not the only factor which causes change. There are also *changes in actual experience* which may not come to us by remote communication or by word of mouth, but in the very business of living. Such changes include changes in economic conditions, floods, earthquakes, an outbreak of some infectious disease, the evacuation of slum children and so on. An example of research into the effects of unemployment on attitudes is that carried out by M. O. Hall[1] on employed and unemployed engineers in or near New York. He found, as one might expect, that 'occupational morale', i.e. the attitude towards such propositions as 'Ambition is all right for youngsters, but a man gets to realize it is all the bunk', was lowest among the men who were in the worst economic positions. The unemployed groups were naturally less conservative than the employed. Such an effect of unemployment and distress is a commonplace. It is widely held that prosperity is a bulwark against Communism or, *per contra*, a condition in which men at last come to their senses.

(3) *Changes in Practice.* We may divide behaviour into symbolic and non-symbolic, roughly corresponding to the distinction between what we say and what we do. It is important to recognize, as LaPiere and Farnsworth[2] point out, that the content of these two kinds of behaviour sometimes conflict: the verbalizations elicited in one

---

[1] Hall, M. O. 'Attitudes and Employment.' *Arch. Psychol.*, 1934. No. 165.
[2] op. cit.

social context do not always enable us to predict with accuracy the non-symbolic behaviour in another, and vice versa. Sometimes this is conscious, sometimes it is not. Sometimes our actions are more reputable than what we say, sometimes they are less reputable. All this is a matter of common experience and provides us with pleasurable opportunities for criticism. On the other hand it is equally obvious that there is a close correspondence between what we do and what we say; in fact the occasions when the correspondence breaks down are commented upon precisely because of their comparative rarity. This being so it is not surprising that when circumstances arise which cause people to act differently they gradually get used to the new ways and change their attitudes accordingly. We have already referred to the grumbles about compulsory education; people were compelled to send their children to school, often against their will, but now that this has been going on for over eighty years the attitude of the public towards education has changed. Undoubtedly large-scale changes in regime are ill-received by many people at first, and the older ones may never get over it', but the younger members of the community soon adjust themselves and—this is our contention here—the very fact of acting out the new modes of behaviour, though not the only factor by any means, helps to bring about a change in attitude.

It was found many white American soldiers changed their attitude towards Negroes after fighting side by side with them in companies containing Negro platoons.[1] It appears that the National Maritime Union of seamen in America has always insisted on equal rights for coloured men, even to the point of expelling white seamen who refuse to sail with Negroes under conditions of equality. An investigation carried out among seamen in New York City in 1946 revealed that the prejudice against Negroes was significantly lower among members of the National Maritime Union than among members of other unions, and that it was lower for those who had sailed five or more times with Negroes than in the case of those who had only shipped once or twice with a mixed crew.[2]

Of course it may be argued that the policy of the union selected seamen with low prejudice, and that we do not know how long the change of heart lasted when the soldiers came back from the war, so that such cases as these, taken by themselves, do not weigh very

[1] U.S. War Department Report, No. B-157. Summarized in *Readings in Social Psychology*, p. 542.
[2] Krech, D. and Crutchfield, R. S., op. cit., p. 514.

heavily. They should not, however, be lightly dismissed. We cannot divide people up into an active part and a thinking and feeling part standing one against one another. We should rather put it that when a man voluntarily or involuntarily changes his habits and mixes with different people, his world is by so much changed. A constituent in the 'new world' may, in a perfectly obvious sense, be the same as a constituent of the 'old world' but its *role* may have changed and that is very often what matters. The Negro seen as a mate is significantly different from a Negro seen as an economic rival. A workman raised to the position of foreman takes a new view of administration and discipline. In fact *one* of the ways of changing people—not always successful to be sure—is to induce them to *do* something different as William James reminded us long ago.

The reason why this effect of change of practice has been elaborated is because of its practical application in the reduction of inter-group tension[1] and in other fields as well.

(4) The final factor responsible for change is one we have discussed before: leadership. The writings and utterances of politicians, publicists, playwrights, moralists, scientists and religious teachers have their effect from time to time, though not by any means as often as they would wish. We have already mentioned the controversy about the 'great man', as the exponent of what is already there or the innovator. He is both in the sense that if the climate of opinion is entirely uncongenial to his message it will wither, and yet his message *may* completely change our perception of the world and our attitude towards it. We have only to think of Marx and Engels and Freud to appreciate that. The great religious teachers, too, must have spoken to men ready to listen; we know that the ethical teaching of Jesus of Nazareth was already in process of formulation before he was born.

Before leaving 'Public Opinion' there are three features of it to which we must refer: its 'language', its cumulative history, and one of its methods of propagating news.

The linguistic feature is the tendency to develop convenient models by means of which we are able to classify unfamiliar particulars and thus adjust ourselves to them. These models are called 'stereotypes' and ever since Walter Lippmann[2] called attention to them in 1922 they have been the subject of a considerable amount of discussion.

---

[1] cf. William, Robin M. 'The Reduction of Inter-group Tension', 1947. Soc. Sc. Res. Council, N.Y. *Bulletin* 57, p. 69.
[2] Lippmann, W. *Public Opinion*. Harcourt Brace, 1922.

We respond to the present in terms of its similarity with the past and in our world of impersonal contacts we develop private stereotypes as rough and ready methods of pigeon-holing. The 'dear old man', the 'chits of girls' in government offices, the 'prim old maid' the 'nosey rozzer' are all of them stereotypes in which individual differences are masked by identity of role. Our outfit of stereotypes is enriched, and in a subtle way impoverished, by the uses we get from tradition, from conversation, from books and from cartoons. Thus all Jews are wily, all natives are 'like children', all Scotsmen are dour, all Chinese inscrutable and, in some circles, all nonconformist grocers put sand in the sugar. It all comes about in the interests of order and as a method of providing ourselves with frames of reference into which we can fit new presentations with ease. The function of stereotypes is quite clear. It is a great saving of energy if we have a stock response to a variety of stimuli. If, in our brief contacts, whether direct or indirect, we had to weigh up the merits of each case, and consider the difference between, say, one business man and another we should soon get muddled. It is much easier to think of all business men as 'hard-faced oppressors of the workers' than to be forced to judge some of them favourably and condemn only a few.

The net result of this saving of energy is, however, often deplorable, and that is why the word 'stereotype' has on the whole a pejorative sound. Doubtless if all our stereotypes were in terms of approval, like the stereotype of 'workers' in left-wing circles, we should often be taken in but we should at least tend to behave decently. Unhappily most of our stereotypes are unpleasant and provide us with targets for abuse and socially acceptable objectives of aggression.

Among the experiments on stereotyping mention must be made of the pioneer study of S. A. Rice.[1] He showed a group of students pictures of Herriot, Krassin, a bootlegger, a steel magnate and five more, and he provided them with a list of terms such as labour leader, senator, financier, Bolshevik, etc. The subjects were to say which term applied to which photograph. Krassin, portrayed with winged collar and Van Dyke beard was judged a senator or a premier far more often than a Bolshevik. They guessed right more often than not about the bootlegger because he was photographed in a heavy overcoat with a turned-up collar, wearing a cap, and smoking a cigar, but some of the subjects thought he was a manufacturer.

Another method of investigation is that employed by Katz and

[1] Rice, S. A. *Quantitative Methods in Politics.* Knopf, 1928.

Braly.[1] They gave a list of characteristics and asked the subjects to say which applied to particular national groups. A high proportion voted the Germans 'scientifically-minded', Negroes 'superstitious', Turks 'cruel', and English 'sportsmanlike'.

Newspapers and magazines have been combed for evidence in America,[2] to show how stereotypes are reinforced by what we read and also what we see on the stage. A study of rapid change in stereotyping when political conversion demands it, is that of Whitman Barrow[3] who compared the image of the United States presented to the readers of *Izvestia* during the period January–June 1945 with that depicted between January and June in 1947. In the earlier period the Americans were praised for their war effort, in the later one they were abused for their imperialism. Similar quick changes could be found in the newspapers of other countries if we compared their references to the U.S.S.R.

From this it will be seen how heavily reinforced stereotypes are, how convenient they are not only as energy-saving devices but also for purposes of propaganda, and therefore how hard they are to break down.   They may change their colour, but they remain global images for focusing praise or blame without awkward discrimination.

The 'cumulative history' of public opinion has to be recognized if we want to understand how it develops. Public opinion at the present time, in all its large, and small-scale, manifestations, is the resultant of a long history, the beginnings of which we can never discover. Ever since our remotest ancestors communicated in symbols it has a continuous history of innumerable conversations, writings and speechmakings. It has been shaped down the ages by the four factors noted above, by new events, by changing circumstances of living, by changes in conduct and by influential men and women. In order to understand the attitude of English social classes towards one another now, we have to remember that for hundreds of years our aristocracy has received recruits from below, and that younger sons and their descendants have had to fend for themselves. To understand public opinion in Canada now we have to consider the history of the relation between the French and English Canadians. To appreciate the attitude

[1] Katz, D. and Braly, K. W. 'Racial Stereotypes of One Hundred College Students.' *J of Abs. and Soc. Psychol.*, 1933, 28, p. 280.
[2] cf. Klineberg, O. 'Tensions Affecting International Understanding.' Soc. Sci. Res. Council, *Bulletin*, 62, 1950, p. 94.
[3] Barrow, W. 'Izvestia looks inside U.S.A.' *Pub. Op. Quarterly*, 1948, 12, p. 430.

of the French towards the Germans we have to remember their conflicts. According to Tannenbaum[1] the attitude of the white Americans towards the Negroes is different from that of the Brazilians because in the latter country the conquerors had a tradition of slave law which made the slave a 'beneficiary of the ancient legal heritage', whereby slavery became 'a mere matter of an available sum of money for redemption'. In North America, on the other hand there was no such provision and the only way of dealing with the Negro slave was to make him a chattel, which placed him on a lower moral and biological plane than his owner.

With different histories behind them, and different predicaments confronting them, it is not surprising that publics differ in their opinions about the 'same thing'. It was found, for example, in 1946 that sample populations in the United States, Great Britain and Australia responded differently to the question: 'Do you believe Russia is just building up protection against being attacked—or is she trying to make herself the ruling power of the world?' 48 per cent. of the Australians and 58 per cent. of the Americans plumped for the second alternative; only 26 per cent. of the British took the same view.[2]

One point about public opinion, which has been mentioned from time to time in this account of it, deserves to be emphasized. We must avoid the mistaken view, which language imposes on us, that public opinion is a body of dispositions lying in wait for events or cross-questions to stimulate them into activity, as though the events and questions were neutral. The events and the questions are themselves apprehended in terms of the existing attitudes of those in whose lives they take their place. They are perceived as they are because the attitudes are what they are.[3] We do not hear of an event in cold blood, as it were, and then after a pause take an attitude. The very interpretation of the words we hear is coloured by the attitude in which we are when we hear it. We may hear it in a neutral attitude and having heard it our attitude may change. We may hear it in an attitude with which what we hear conflicts, we are surprised and, again, we may change our minds. But if what we hear is vague we may, and frequently do, interpret it to suit our attitude and even add a bit here and there for the sake of plausibility. It is obvious that this sets limits and dictates techniques to the propagandist as we shall see later.

[1] Tannenbaum, F. *Slave and Citizen*. Knopf, 1947.
[2] Klineberg, O. *Tensions Affecting International Understanding*, p. 131.
[3] For an elaboration of this hypothesis see Krech and Crutchfield: *Theory and Problem of Social Psychology*, McGraw-Hill, 1948.

Rumour. The propagation of news through the medium of conversation has one form of special interest and that is: rumour. It is perfectly plausible to call any story that passes from mouth to mouth a 'rumour' because in the passing it is liable to undergo certain changes. There is, however, convenience in keeping to the slightly disparaging sense of the word, and to contrast stories that *merely* pass from mouth to mouth, with those which are also checked against some official verification.

One of the most interesting experimental investigations into the changes which take place as a story passes from one person to another is to be found in Bartlett's *Remembering*.[1] He performed a series of experiments which can easily be repeated in the form of a parlour game. Take a simple drawing or a story and let a person look at it for a short time, or read it, as the case may be, then tell him to reproduce it and hand his reproduction to the next person. He repeats the process and *his* reproduction is handed on until you have the series of reproductions of the whole group and then, when they are spread out, you can see the progressive changes that have been made. In the picture there is a tendency for meaningfulness to creep in, for peculiar elements either to disappear or to be exaggerated, and for a somewhat formalized version, which may be quite unlike the original, to become relatively stable. Much the same happens with stories. Again, the end products tend to be more rational than the originals, if, as was the case with Bartlett's material, they are bizarre. On the whole there is simplification, while certain incidents tend to become dominant.

Much the same result was found by Northway[2] and by Allport and Postman in their *Psychology of Rumour*.[3] They speak of 'tendencies to level, to sharpen, and to assimilate to personal and cultural contexts'.

So much for the formal changes. The problem of rumour, however, is not only concerned with them. The story itself, if it is to live in competition with other stories, must have some dramatic quality, it must have an air of authenticity, and it must have some relevance to the social context in which it is to spread.

LaPiere and Farnsworth,[4] directing their attention as they always do to the social situation itself, point out that rumour battens on conversational rivalry. This is because, in a congenial situation, conver-

---

[1] C. U. P., 1932. cf. *Readings in Social Psychology*, p. 69.
[2] Northway, M. L. 'The Influence of Age and Social Group on Children's Remembering.' *B. J. Psych.*, 1936, 27.
[3] Holt, 1947.   [4] op. cit., p. 412.

sation is the principal activity 'and rivalry stimulates each individual to do his best, which means doing such things as introducing a topic which is of general interest to the members of the group, telling a better story than the one just told, or adding details to that story.' This bid for transient leadership partially accounts for the inclination to embroider with gay colours, and to avoid spoiling a good tale for the sake of a few facts. It also accounts for the way in which phrases which tone down the factual appearance of the story get left out.

Naturally people like stories which fit in with their preconceived ideas and attitudes. In an experimental study by G. H. Smith,[1] for example, it was found that when confronted with a set of pro-Russian and anti-Russian statements, students who were themselves pro-Russian believed the former, while students who were anti-Russian believed the latter.

We associate rumour and its spreading with times of crisis; and not only with crisis, but also with the unknown. If a new-comer arrives in a village he will be talked about, and before he knows where he is the confirmed bachelor will find himself divorced and possibly a fugitive from justice. It is the unknown round which rumour centres, not only for the obvious reason that *ex hypothesi* there is no official information, but for a more significant reason. We come again to our 'frames of reference'. Faced with the unknown, the mysterious, the only way to cope with it is to fit it into some scheme or other. If there is no official one, we make one up. That is why rumour spreads in times of crisis, or aboard a ship bound for a destination unknown to the passengers. The need for a stable frame of reference *is* a crisis situation. People do not know, as they say significantly enough, 'where they are'. The function of rumour is not merely to give a conversational claimant the chance to take the lead, rumour also serves to provide a sense of 'knowing' in a situation in which official knowledge is not available. If we are in need of allied help and wonder what we are going to do without it, a bit of white paint on a station platform may soon look like Siberian snow, and we are comforted to hear that train-loads of brave Russian soldiers have come to our rescue. If there is a critical contest going on in our minds between the peaceable principles which we have been taught and the attitude of hostility expected of us in war-time, we are liable to feel 'at sea' and uneasy. If, under these circumstances we 'know for a fact' that our enemies are responsible for such

---

[1] Smith, G. H. 'Beliefs in Statements labelled Fact and Rumour'. *J. Abs. and Soc. Psych.*, 1947, 42, p. 80.

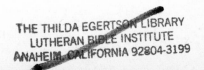

barbarities as make them unworthy to live, then, as we say, 'there can be no question about it', which is just what we want.

Rumour, then, manifests certain formal modifications as the story spreads abroad; it spreads at all, partly because people like to show themselves 'in the know', and partly because 'knowing' is comforting in an unstable situation. During the World War I 'rumour clinics' were established in America to find out what rumours were current. Then attempts were made to counteract them. It has, however, been somewhat sourly observed that the 'rumour clinic', particularly when it makes use of the radio, 'spreads more rumours than it kills'.[1]

Assessing Public Opinions. We must now turn to the problem of assessing public opinion and attitudes. When this is done on a large scale the techniques of Public Opinion Polls are used. These organizations have multiplied enormously during the last few years. In America there is the National Opinion Research Centre, the American Institute of Public Opinion—the Gallup Poll, the Fortune Poll (Elmer Roper). In England there is the British Institute of Public Opinion.

For opinion research in other countries the student should consult the *International Journal of Opinion and Attitude Research* which first appeared in 1947.

The questions asked may be provided with appropriate multiple answers, such as 'Yes', 'No' and 'Don't know' or they may be 'open-end' questions which allow of a more elaborate answer. Obviously the opportunities of questioning will partly determine the type of question used. The first type can be answered in a trice, the second requires something approaching an interview. Both types can be combined; the 'open-end' question may be used in a pilot survey, which helps to determine the multiple-answer question. A small sample of those who have been 'polled' in the survey proper may then be further questioned with the 'open-end' method. The phrasing of questions is an important matter especially when it is about a subject on which people are likely to feel impelled to give a 'respectable' answer, such as questions about cleaning their teeth and going to church.

The 'population' questioned depends on what one wants to find out. One may want to assess the attitude and likely behaviour of the adult population of a country or to discover the prevailing habits of house-wives. Any 'population', however, raises the problem of sampling. If the 'opinion' of the population as a whole is wanted, a 'quota' sample

[1] Krech, D. and Crutchfield, R. S. op. cit., p. 415, n. 8.

may be questioned. The 'quota' sample is made up of people having characteristics which are deemed relevant to their attitude on the question they are going to be asked. The proportions in which these characteristics are represented in the sample correspond to the proportion in which they are represented in the larger population to which inference is going to be made. The relevant characteristics are usually age, sex, geographic location, and socio-economic status. The number of persons who have to be questioned is surprisingly small, a sample of 500 often giving about as good a basis of inference as one, two or three times the size, though the numbers required will of course, depend upon the nature of the enquiry.

Another device for assessing the attitudes of special groups of people is to use panels of respondents who are prepared to give their views on expert or general questions. The same people may be invited to answer questions on the same subject at intervals and thus we may gauge the effect of changing events upon the section of the public they represent.

In this country Mass Observation was established in the 1930's employing somewhat less formal methods with a panel of correspondents and observers who take note of spontaneous conversation as well as the answers to questions.

The reliability of the inferences which are drawn depends on the reliability of the sample, on the honesty of the answers, and on the maintenance of the relevant conditions under which the answers were given. Assuming that your sample is statistically valid, that the questions are unambiguous, you may infer that to-morrow or next week the corresponding proportion of the public you have sampled will say the same kind of thing or behave in a certain way unless there has been some change of external circumstances which alter the situation. It is here that difficulties arise at election time. You take your poll, and if the election is to-morrow you may predict with considerable accuracy but if the poll does not take place until next month something you have not bargained for may occur to upset your calculations; it might be the actual publication of your prediction.

The value of Public Opinion Polls as distinct from their accuracy, is a disputed matter. For the purposes of market research and such-like special interests they are obviously useful. It is the polls on matters of political policy that come in for criticism. In favour of the polls it is said that they help to tell us what other people think and thus widen our understanding of our neighbours. It is also said, perhaps with greater plausibility, that by means of public opinion polls people in executive authority are able to keep their fingers on the public pulse, and therefore be better placed to satisfy their requirements. Against the polls it is urged that, unless they are carried out and presented with proper statistical safeguards, they mislead the public and their representatives.[1] Even if they are not misleading, may they not, it is asked, emasculate leadership and impede independence of thought? If the leader wants to continue his leadership he might follow the polls rather than use them as a guide to the putting into practice his own policy more efficiently. The danger is no doubt there, and we all know that the seats in the bandwagon are well upholstered, but so far there is no evidence on either side of the Atlantic of a slavish acceptance of Mr. Gallup's verdicts as pointing the way to salvation.

---

[1] cf. Young, K. op. cit., p. 455.

CHAPTER VII

ATTITUDE RESEARCH

THE assessment of the attitudes of individuals and small groups presents special problems. It is of the order of laboratory research, while public opinion polling is field-work. Of course the technique used in attitude research may well be used in Opinion polls, but the purpose of the former is seldom the same as the purpose of the latter. The distinction is important because it is not always borne in mind, even, one suspects, by some of the investigators themselves. Hundreds upon hundreds of students have answered attitude questionnaires; indeed even the most hardened reader of journals may be forgiven if he sometimes finds an incipient yawn to stifle. But from few, if any, of these studies, can an inference be drawn to a wider public, because the samples are not representative. Attitude research is concerned with different matters: (1) the construction of questionnaires, (2) the nature of the attitudes measured by them, (3) the factors that have influenced these attitudes, and (4) the ways in which they may be changed.

1. There are, broadly speaking, two types of questionnaires. One is designed to measure attitudes of like or dislike towards other groups—'social distance' as it is sometimes called; the other to measure attitudes or complexes of attitude towards issues such as war, religion, communism, or companionate marriage.

A preference ranking can, of course, be obtained by asking the subject to list a series of items in order of preference. Another, and more satisfactory method is that known as the method of paired comparisons. Each item is shown with every other, and a score of preference results from which a rank order can be constructed. This method was used, for instance, by Guilford[1] who investigated the nationality preference of about 1,100 students in seven colleges. The English, German, French and Swedish come top in that order, and Hindus, Negroes, Chinese and Turks come last. This was somewhat similar to the results

[1] Guilford, J. P. 'Racial Preferences of a Thousand American University Students.' *J. Soc. Psychol.*, 1931, 2, p. 179.

of a study by Thurstone[1] in 1928. He used a different method of scoring and was able to measure not only the order, but the distance between the nationalities. According to his calculation his subjects put the English several rungs down the ladder from themselves, then at about the same distance from the English they put the Scots, but the Irish are only a little way farther off.

These methods, however, are not questionnaire methods. Bogardus[2] was the pioneer here, with a series of questions about each of forty different nationalities, which he put to 1,725 Americans. The questions are in the form of categories of distance: (1) admit to close kinship by marriage, (2) admit to my club as personal chum, (3) admit to my street as neighbour, (4) admit to employment in my occupation, (5) admit to citizenship in my country, (6) admit as visitors only to my country and (7) exclude from my country. As an illustration let us take the Swedes. 45·3 per cent. would accept them as kin, 62·1 per cent. as chums, 75·6 per cent. as neighbours, 78 per cent. as co-employees, 86·3 per cent. as fellow citizens, 5·4 per cent. only as visitors and 1 per cent. would exclude them altogether. The Turks fare much worse, as they always do on all the ranking systems in America; they have an 'unspeakable' stereotype, though (or perhaps because) very few Americans have ever clapped eyes on one. At any rate only 1·4 per cent. could stand them as kin, 10 per cent. as chums, 11·7 per cent. as neighbours, 19 per cent. as fellow-workers, 25·3 per cent. as fellow citizens, 41 per cent. would have them as visitors only, and 23·4 per cent. would not have them in the country at all.

Two hundred and two of Bogardus's sample were Negroes and Mulattoes. Their preferences were different. The French fare best after the Negroes and Mulattoes themselves, then the Spaniards, English, Canadians, Mexicans in that order, leading up to White Americans whom 6 per cent. would be prepared to harbour as relations.

The Bogardus social distance scale produces remarkably consistent results in America, both geographically and over a period of time. One general factor would seem to be a distaste for foreigners. E. L. Hartley[3] used the Bogardus distance scale with the introduction of three purely imaginary nationalities: the Danireans, the Pireneans, and the Wallonians. At one University the Chinese and Arabs were thought less well

[1] Thurstone, L. L. 'An experimental study of Nationality Preferences.' *J. Genet. Psychol.*, 1928, 1, p. 405.
[2] Bogardus, E. S. *Immigration and Race Attitudes.* Heath & Co., 1928. Condensed in *Readings in Soc. Psych.*, p. 503.
[3] Hartley, E. L. *Problems in Prejudice.* King's Crown Press, 1946.

of than the Pireneans and Danireans, but rather better liked than the Wallonians. At other Universities a different place was allotted to them. A manipulation of the results seemed to show that some people were more hostile to foreigners in general than others, from which Hartley concluded that 'the degrees of tolerance expressed by individuals is a generalized function of the individual and is not completely determined by the specific group towards which the attitude is directed'. Anyway, none of them had ever heard of a Pirenean before.

A somewhat similar social distance scale was applied by S. C. Dodd[1] to some 170 freshmen of different nationalities in the American University of Beirut. They were asked to indicate the degrees of intimacy they would tolerate with fifteen national, eleven religious, three educational, and five economic groups. The variety of preference was, as one might expect, very great, but it is interesting to note that 'attitudes associated with religious affiliation towards those of other faiths seemed to transcend in strength those identified with all other groupings'.[2]

The measurement of attitudes towards general issues is a rather more complicated business. It involves the collecting and evaluation of appropriate statements with which the subject has to indicate his agreement or disagreement. Supposing you are trying to measure a person's attitude toward war, you have to find a set of statements ranging from those with which only the most bellicose would agree to those which appeal only to the ardent pacifist, with intermediate positions between the extremes. The ideal would be a scale of 'equal appearing intervals', and it is this kind of scale that Thurstone devised. The technique is as follows. First you collect or make up some 100 statements which you think cover the range from one extreme to another. Next you persuade some 200 or 300 judges to sort the statements into eleven piles, the ones most favourable to, say, war or the church, are placed in pile 1, those least favourable in pile 11 and the others on some intermediate pile. Every statement is now given a position 200 or 300 times, and you can easily discover its 'median' position, which is the one where half the judges consider it more favourable and half less favourable than that particular position. You are now faced with an obvious difficulty; in some cases the judges will agree fairly well, in others they will disagree and

---

[1] Dodd, S. C. 'A Social Distance Scale in the Near East.' *Am. J. of Sociol.*, 1935, 41, p. 194.
[2] Murphy, Murphy and Newcombe. op. cit., p. 1,010.

the range of piles on which the statement has been placed will be large. This means that that particular proposition has an ambiguous value and must be rejected. It is easy enough to measure the dispersion of allocations and to choose those with a small dispersion, and exclude the others. Now you have a number of judgments left, each with their median scores between one and eleven, and you can pick out about twenty-two statements whose scores differ by about the same amount. The score of any subject who registers his agreement with any of the statements is either the arithmetic mean of the scores of the statements he endorses or the median of his endorsements.[1]

One complaint against scales constructed by this method is that some people endorse statements in various positions on the scale, that is to say their last endorsement along the scale does not imply endorsement of all the statements up to that position. Guttman[2] suggests that this must mean that more than one attitude is operating. He has therefore devised a technique for purifying scales so as to achieve unidimensional ones. Unfortunately this may lead to a group of statements closely centred round one theme and this may prejudice its usefulness, because, after all, when one is testing a subject one does at least want to secure and keep their interest and this is not easy to do if you keep on asking him whether he agrees with statements which vary very little in content.

Another complaint is that the Thurstone method is time-consuming and requires the collaboration of too many preliminary judges. Lickert,[3] therefore, suggests the employment of a simpler method. He too takes a number of statements thought relevant to the attitude to be measured. The subjects have to indicate for each of them whether they: strongly approve, approve, are undecided, disapprove, strongly disapprove. The score for each individual is the summation of the categories he registers, numbered 5, 4, 3, 2, 1. The next step is to see how far the judgments on each statement correlate with the total score and eliminate those which do not show a substantial agreement. Tried out on the material of a scale to measure attitude towards war, constructed by Thurstone and Droba, Lickert found that his method

---

[1] Accounts of this technique will be found in many text-books on Social Psychology. There are particularly clear ones in Bird's *Social Psychology*, p. 151 f. and Krech, D. and Crutchfield, R. S. *Theory and Problems of Social Psychology*, p. 214 f.

[2] Guttman, L. The Quantification of a Class of Attributes: a Theory and a Method of Scale Construction in Horst, P. *et al. The Prediction of Personal Adjustment.* Soc. Sci. Res. Council. No. 48, 1941 and 'A Basis for Scaling Qualitative Data.' *Amer. Sociol. Rev.,* 1944, 9, p. 139.

[3] Lickert, R. 'A Technique for the Measurement of Attitudes.' *Arch. Psychol.,* No. 140, 1932.

correlated highly with the results obtained by the Thurstone method.

By one method or another a number of attitude scales have been constructed to measure attitudes to the Church and anti-Semitism, attitude towards Negroes, attitudes to war, conservatism, and radicalism.

The question is sometimes raised as to whether these verbal tests really test attitudes effectively. Several issues are involved here. In the first place there is the simple issue of wilful cheating. So far as this is concerned there seems to be agreement that people take the questions seriously, but when delicate issues are at stake the safeguard of anonymity must obviously be used. Another and more important issue is one we have already touched on when considering Opinion Polls: does a verbal test give any indication as to how the people tested would behave under other circumstances? Sometimes it is possible to have a rough check on the results of the verbal test if they can be correlated with a person's political and religious affiliations.

However, one must always bear in mind that a person's conduct is always influenced by the social situation in which he is, and this means that inferences from an attitude test are bound to be precarious. Children's verbalization about honesty and dishonesty do not, alas, always entitle us to predict their behaviour in situations where dishonesty provides a solution to their problem. LaPiere[1] conducted an investigation into the race prejudice of the English and French in which he found that the French were less prejudiced than the English. He also found, however, that hotel-keepers and restaurateurs often expressed racial prejudice, but nevertheless received coloured guests.

Of course there is a considerable amount of consistency between what we say and what we do but one cannot always foresee the special features of the social situation which will make all the difference in overt behaviour.

These formal questionnaire methods are not the only ones used in the study of attitudes; projection techniques and clinical interviews are also employed. Proshansky,[2] for example, gave his subjects pictures to interpret in his investigation into attitudes towards labour and found that the same picture would be 'seen' differently by people holding attitudes sympathetic or the reverse towards labour problems. The use of the clinical interview and projection technique are illustrated by a study of anti-Semitism undertaken by Frenkel-Brunswick and

[1] LaPiere, R. T. 'Race Prejudice: France and England.' *Social Forces*, 1928, 7, p. 101.
[2] Proshansky, H. M. 'A Projective Method for the study of Attitudes.' *J. of Abs. and Soc. Psychol.*, 1943, 38, p. 39.

Sandford[1] in the University of California. The results of this investigation are of great interest. They show how much our attitudes towards other 'races' are influenced by unconscious motivations, repressed aggressiveness, and attitudes towards parents. Broadly speaking the highly prejudiced had not solved their intimate problems as efficiently as the more tolerant. 'Ethno-centrism' may, indeed, be a neurotic symptom.

2. As to the nature of attitudes the point of interest is not so much the definition of attitudes which is a fairly simple matter, as the relation between an attitude towards one topic and an attitude towards another. Are there, in fact, constellations of attitudes? In the first place it depends on the topic. If, for example, you were to have two sentences: 'Negroes ought to be segregated in trains' and 'Negroes ought to use separate public conveniences', it would not be surprising if both evoked the 'same attitude' of prejudice against the Negro. To avoid language which implies that an attitude is a thing inside us, we may say that with respect to any topic of fairly narrow range a group of propositions can be compiled such that assent or dissent to any one is very likely to be accompanied by assent or dissent to all the others. They must all, however, be of the same generality or specificity. Cherrington,[2] for example, found that the internationalist scores of his subjects varied according to the specificity or generality of the questions asked before and after lectures, conferences, and/or a summer at Geneva. A difference remained, though internationalism was increased.

This, again, is not surprising, partly because of our lack of logic, but partly because 'circumstances alter cases'. Another source of high correlation between attitude scores may come from people who have been brought up in an environment in which two attitudes, say very favourable towards the Church and very unfavourable to Communism are part of the atmosphere of the environment. This, indeed, was found by Newcomb and Svehla[3] in their elaborate study of inter-family resemblances in attitudes. They found that 'in families where parents agree closely and where their church and communism scores are closely correlated, the children show a reliably higher church-communism correlation (.74) than do unselected children.'

[1] Frenkel-Brunswick, E. and Sandford, R. N. 'Some Personality Factors in Anti-Semitism.' *J. Psychol.*, 1945, 20, 271, and the 'Anti-Democratic Personality.' *Readings in Soc. Psychol.*, p. 531.

[2] Murphy, Murphy and Newcomb. op. cit., p. 954.

[3] Newcomb, T. M. and Svehla, G. 'Inter-family Relationship in Attitudes.' *Sociometry*, 1937, cf. Murphy, Murphy and Newcomb. op. cit., p. 1,037.

All this is obvious enough and it is not of great importance. What is more interesting is the question: are there constellations of attitudes which merit some general name such as 'conservative' or 'radical'? Attitude tests which claim to measure 'radicalism' have been constructed, but they have come under a fire of criticism from, for instance, Quinn McNeman,[1] who complains that: 'Not only do various scales constructed to measure conservatism-radicalism seem, by inspection, to be getting at different things, but even within a given scale there may be a mixture of kinds of "conservatism-radicalism".' This confusion is partly due to the general ambiguity of such popular terms as 'conservatism' and 'radical'. It is more prudent to see whether there are any clusters of proposition, not dealing with the same subject matter, but such that they all tend to be either accepted or rejected together.

A method of finding this out is the method of 'factorial analysis', which is an extension of the mathematical measurement of correlation. You give a number of tasks to your subjects—in this case requiring them to register their agreement or disagreement with a set of propositions. You then inter-correlate all the results. This provides you with a table of correlation between every pair of questions. As an example we can take H. J. Eysenck's investigation published in the *International Journal of Opinion and Attitude Research*[2] in 1947. His questions consisted of forty statements. Among them are No. 1. 'Coloured people are innately inferior to white people'; No. 12. 'Ultimately, private property should be abolished and complete socialism induced;' 13. 'Conscientious objectors are traitors to their country, and should be treated accordingly'. Now the correlation between 1 and 12 was $- \cdot 31$, between 1 and 13: $+ \cdot 39$ and between 12 and 13: $- \cdot 33$. That is to say, a person who accepts No. 1 is likely to reject No. 12 and accept No. 13, though it clearly does not happen in every case. The examples given are, on the whole, what we might expect. The other seventy-seven statements dealt with abortion, Jews, companionate marriage, equal pay for men and women, and so on. It may be seen from these instances that it is on the cards that there are, indeed, groupings of topics about which people tend to feel alike. The next task is to apply the mathematical technique of factorial analysis[3] to the whole table. By this technique items that 'go together' are grouped in such a way that

[1] McNeman, Q. 'Opinion—Attitude Methodology.' *Psychol. Bull.*, 1946, 43, p. 289.
[2] H. J. Eysenck. *Primary Social Attitudes*. op. cit., 1947. Vol. 1, p. 49.
[3] cf. Burt, Sir C. *Factors of the Mind*. Univ. of London Press, 1940.

we can express ourselves by saying that one 'factor' is at work, though it must be remembered that this is really only a device for talking about the 'going together', which is what we are really concerned with. When one 'factor' has been 'extracted' we can by further manipulation remove its influence so as to see whether another factor is also operating. We can then remove that and see whether that leaves another grouping and so on.

Eysenck 'extracted' two factors of significance, both of them bipolar, i.e. indicating two opposed attitudes. 'On the one hand, we find a belief that private property should be abolished, that the death penalty should go, that Sunday observance is old-fashioned, that Jews are valuable citizens. . . . On the other hand, we have a belief that nationalization is inefficient, that compulsory religious education is desirable, that Jews are too powerful in this country. . . .' This factor Eysenck calls 'R'. He gave his questionnaire to subjects who avowed themselves Conservative, Liberal or Socialist and the difference in their agreements and disagreements with the statements does lend some colour to the use of the expression 'Radicalism-Conservatism' as an appropriate name for this 'factor'. The second factor is not nearly so easy to name. 'Here we have,' he writes, 'on the one hand a belief that we must go back to religion, that birth control is illegal, that the double standard of morality is bad, that religious education should be made compulsory, that our evils have moral causes, that we should give up our sovereignty, abolish the death penalty and attempt to cure criminals rather than punish them. The opposing set of beliefs approves of companionate marriage, wants to alter divorce, licensing and abortion laws, considers the Japanese cruel by nature, the Jews too powerful, war inherent in human nature, Sunday observance old-fashioned, compulsory sterilization desirable, women and coloured people inferior, and C.O.s traitors to their country.' Such a pair of contrasting groups is very odd. 'There is,' says Eysenck, 'no convenient label in common language for this factor.' There certainly is not. Perhaps, he suggests, it might be called 'theoretical/practical', or it may be an instance of James's 'tender-minded, tough minded' distinction, though neither of these expressions is really very satisfactory. Eysenck labels it 'T'. He also gives evidence that after the two 'bi-polar factors' are removed, there are two other 'factors', one uniting 'conscious feminist' approvals and disapprovals, the other, 'humanitarian ones'.

This example of the application of 'factor analysis' to the study of attitudes shows the advantages, and the difficulties of the method. Some 'progressive' factor has been detected by other investigators,[1] and usually the groupings and contrasts are fairly intelligible. Sometimes, however, it happens, as we have seen, that groupings emerge which are not easy to interpret. At the same time factor analysis is the only efficient technique for bringing out of a complicated system of correlation the ones that are grouped together in agreement and disagreement.

Hadley Cantril,[2] using a questionnaire about wartime issues, claims to extract three 'factors : reasoned determination to achieve the objective; confidence in leaders; and satisfaction with traditional values.

3. The next question with which the study of attitude is concerned is the question of what circumstances influence attitudes. This is obviously closely connected with the next subject to which we shall have to turn: how attitudes can be changed, but for convenience we separate the two topics, and consider first the more general question.

Taking a broad view of the whole subject it can, of course, be said that the attitudes we have are determined by the culture in which we live, but that does not tell us more than that we should expect people of different cultures to feel differently about certain very general issues. Within any given culture, however, there are plenty of differences. Can anything be said about the circumstances which have caused these? The answer is: not very much, because any given person's attitudes are a product of what has been put before him and his own responses to it.

High correlations have been found by Newcomb and Svehla, in a research to which we have already referred,[3] between the attitude of children towards religion and communism and that of their parents, particularly when the parents agree in their attitudes towards both topics, but they did not, in this investigation, show so high a correlation with their parents on the subject of war. It may be that the phrase 'brought up to believe' this or that covers certain topics but not others. One can envisage households in which there is a strong pro-Church and anti-communist atmosphere, which may be absorbed by the children; one can envisage strongly pacifist homes with the same result. On the other hand it may be (and this is a subject for further investigation) that attitudes towards war, an eventuality which impinges differently upon the young from the way it presents itself to the

---

[1] cf. Vernon, P. E. *The Assessment of Psychological Qualities by Verbal Methods.* Ind. Health Research Board. Report No. 83, H.M.S.O., 1938, p. 34 f. and p. 108.
[2] *Gauging Public Opinion*, Princeton, 1945.   [3] p. 110.

old, are not usually the subject-matter of parental indoctrination. In the same investigation it was found that on the whole parents agreed most in religion, and that siblings did not agree with one another as much as they did with their parents. The correlations were slightly higher at the lower occupational levels than in the higher ones, and decreased a little with increasing age.

All this fits in with our expectations, but it does not always work as Hirschberg and Gilliland[1] found when they administered Thurston's 'Attitude toward God' scale, Stayner's 'Opinions about Depression' scale and Lomas's 'Attitude toward the New Deal' scale to 200 students and their parents. They found a correlation of only $+\cdot 29$ in attitudes towards God, $+\cdot 59$ in attitude towards the New Deal and $+\cdot 42$ in attitude towards the depression. Perhaps the four years that have separated the two investigations have made the difference, more likely it is a difference in the samples used, and the issues involved. It is found that on the whole if parents are internationalist-minded, or if one or both are foreign born, the children are likely to be internationalist.[2] Morgan and Remmen,[3] who attempted to find out how the depression had influenced student opinion, found that they were more liberal in 1934 than in 1931 and that the correlation between them and their fathers was $\cdot 68$, the students being more 'liberal' than their parents. The same thing has been found elsewhere: e.g. by Stagner,[4] who found that, in spite of a 'liberal' shift, the children still stuck to the political party of their parents. The significance of this last allegiance can only be appreciated when we know more about the role of the political parties in America as compared with this country. Furthermore some slight evidence has been brought forward[5] to show that extreme radicalism tends to go with a high degree of antagonism against the father.

Finally we must mention the work of the Horowitzes.[6] They reported that in a Tennessee village the smallest children played freely with members of either race, so that any idea of a 'natural' antipathy goes by the board. They found, however, that playing with Negro

---

[1] Hirschberg, G. and Gilliland, A. R. 'Parent-Child Relationship in Attitudes.' *J. Ab. and Soc. Psychol.*, 1942, 37, 125.

[2] Krech, D. and Crutchfield, R. S. op cit., p. 180.

[3] Morgan, C. L. and Remmen, H. H. 'Liberalism and Conservatism of College Students as affected by the Depress.' *Sch. and Soc.*, 1935, 41, p. 780.

[4] Stagner, R. 'Trends in Student Political Thought.' *Sch. and Soc.*, 1936, 44, p. 602.

[5] Murphy, Murphy and Newcomb. op. cit., p. 941.

[6] Murphy, Murphy and Newcomb. op. cit., pp. 239 and 371 discuss an unpublished study. Also Horowitz, E. L. 'Development of Attitude towards Negroes.' *Archives of Psychology*, 1936, No. 104. cf. *Readings in Soc. Psychol.*, p. 507.

children soon earned them a 'whipping,' and on cross-questioning the children readily admitted that their parents forbade them to play with Negroes, warning them against all kinds of ills if they did. In the later investigation on children in New York, Georgia and Tennessee this was confirmed. The method here was not observation of behaviour; pictures of white and coloured children were presented to the little subjects and they had to rank them by the paired comparison method, and pick out the ones they would like to play with, etc. The children examined had sometimes had pleasant experiences with Negro children, but it seemed to make no difference; 'The attitudes,' says E. L. Horowitz, 'are chiefly determined not by contact with Negroes, but by contact with the prevalent attitude towards Negroes.' To which we may add a story told by Sherif. 'One day a little girl answered the door and then ran to her mother saying that a lady wanted to see her. Her mother went to the door and when she returned she said, "That wasn't a lady, dear. That was a Negro. You mustn't call Negroes 'ladies'."' Such an experience is likely to be even more potent than a 'whipping', and when such experiences do not occur we may expect a lessening of anti-Negro prejudice. We cannot therefore be surprised that in the Horowitz material: 'A small group of communist children tested in New York City showed no apparent prejudice against the Negro.'

It is well known that the prejudicial attitude against Negroes is extremely strong and widespread in America. This is because it is inculcated not only by verbal indoctrination but also by actual disciplining of conduct and by the fact that the attitude finds support almost everywhere, both in the sorts of things said by white people about Negroes, and also by the very spectacle of Negroes living in conditions conspicuously less commodious than the whites. Such all-round corroboration makes for a formidable amount of reinforcement.

Other attitudes met with in the home are by no means universally supported, and therefore the attitude of a child with respect to a given topic may very well differ from that of his parents. To begin with, most attitudes find their expression verbally rather than in other forms of overt conduct. The child hears expressions of disapproval against war, but it does not have to do anything about it. In other words the child does not 'understand the meaning of' issues like war and communism in the practical kind of way that he understands about not playing with a Negro child. We can therefore understand the relatively high correlation between children's attitudes towards the Church and those of their parents—there is, after all, Church-*going*.

On the other hand the child comes across other attitudes about war, church, communism, and the like, held by boys and girls and adults with whom he is allowed to consort. Therefore the influence of the parents on such matters is not without its rivals, and personal factors come into play. An attitude towards a subject may be accepted precisely because it is *not* that of the parents. It may also be accepted because it fits in with some acquired emotional disposition, as we saw in the case of Frenkel-Brunswick and Sanford's study of Anti-Semitism.[1]

Krech and Crutchfield[2] discuss a thesis by E. L. Queener on internationalism. He compared attitudes on internationalist issues with the general life history of his subjects and found that in some cases sheer adaptability to the dominant group played a part and sometimes more recondite 'personality motifs'. In a study of anti-Semitism in a London borough it was found that pronounced anti-semitic attitudes were associated with personal maladjustment.[3]

Many studies have been made to find out whether sex or age are correlated with attitude.[4] Girls for example are reputed to be more religious and less 'liberal' than boys. Such generalizations, however, do not have much value. Attitudes are not things which are sex-linked, or automatically change with age. They are acquired in the process of social intercourse. If the role of a girl is different from that of a boy, then the attitude of the girl towards a *relevant* issue will probably be different from that of the boy. Such sex-differences as there are cannot therefore be universalized; they are tied to the relevant cultural circumstances appertaining when the investigation took place.

The same is true of age. Common observation, as well as laborious study, shows that in some societies adolescents are more 'liberal' than their parents. We think of adolescence as a time when traces are kicked over. However, experience in Germany under the influence of National Socialist doctrine should make us pause. In a society in which it is traditional for young people to think of adult views as 'old fashioned' they will be subtly encouraged to be 'new fangled'. Hostility to the home may play its part, but a persistent climate of 'progressiveness' is probably more important, taken in conjunction with the surrounding circumstances, such as the chances of getting jobs and the particular

[1] cf. p. 110.   [2] op cit., p. 155.
[3] Robb, J. H. 'A study of Anti-Semitism in a Working Class Area.' Ph.D.Thesis. Univ. of London.
[4] cf. Murphy, Murphy and Newcomb. op. cit., p. 914 f. Bird, C. op. cit., p. 177.

prestige-giving opinion of the moment. On the other hand the need for a feeling of security, the pleasure of playing a part in a noble enter-prise, and the general enjoyment of large-scale conformity, may be harnessed to attitudes far more 'conservative' than those of the adult generation. There is no youthful liberalism which sets in with the physiological changes of puberty; what will set in is a function of a number of variables which are extremely difficult to identify.

So far as intelligence and attitude are concerned, much the same considerations apply. 'Religious and political radicalism . . . do show consistent though usually low positive correlation with the common measure of intelligence.' So write Murphy, Murphy and Newcomb,[1] but they interpret this finding in terms of cultural circumstances. 'This may mean no more' they say, 'than that those with greater capacities are more sensitive to currents moving in a particular place and time.' On the whole what is called 'radical' in these studies is a readiness to consider complexities in the social fabric and difficulties in traditional opinion, which the 'conservative' is inclined to disregard. This, however, can only be done if an enquiring mind is rewarded, or at least not penalized. It may take more wits to be 'radical', but if there is no opportunity for discussion one's wits may be used for other purposes.

More significant as determinants of attitudes are such characteristics as socio-economic status. On many issues this makes but little differ-ence, but Stagner[2] found, as we should expect, that business men made higher 'Fascist' scores than professionals and members of labour or-ganizations, while L. D. White[3] found that people of low economic status, and also those who were foreign born, showed a preference for public employment as compared with private employment.

In the matter of 'race' prejudice, the evidence concerning the in-fluence of actual contact is somewhat contradictory. In the first place a strong feeling against a 'race' can certainly be expressed on a basis of no experience whatever. The experiment of Hartley has shown that. On the other hand Campbell[4] reported that among his subjects in an investigation into attitudes towards Jews: 'People who had had no contact with Jews seldom expressed hostility toward them.' The fact is that contact as such is ambiguous; what matters is the nature of the

[1] op. cit., p. 931.
[2] Stagner, R. 'Fascist Attitudes.' *J. Social Psychol.*, 1936, 7, pp. 309 and 433.
[3] The Prestige value of Public Employment in Chicago. *Univ. of Chic. Soc. Sci. Studies*, 1929.
[4] Attitude towards Jews in *Readings in Soc. Psychology* (ed.) Newcomb, T. N., p. 521.

contact. Allport and Kramer[1] found that prejudiced subjects reported
that they had had unpleasant experiences with minority-groups. This,
however, is not the only thing that matters. If there is no prevalent
attitude towards any minority-group it is possible that friendly or
unfriendly contact with members may result in a general attitude
towards the group. Such a situation of complete neutrality, however,
is probably rare. In the absence of specific feelings about a given group
there is usually a general feeling for or against minorities, especially
racial ones, as such, or towards foreigners as such. It is in terms of this
that contact with a foreigner is experienced, and the friendliness or
otherwise is likely to be interpreted as confirming one's general attitude,
or as an exception. This holds the more in cases where there is a prevailing attitude; the experience of contact is, as it were, *through* the
attitude. If the prejudice is initially weak, friendly experience might
reverse it, especially when the experience means seeing the member of
the group against which the prejudice is directed in a new light,
as in the case of soldiers fighting with Negroes in the war.[2] If the attitude is strong then even what to outside observers appears to be a
'neutral' contact, is quite likely to be experienced as a hostile one, while
friendly contacts may well be forgotten and unfriendly ones exaggerated. The point is that hardly any contacts with other people are
what one might call 'attitude-free'.

The general upshot of this discussion is that the *initial* basis of attitude
formation lies in the home. With young children this has a powerful
effect and one proportionate to the pungency of the home attitude
with regard to any given issue. In the home itself, however, the personal factor plays its part and as the child moves into the orbit of other
institutions and associations new pressures are put upon him, and new
possibilities of satisfying his own private needs open up. His development, however, is a continuous one and each new experience is what
it is because of the attitude in which it is met. The effect of the new
experience will be a function of the strength of the attitude aroused,
the nature of the stimulus itself, and the prevailing atmosphere of
opinion which forms its context.

In 1935, Sims and Patrick[3] gave the Hinkley 'Attitude Toward the
Negro' test to a group of students in a Northern University, a group

---

[1] Allport, G. W. and Kramer, B. M. 'Some Roots of Prejudice.' *J. Psychol.*, 1946, 22,
p. 9.
[2] cf. p. 95.
[3] Sims, V. M. and Patrick, J. R. 'Attitudes towards the Negro of Northern and Southern College Students.' *J. of Soc. Psych.*, 1936, 7, p. 192. cf. *Readings in Soc. Psychol.*, p. 358.

of students coming from southern homes and studying in a southern university, and a third group of students from the north studying in the same institution. The northern students in the north were least prejudiced, the southern students in the south were most prejudiced, but the interesting thing is that the northern students in the south became more prejudiced the longer they were there.

Bennington College is a progressive institution in which 'No phrase was more constantly on the lips of its members than "the college community".' The student body of some 250 young ladies was intensively examined between 1935 and 1939 by T. N. Newcomb.[1] He concentrated upon their attitudes towards public affairs and showed by a questionnaire, on 'Political and Economic Progressiveness' and 'Information about Political Affairs' that in general there was a marked and progressive increase in non-conservativism, when one compared 'Freshmen' with the 'Sophomores' and the 'Junior-Seniors'. Such a change was more marked in Bennington than in two other colleges with which it was compared. The strongly self-conscious progressive atmosphere did its work.

This, however, was not all. The general conclusion masked individual differences. A group of students, some of them conservatives and some not, some recognizing their agreement or disagreement with the tone of the place and some not, were interviewed and typical individual adjustments were revealed. For example one conservative, well aware of her negative attitude, observed: 'I wanted to disagree with all the noisy liberals, but I was afraid and I couldn't. I found I couldn't compete so I decided to stick to my father's ideas.' She knew where she stood, but 'Q 47' did not realize how conservative she was, and yet she was judged 'stubborn and resistant': 'I'd accept anything,' she said, 'if they just let me alone.' On the other hand, among 'good group members', 'M 42' told of how: 'My family has always been liberal, but the influences here made me go further,' while 'H 32' said: 'I accepted liberal attitudes here because I had always secretly felt that my family was narrow and intolerant, and because such attitudes had prestige value.' One sees the interaction of the climate of opinion in the community as a whole and the attitudes of the individuals, each individually motivated. The group may act as a positive or negative 'reference group' (as Sherif calls it), and other groups, the home, or a

---

[1] Newcomb, T. N. *Personality and Social Change.* Dryden Press, N.Y., 1943; and 'Influence of Attitude Climate upon Some Determinants of Information.' *J. of Ab. and Soc. Psych.*, 1946, p. 291. cf. *Readings in Soc. Psychology*, p. 345.

special circle of like-minded dissidents, may also play their part as 'reference-groups', so that the reference of an attitude negatively to, e.g. the home, may lead to its reference positively to the college, or vice versa.

These two studies both bring out the importance of a specific institutional 'tone' upon the new-comer who has to adjust himself; the Bennington study emphasizes the personal element in each adaptation.

4. Since the acquisition of attitudes is a matter in which the pressure of other people's utterances, an individual's own peculiarities, and the particular context of the moment are all involved, it is clear that no one method of changing attitudes is universally effective. Only the most general advice can be given, leaving the particular means to be chosen with reference to the particular change which is to be brought about.

There have been enormous numbers of experiments on changing the attitudes of schoolchildren and university students. The method of experimentation is quite straightforward: a test is given to a group, the group is then subjected to 'treatment' and is then re-tested to see whether the 'treatment' has been successful. Usually the conduct of the experimental group is compared with a 'control' group which has not been through the experimental mill. The literature on the subject is voluminous and not all of it can be said to hold the interest which it sets out to capture. Happily the invaluable Murphy, Murphy and Newcomb have listed the principal researches in their book on *Experimental Social Psychology*.[1] This carries us up to 1936 and later work has been classified by Arnold Rose,[2] and a short list will be found in R. W. William's monograph on *The Reduction of Intergroup Tension*.[3] Schoolchildren, university students and anyone else conveniently accessible have been lectured at, discussed with, and subjected to a variety of other experiences with the not unexpected result that sometimes the method chosen works, sometimes it does not.

As examples of the kind of experiment conducted we may take the following. W. K. C. Chen[4] chose statements favourable and unfavourable to the Japanese side in their conflict over Manchuria in 1931. These statements were presented to the subjects for agreement or disagreement and then they were divided up into groups some of which had pro-Chinese and other pro-Japanese propaganda, while others just

---

[1] Pp. 948–951, 956–959.
[2] 'Studies in Reduction of Prejudice.' Am. Council on Race Relations, 1948.
[3] Soc. Sci. Research Council, N.Y. *Bulletin* 57, 1947, pp. 28–30.
[4] 'The Influence of Oral Propaganda Material upon Students' Attitudes.' *Arch. Psychol.*, 1933, 23. No. 150.

had 'neutral' material put before them. The propaganda was found to be effective when the subjects were re-tested.

The influence of films has been investigated by Peterson and Thurston,[1] who found that more often than not they made a difference, but the difficulty is that the general climate of opinion in which the children lived is very difficult to assess, so that we cannot say why some films worked and others did not. According to another pair of investigators[2] in the same field 'the movies tend to fix and further establish the behaviour pattern and type of attitudes which already exist', and that sounds a very plausible statement.

A bold experiment was carried out in the city of Allentown, Pennsylvania by the Socialist Candidate in an election.[3] He drew up two kinds of election appeal, one alleged to be 'rational' the other 'emotional'. He distributed the 'emotional' one to three wards of the city and the 'rational' one to four wards, leaving twelve wards as controls. Of course all sorts of factors influence voting, but it still remains that the increase in the Socialist vote in the 'emotional wards' was greater than in the others.

Finally there have been a number of experiments on the importance of 'prestige suggestion'. In one of them[4] the investigators took four groups and asked them to rank ten professions for intelligence required and for social usefulness. One group just did their ranking, the others were told the (fictitious) judgments of five hundred other students. The judgments of the three experimental groups were in accord with 'majority' suggestions. In other experiments the influence of an authoritative personality as having agreed with this, that, or another judgment is measured.

There are two ways of interpreting 'prestige suggestion', both of which have their force. Sherif[5] stresses the importance of 'frame of reference' and 'reference groups' as being necessary for a feeling of confidence. For him the 'majority opinion' and the 'celebrated name' are, as it were, refuges or sources of stability, though it is true that judgments said to be supported by disapproved-of groups tend to be

---

[1] Peterson, R. C. and Thurston, L. L. *Motion Pictures and the Social Attitude of Children.* McMiller, N.Y., 1937.

[2] Shuttleworth, F. K. and May, M. A. *The Social Conduct and Attitude of Movie Fans,* 1933.

[3] Hartmann, G. W. 'A Field Experiment on the Comparative Effects of "emotional" and "rational" Political Leaflets in Determining Election Results.' *J. Ab. Soc. Psych.,* 1936, 31, 99.

[4] Asch, S. E., Block, H. and Hertzman, M. 'Studies in the Principles of Judgments and Attitudes I.' 1938. *J. Psychol.,* 1938, 5, p. 219. II. 1940. *J. Soc. Psych.,* 1940, 12, p. 433.

[5] *Outlines of Social Psychology,* p. 235.

rejected. This, however, is what one might call an inverted refuge—
you know at least what *not* to say. Krech and Crutchfield,[1] on the
other hand, applying their view that material positively *looks* as it does
because it is received in, or through, an attitude, make the point that
hearing about the judgments of others, whether of a sheer number of
others or of a distinguished other, makes the thing you have to judge
yourself *look* different. Thus in an experiment by Lewis[2] the experimental subjects were told how various political leaders had rated a
group of slogans; the 'control' group were just asked to rate them
without any clues. One of the slogans was: 'Balance the Budget'. To
the control group this meant: 'Abolish relief,' to the communist group,
who were told that Browden had rated it high, it meant: 'Lower war
appropriation' (this was in 1938–9) 'and give more relief money.'

Each of these views makes an important point: on the one hand when
the matter is somewhat vague and admits of several interpretations we
like to have support, and on the other hand the support to which we
cling gives a more definite *look* to the material.

What has been said provides the clue to effective propaganda: i.e.
the conscious attempt to make people think, feel and act in certain
ways.

To begin with the 'audience' addressed already has its attitudes, its
ways of 'seeing things' in terms of them, its beliefs, its standards of
reference, groups of which it approves, groups of which it disapproves
and so forth. It is clearly fatal for the propagandist to be ignorant of
these, because whatever he says he will be heard or read in terms of
them. No technique, whether argument, emotional appeal, reference
to authority or anything else, is of the slightest use if the initial attitude
situation is fundamentally hostile. 'Communist propaganda in the
United States', wrote Albig in 1939,[3] 'has often failed to consider the
widespread aversion of masses of Americans to the identification of
themselves as "the proletariat".' Justification of your appeal by reference to its 'innate' plausibility is mere ineptitude.

From this it follows that the new 'suggestion' must link up with what
is already there. If possible you link your suggestion with an existing
need. You will have a better chance of getting what you want across
if you fasten on a topic which is rather vague than if you concentrate
upon one which is already clear-cut and try to change attitudes via

[1] op. cit., p. 337.
[2] Lewis, H. B. 'Studies in the Principles of Judgments and Attitudes IV.' 'The Operation of Prestige Suggestion.' *J. Soc. Psych.*, 1941, 14, p. 229.
[3] op cit., p. 317.

that. Naturally you will exploit the current emotional language and stereotypes, and make use of the familiar techniques of 'name-calling', 'testimonials', 'glittering generalizations', and the 'plainfolks appeal' which were recommended by the Institute of Propaganda Analysis in the 1930's.[1] Whether you use 'emotional' appeals or appeals couched in the form of argument will depend upon your audience, your topic, and your purpose. In addition to this it is well to bear in mind the 'boomerang' effect of propaganda. We must remember that we are all 'propaganda conscious' in the sense that we put up a resistance if we feel we are being 'got at'.

By playing upon the existing attitude complex you may make your audience *see* things as you wish them to see them, but more is required. It is also desirable to get your views linked up with the groups which serve as 'references' to their members. This explains the importance of 'Group Discussion', stressed by Lewin and already mentioned.[2]

But it is not only 'group-discussion' as a device that we have in mind. It is the linking up of the new attitude with such prestige groups as the Church, the political party, the nation and so forth. What one wants to aim at is—to use Sherif's expression again—a new 'ego involvement'. He quotes[3] the analysis R. K. Merton[4] made of a War Bond Drive on the Columbia Broadcasting System in which Miss Kate Smith made appeals throughout the day. According to Merton, the ones that went down best were the 'sacrifice theme' and the 'participation theme'. He quotes two listeners saying: 'Well, Dad, we *did* something. I was part of the Show,' and: ' We felt that others had been impressed and bought a bond. And the fact that so many people felt the same way made me feel right—that I was in the right channel.' While it is true that Americans do not seem to suffer from the inhibiting shyness that glues the tongues of other people, the sentiments are not unfamiliar.

'Re-education,' say Lewin and Grabbe,[5] 'influences conduct only when the new system of values and beliefs dominates the individual's perception. The acceptance of the new system is linked with the acceptance of a specific group, a particular role, a definite source of authority as new points of reference.'

Undoubtedly the *malaise* of so many people at the present moment

[1] Young, K. op. cit., p. 508.   [2] p. 32.   [3] op. cit., p. 311.
[4] Merton, R. K. *Mass Persuasion, the Social Psychology of a War Bond Drive.* Harper, 1946.
[5] Lewin, K. and Grabbe, P. 'Conduct, Knowledge and Acceptance of New Values.' *Journal of Social Issues*, 1945, I, p. 53.

is partly due to the fact that they have to fumble out their opinions and attitudes very much on their own, they do not see any role clearly before them, the 'news' is not easy to interpret, and they are not strengthened by an 'involvement' in any group with a clear view which they can share. There is, of course, one group with a very clear view, and those involved in that continually say how invigorating such membership is, but for many people the groups to which they do feel themselves affiliated are divided in their views and therefore give no single-minded support. The situation is therefore one of interest to students of propaganda. The difficulty which faces the propagandist, of course, is that they have to address themselves to a complex attitude pattern. Granted most people like being given what they call a 'lead', they do not all fall for the same leader. It is a sombre thought, but a 'Pearl Harbour' would be—for the propagandist—a godsend.[1]

---

[1] For further reading on Propaganda see Dobb, L. W. *Propaganda, Its Psychology and Technique*. Holt, 1935. Lambert, R. S. *Propaganda*. Nelson, 1938.

PART II

THE INDIVIDUAL AND SOCIETY

CHAPTER VIII

SOCIAL DETERMINATION OF FACULTIES

IN this part we shall be concerned with the growth and development of the individual and his faculties in so far as it is determined by his social contacts.

In this chapter we shall consider social influence on intellectual capacity, perception and memory.

Society and the Self. Before embarking on particular aspects or faculties such as these, however, we must turn our attention to a far more fundamental matter: the very existence of persons as we know them. Here we skirt the whirlpools of philosophical controversy which have been set boiling afresh by the volcanic eruption of Professor Ryle.[1] He has called into question the plain man's concept of the mind as a ghost which inhabits the bodily machine, and it will soon be apparent that certain social psychologists have independently raised the same issue, though in a somewhat different form.

The simple image which imperceptibly forms in our minds is of an individual with all his faculties having to adapt himself to the society in which he is born. We think of him much as we remember our own experience when we have joined a society and have had to take cognizance of its habits so that we can fit in. We picture little Shirley and little Raymond similarly adjusting their conduct to, say, the complexities of the lower-middle-class culture-pattern. They say to themselves in our imagination: 'What must *I* do now, so that they will like *me?*'

If, however, we pause to reflect a moment, we can see that this ascription of a ready-made 'I' and 'me' is of very doubtful validity

[1] *The Concept of Mind.* Hutchinson, 1949.

Surely the 'I' and 'me' imply a separation from 'you', 'him', 'her' and 'them'. How did little Shirley and little Raymond acquire their Shirley-hood and Raymond-hood? Must it not have been out of, and by means of, social intercourse with other human beings? Something that we can call 'awareness' or 'consciousness' of course we can allow them from the start. They are capable of selecting stimuli to respond to, and we can contrast that of which they are unaware with that of which they are aware, and times when they are conscious with times when they are not. But we can use those words intelligibly of any animal, insect or bird. We do not thereby mean that they are conscious of themselves as acting, that they refer experience to themselves, or that they have those private conversations with themselves which we indubitably learn to have.

Pursuing this line of thought we cannot help sympathizing with George H. Mead when he exclaims: 'It is absurd to look at the mind simply from the standpoint of the individual human organism; for, although it has its focus there, it is essentially a social phenomenon.'[1] Several American writers have emphasized the social origin of *self*-consciousness, but Mead is the one who has made the most careful analysis of the problem, and put forward the most detailed suggestions as to how it is to be solved. His work is not as well known in this country as it should be, and it is hoped that the following account of his theory will send readers back to the original, because it is impossible in a short space to follow up all the problems which he raises.

To begin with, Mead, though no narrow behaviourist, approaches the problem from the standpoint of behaviour, and the first point to be made is that all social intercourse, whether it be of ants, cats, dogs, birds or human infants involves mutual adjustment. Each participant responds to the movements, posture and gesture of the other. In a dog-fight each dog's movements are a response to those of his enemy. So it is with cats playing, birds feeding their young, and infants reaching for the breast; each single movement of the one party is what it is because of the position, movement, or posture of the other, and vice versa. How this inter adjustment comes about we need not ask, we can take this as our starting point, noting two things: (1) throughout a vast range of the animal kingdom there are certain performances such as copulation and the care of the young which are social in the sense that two inter-adjusting organisms are involved, and (2) that in such performances we need not assume *self*-consciousness at all.

[1] *Mind, Self and Society.* Univ. of Chicago Press, 1934, p. 133.

The next point is that by association, or conditioning, certain gestures or movements become signs of future movements so that anticipation is possible, and also certain gestures, barkings, mewings, squawkings, or human wailings, may be followed by satisfaction, and gradually become learnt as ways of inducing the other partner to cooperate. Thus the human infant acquires a repertoire of gestures and cries by means of which *in fact* (though not in design) he indicates his needs, and learns the signs of coming joy or pain from his mother's face and the movements of her hands. And still there need be no *self-consciousness*. All this learning of signs of pleasure or pain goes on throughout our lives and for a great part of the time we respond more or less appropriately to such stimuli without reflection.

But for human beings at any rate other possibilities loom ahead. Into what Mead calls the 'conversation of gestures' at the non–deliberate level comes something else. A gesture is an habituated movement acquired by its maker, it is responded to as a conditioned stimulus by the partners in the social act who witness it, but it is, in Mead's term, not yet 'significant'. It becomes 'significant' when it 'answers to a meaning in the experience of the first individual and . . . also calls out that meaning in the second individual'.[1] I may learn to hold out my hand to a visitor and then do it automatically, but supposing I have had a quarrel and then, when I meet my erstwhile adversary, hold out my hand to him, my meaning is: 'Shake!' The meaning of my gesture is his holding out his hand that it should be clasped by me. Now how do I acquire not only the habit of holding out my hand, but the meaning of my action in this context when I do it deliberately? It cannot be, Mead argues, on a basis of spontaneous imitation that we communicate, firstly because the tendency to imitate has, to say the least of it, been grossly exaggerated, and secondly because (quite apart from this example) we usually intend to invite our partners in the exchange to do something different from what we ourselves are doing. How, then, do we pass from non-significant to significant gestures? Here it is that Mead takes his bold step, upon which his whole theory rests. Let us state it in his own words: 'When, in any given social act or situation, one individual indicates by a gesture to another individual what this other individual is to do, the first individual is conscious of the meaning of his own gesture—or the meaning of his gesture appears in his own experience—in so far as *he takes the attitude of the second individual towards that gesture*, and tends to respond to it implicitly

[1] ibid., p. 46.

in the same way that the second individual responds to it explicitly.'[1] This is the heart and centre of the whole business. The gesture we make evokes in some incipient and adumbrated manner the response we intend to elicit; we 'take the attitude of the other'.

Let us leave the matter here for a moment and consider a special form of 'gesture': the vocal gesture, or speech. This has, as has often been noticed, a special quality: the speaker hears himself. The child develops a repertoire of vocalization accumulated from the rewarded elements of its spontaneous babbling and the cries associated with certain satisfaction to come. And all this occurs on what Mead might call a 'non-significant' level. But when significance comes in, then the word I utter as a command or request (and it is here, and not in intellectual discourse that language begins) is heard by me and, according to Mead's theory, *elicits in me* the attitude of the other. 'You ask somebody to bring a visitor a chair,' says Mead by way of illustration. 'You arouse the tendency to get the chair in the other, but if he is slow to act you get the chair yourself. The response to the vocal gesture is the doing of a certain thing, and you arouse that same tendency in yourself. You are always replying to yourself, just as other people reply.'[2] And interestingly enough, he reminds us of the difficulties of teaching someone to do something you can do yourself, because you are itching to do it all the time.

We can now take another step. Since you arouse in yourself the response of the other, you prepare yourself in advance to meet it when it comes, and to whatever does come you react, arousing the response to that and preparing yourself still further. But then, supposing you say the word of command to yourself and not aloud, and still arouse the other's response in yourself ('taking the attitude of the other'), you may—may you not?—refrain from uttering the word out loud. 'Oh, no, he will do so-and-so, if I say . . . and I don't want him to do that.' Are we not approaching internal conversation? 'The individual,' says Mead, 'comes to carry on a conversation of gestures with *himself*. He says something, and that calls out a certain reply in himself, which makes him change what he was going to say.'[3]

We have at last arrived, or almost so. We were looking for that element in our social contacts out of which *self*-consciousness is born. It is the self as object that we are seeking. Well here, according to Mead, it is, or, rather, here are its beginnings. It is, paradoxically enough, out of the reference to others that *ourselves* are generated.

[1] ibid., p. 47 (my italics).   [2] ibid., p. 67.   [3] ibid., p. 141 (my italics).

The theory is a bold one, but its ingenuity can be realized if we appreciate the nature of the problem. Once you reject a kind of primal self-hood in everyone, then you are left with conscious, but not *self*-conscious, reacting organisms. Where does the reflexive element of 'self' come in? Something must occur to present myself to myself as different from others and yet—and this is of major importance—to enable me to guide my action with respect to others. The reflecting in my person of the anticipated response of the other, for Mead, does the trick.

The notion of 'taking the attitude of the other' is by no means free of difficulties, and worse is to follow, but Mead has at least presented, and taken up, the challenge.

Furthermore, his theory, as we shall see in a moment, has its points. In the course of its development one thing may soon become apparent. According to his view we start off 'taking the attitude of the other' in bits, as it were. First in single interchanges, then in long and controlled pieces of social action, and then towards persons, because we shall build up systems of expected responses, characteristic of different people. 'We divide ourselves up in all sorts of different selves with reference to our acquaintance.'[1] Well—we do. We 'take the attitude' of a whole lot of others from time to time, putting on our 'acts', as schoolmaster, friend, pub-crawler, or lover, playing our part with reference to the anticipated responses of the persons we are with at the moment.

And as children we develop our 'selves' in play. Not in mere jumping and gambolling, but in 'playing at' something—being a policeman, a shopkeeper, the guard of a train. Do we not then often act out the role of the other, selling and responding with the gesture of buying, being the guard and responding with the action of passengers, which we call forth by our speech as guard?

Now, however, comes a difficult move. We are not really inconsistent chameleons, changing our responses with every person we meet. Of course, there are such, and one can see that the 'divided personality' has its place in Mead's scheme, but most people are better integrated. They do not only have their line with X, their line with Y, and their line with Z; they have their roles as citizens.

We can best understand how Mead deals with this, if we take his advice and consider what happens when we play an organized game. The rules of the game schematize the expected response of the players.

[1] ibid., p. 142.

Any given player must 'take the attitude of the other' to whom he is at the moment throwing or kicking the ball, and he must 'take the attitude of the other', the enemy, who is trying to intervene. Co-operative game-playing is an impossibility if this is not done. All the time each player is controlling his activity with respect to the antici-pated response he expects and therefore he must adjust in advance. But a game is not a mere set of interchanges, where the ball is at any given moment, it is a co-operative enterprise which every player on the field must understand so as to frame his own private policy and play his role *vis-à-vis* the role of *all* others.

How does this come about? The answer is clear, but its full implica-tions are extremely obscure. The answer is that the player takes the attitude of a *generalized other*. All the attitudes of the other players and the expected responses, and the logic of the game are absorbed in the 'generalized other'. This second notion is a kind of abstract synthesis of the first, the 'attitude of the other', but whereas one might picture a neural basis for the reflected response in oneself of the answer to a particular gesture, and even a state of readiness for a system of ex-pected responses in a social situation, what the physiological formula-tion for the 'generalized other' could be is very difficult to see. This, however, is not an insuperable difficulty. Why should we not use the concept or model of the 'generalized other' if it is useful and simply say that we cannot express what we want it for in neuro-muscular language?

However that may be, the game situation is a mere illustration lead-ing up to the statement: 'The organized community or social group which gives the individual the unity of self may be called the "general-ized other".'[1] And, again: 'In the full development of the individual's self that self is constituted not only by an organization of . . . particular individual attitudes, but also by an organization of the social attitudes of the generalized other or the social group to which he belongs', so that he becomes 'an individual reflection of the general systematic pattern of social or group behaviour'[2].

It must be emphasized that the moulding of conduct by the 'general-ized other' must not be looked at, as it were, from outside. It is *'taken'*, as Mead puts it, by the individual, it is, as the Freudian might put it, 'introjected'. In fact in some respects the generalized other is very like the Freudian super-ego. The thing to remember is this: our unre-flective conduct is, much of it, shaped by society and enters into our

[1] ibid., p. 154.   [2] ibid., p. 158.

system. The 'generalized other' of Mead, strictly speaking is operating only when we act with reflection: 'If I do that, then *people will say.* . . .' It operates in us—indeed it *is* part of us—when we have moral arguments with ourselves. The 'generalized other' puts the conventional point of view, the reaction likely to be called forth by our proposed conduct, and *actually* called forth in incipient form in us when we phrase our proposal. There is not a proposal, *then* a phrasing of it; the phrasing of it *is* the proposal, to which the generalized other in us responds. We may give in, we may not.

We have now, it will be observed reached something else. We have just talked about what we might call the consolidated 'other', dialectically developed in our interaction with individual persons and, if the distinction be not misleading, with people in general. This is addressed by proposals. The single self, as seen from the *outside*, is from the *inside*, split into the reflexive aspects of 'I' and 'me'—'I', and the self as object. The 'me' is that group of organized attitudes to which the individual responds as an 'I',[1] and the organized attitudes, let us not forget, are the potential responses of 'others' which have by this time systematized themselves inside us. But what about the 'I'? This has emerged as the correlative of the 'me', but it is not the same as the 'me'. It is never an object until it has performed, and then it is a 'me' in memory. 'The "I" of this moment is present in the "me" of the next moment.'[2]

It is one of the great merits of Mead's theory that he leaves room for spontaneity—too much room, may be. Anyway proposals are made, situations are faced, desires are expressed by the spontaneous 'I', and they call forth, save in purely automatic or impulsive action, or when we are, as we say, 'lost' in some 'enthralling' enterprise, a response in the 'me', which is now the systematized residues of previous responses. But what the 'I' will propose, or do, or desire, 'He does not know and nobody else knows'.[3] The action of the 'I' cannot be calculated. 'It is only after we have said the word we are saying that we recognize ourselves as the person that has said it, as this particular self that says this particular thing; it is only after we have done the thing that we are going to do that we are aware of what we are doing.'[4]

This is a hard saying, but it has advantages. It puts the 'I' out of access, which it always is. It provides for the freedom required by reason, though it involves endowing the 'I' with certain abilities which make its proposals not wholly inconsequent. It lays the 'ghost in the

[1] ibid., p. 186.   ibid., p. 174.   [3] ibid., p. 176.   [4] ibid., p. 203.

6

machine', because the 'I' is no homunculus that consults its ideas and then speaks or acts; it speaks, it acts. However, Mead does seem to have over-emphasized its unpredictability, and he, himself draws a distinction between the artist, the creative scientist, and the moralist—whose 'I' produces something new, with the conventional man who always gives way to his 'me', wincing at the response of the 'generalized other'. In all people the 'me' must hold sway, but in some people it holds less sway than in others.

For all that, the 'I' has direction. It seeks 'self-expression', and there is always a conflict going on, sometimes on a large scale, sometimes on a small one, between the spontaneous 'I' and the conventional 'me'. The strong 'I' then turns, says Mead, to a wider society, enlarging the scope of reason beyond what his 'me' has hitherto accepted, or enlarging the scope of morality beyond his local group.

In all this it will have been seen that for Mead, social relations and the 'conversation of gesture' are prior to the development of selves. That is why we had to start with social conduct at the animal level. As he puts it: 'There would be no call for assistance if there was not a tendency to respond to the cry of distress.' It will also be noticed that the conception of the 'generalized other', which is in *all* members of society forms the basis for coherent social co-operation, while the spontaneous 'I' accounts for social change.

Society then is a system of selves, each with its own unique individuality, reflecting the reactions of others from its own point of view. Mind is internal conversation, language is essential to thought, and the 'process of relating one's own organism to the others in the interactions that are going on, in so far as it is imported into the conduct of the individual with the conversation of the "I" and the "me", constitutes the self'.[1] The notion of 'ego-involvement' is no mystery, save as 'involved' there is no 'ego'.

Some of the difficulties in Mead's story have been indicated. The nature of the 'generalized other', and the source of the 'I's' rationality and moral vision are obscure. For all that, his theory brings to notice the problem which other people will have to solve if any adequate account of the social nature of man is to be worked out. It is not suggested that Mead is the only social-psychologist to think along such lines. Other American writers such as William James, Cooley, Royce and J. M. Baldwin, who spoke of the 'dialectic of personal growth' were groping after the same kind of solution. Piaget in Switzerland

[1] ibid., p. 179.

too, emphasized the importance of games in the growth of a sense of personal responsibility. In what Mead contemptuously refers to as 'the more or less fantastic psychology of the Freudian group', the intro-jection of external standards has received full recognition, while the concept of role-taking is a commonplace among the modern cultural anthropologists. And if we look further afield, we can see Lewin's notion of the ego as a 'system or complex of systems, a functional part region within the psychological totality'[1] as extended into a wider setting with Mead's image of the self as 'an eddy in the social current'.[1]

Whatever position we take up about the best formulation of what we refer to as the 'self', it must be agreed that social influences are para-mount in its development. We now turn to a consideration of some of the ways in which its functioning is socially determined.

Society and Perception. Let us start with perception. The faculty of sense-perception might seem at first blush to be a somewhat unpromising field. This, however, is not the case. There seems to be very little evidence that people from different societies have different degrees of sensory acuity. At the turn of the century, Rivers, MacDougall and Myers took part in an anthropological expedition to the Torres Straits, and they took every opportunity that offered to test the simpler peoples by laboratory methods. The same procedure has been used by other psychologists,[2] and all with the same result. *With such tests* the performance of one ethnic group differs but little from that of others, with the sole exception of colour discrimination. Even here it is not always easy to infer from the test situation to 'real life'.

But sheer sensory acuity is not the only factor responsible for the world in which we live. Every animal selects stimuli for attention on a basis of its biological needs, as promises of satisfaction. This will mean that children coming from different cultures will give different struc-tural emphasis to the world they see about them. Even in our own culture this is obvious enough. The shepherd notices differences be-tween his sheep which the ignorant do not, the motor mechanic hears sounds which the mere motorist does not, and the artist sees colours and shapes which the philistine ignores. What wonder then that we hear stories of the perceptual skill of primitive peoples. They are brought up to notice differences which are meaningless to us. Such

---

[1] *Dynamic Theory of Personality*. McGraw-Hill, 1935, p. 56.
[2] For a résumé of the work of Klineberg, O. *Race Differences*, Chapter VII.

powers are revealed by their discriminative reaction; from time to time they respond differently to things or sounds which seem to us alike. In some sense, then, the perceptual world is culturally conditioned. Of course this variety of perceptual worlds must not be exaggerated, otherwise the possibility of inter-communication would be inexplicable. In any case it is by no means easy to decide how far the world does look different to people from different cultures, or with different interests from our own. Of course, if someone says: 'Look!' and then points out something you had not seen before, you suppose that his spontaneous discrimination operated differently from yours. Even then it is doubtful whether you would be satisfied if you could see nothing when he tried to point it out to you, so that it is really more a case of different noticings than different worlds altogether.

But what about the cases quoted by Klineberg?[1] It appears according to Malinowski[2] that among the Trobriand Islanders a child's resemblance to its father is taken for granted, but it is an insult to say that it resembles its mother or any maternal relative, and brothers are deemed not to resemble one another. Now do they *see* resemblances which we do not, or do they merely refrain from any painful reference? We cannot tell. Again Zillig[3] chose out of a class some children who were popular and some who were unpopular. She taught both groups some Calisthenic exercises, coaching the popular ones to make mistakes, and the unpopular ones to perform according to her instructions. When the rest of the children were asked which did the exercise correctly, they almost all voted for the popular group. Again, did they *see* in terms of their preference?

Finally there is the case of the Maori chief who was painted by an English painter. He thought nothing of the portrait: 'That's not what I am,' he said. When he was asked to draw his own portrait he reproduced very little besides his tattoo pattern.[4] Assuming honesty, which is difficult to assess in the first two cases, all these instances can be explained in terms of different noticings. You can look out for resemblances where they 'ought' to be, you can look out for mistakes where you want to find them, and abstract features of a face which are of special interest.

There are, however, cases rather less easily explained. Ansbacher[5]

[1] *Social Psychology*. Holt, 1940, p. 203.
[2] *Sex and Repression in Savage Society*. Kegan Paul.
[3] Quoted Klineberg, O. op. cit., p. 206.   [4] ibid., p. 210.
[5] Ansbacher, H. 'Perception of number as affected by the monetary value of the objects.' *Arch. Psychol.*, 1937. No. 215.

found that for his subjects postage stamps of higher value 'looked' larger than ones of lower value. And then there is the experiment of Bruner and Goodman.[1] They presented coins to be compared in size with grey discs. The coins were uniformly judged larger than the valueless discs which were of the same objective size, and poor children's estimates were more 'out' than those of children from richer homes.

Now judgments of 'big' and 'small' are reference-framework judgments, and here we seem to have examples of the operation of socially determined norms.

Then there is the view that children and the simpler peoples see the world as a more animated place than grown-ups and civilized men do. The child's vision of the world has been investigated by Piaget,[2] who found that his Swiss children tend at an early age to speak of inanimate objects as though they were living things. The animatism and animism of primitive religion has been explained by the fact that the savage sees the world as a system of personal forces. Kelsen[3] goes so far as to suggest that primitive men could not take an impersonal view of the world, but it is not easy to see how he knows.

At any rate we must be careful not to draw the contrast between children and savages on the one hand and our grown-up civilized selves on the other too sharply. When Margaret Mead[4] talked to her little Manu friends about their boats being 'naughty', they thought she was very odd and calmly explained the facts of the case. On the other hand the most civilized of men will sometimes find that physical objects, particularly those constructed of metal, behave towards him with calculated malignancy. It looks as though there was a universal tendency to include physical things in the society of living beings and to respond to them as such. It may be, as Sapir[5] has suggested, that language has its effects in encouraging such personification, but it can scarcely cause them. The danger is that we may select the personification of children and of savages and contrast it with ourselves in our most objective moods, forgetting our own frequent and foolish indignation, and even forgetting our poetry.

Society and Memory.   What about memory? Some of

---

[1] Bruner, J. S. and Goodman, C. C. 'Value and Need as Organizing Factor in Perception.' *J. of Abn. Soc. Psych.*, 1947, 42, p. 33. cf. *Readings in Social Psychology*, p. 99.
[2] *Language and Thought of the Child*. Kegan Paul, 1926.
[3] *Society and Nature*. Kegan Paul, 1946.
[4] *Growing up in New Guinea*. Penguin ed., p. 79.
[5] Encycl. Soc. Sc. Art: *Language*.

the same factors as we have just noticed apply here as well. What we remember is partly determined by our interests, and therefore if our interests are different we are liable to recall different things. Bartlett[1] tells us of a Swazi chief who came to England with some of his tribe. When they got back they were asked about their visit and the one thing that stood out in their memories was the policeman holding up his hand to stop the traffic. May this not be, Bartlett asks, because this gesture is a common form of greeting in Swaziland and it was therefore noticed by the visitors, particularly because it seemed to have such a majestic effect? Bartlett gives further information about the capacities of the primitive peoples he met in Africa to remember. Put through a test, they did no better than white men, but they were able to recall in astonishing detail the characteristics of cattle and the price paid for them, but then, as he says: 'Most Swazi culture revolves round the possession and care of cattle.' It is true that he found differing modes of recall. A Zulu, recalling past exploits, got into an emotional state and relived his past, while the Swazi seemed more collected and cool. Indeed the Swazi mode was recapitulatory, a going through from beginning to end of the material recalled. Recalling learnt material can be improved by practice, and the method adopted in practising is likely to affect the general method of recall. In a pre-literate society memory must be relied on much more than in a literate one. What we would like to know is whether, as seems likely, praise and blame are meted out to children in such a way as to select a method of reporting as the one most socially approved.

The French Sociologist, Halbwachs,[2] has made a careful and elaborate analysis of the influence of group participation and group affiliation on the content of our memories and the facilitation of recall. He seems at times to favour the conception of a 'group memory', but such a notion is unnecessary to account for the way in which our memories of past events are partly determined by the existence of groups with which we identified ourselves on the original occasion, and the way in which recall may be inhibited by loss of contact with them.

Society and the Expression of Emotion. It is clear that the emotional states of rage, fear, anger, sorrow, and so forth, occur in all men on appropriate occasions. They may also occur on what we deem to be inappropriate occasions as well, but

---

[1] *Remembering.* Camb. Univ. Press.
[2] *Les Cadres Sociance de la Memoir.* Alcon, 1925. *Memoir et Société.* In L'Année Sociologique, 1940–48. Paris, 1949, p. 11.

psycho-analysis has shown that when this happens, the responses can be traced to situations, of which we are unaware, in which they would be suitable. Culture influences emotion in two ways. (1) It defines the 'appropriate occasions'. Of course some situations will make all men angry or afraid, but in some societies there are situations which will prompt their members to rage or envy, which would leave members of other societies unmoved. (2) More important is the cultural effect on emotional expression. It looks as though there were 'natural' forms of emotional expression, common to all mankind, but cultural standards can overlay such 'natural' expressions either by inhibiting them, or by encouraging them, or by altering them. Thus, in some societies, including our own, the expression of deep emotion may be considered indelicate, while among war-like tribes the young initiates are expected to face severe pain with indifference. On the other hand, tears may be called for at funerals in circumstances in which there is no reason to suppose that they are prompted by grief. It seems that some primitive peoples can weep at will.[1] Finally, we have those cases where an 'inappropriate' expression is called for, as when the Japanese smile on occasions when we should expect them to display sorrow, or depression. We, too, after all, are expected to look sympathetic, even when listening to the account of Mrs. Smith's operation for the sixth time, and we are expected to look pleased throughout a party at which we are condemned to play progressive games. Such unusual expression of emotion may, of course, be misleading, but on the whole we seem to be able to detect the 'true' emotion, even when it is culturally masked.[2]

Society and Intelligence. Having discussed the influence of society on experience in general we turn to that integrating faculty which lies at the heart of it: intelligence, and in so doing we enter upon a battlefield. The 'nature-nurture' controversy looms up, class prejudice makes itself felt, and the trained war horses of educational psychology paw the ground. We must attempt to disentangle the issues and view some of the evidence, but we have not time to enter into a full discussion of all the problems. We must take for granted the practice of intelligence testing and its history, and refrain from any discussion of the various methods of assessment and the 'thing' assessed. What we are interested in is the part played by the social environment.

[1] Nadel, S. F. *The Foundations of Social Anthropology.* Cohen and West, 1951, p. 66.
[2] Klineberg, O. *Race Differences*, Chap. XV.

It is, however, important to start off with a clear idea of the basic facts. Though the word 'intelligence' is used with many different meanings, largely because it is an approbation term and therefore tends to be applied when praise is thought to be due, it is fairly easy to find agreement about its applicability in cognitive processes. There are verbal and practical problems the solution of which depends not so much on information as on what we often call, 'seeing the point', though, of course, *some* knowledge is required for the very understanding of the problem at all. Now it has been found that a capacity to solve one kind of cognitive problem goes with a capacity to solve several other kinds of cognitive problems, but does not necessarily go with ability to play the piano, or thread a needle. It is therefore natural for us to say that one 'factor' is responsible for this general cognitive ability, while there are special factors of, say, manual dexterity, etc., which are responsible for the specific abilities. It is also plausible to call this 'general ability', which we think of as being responsible for proficiency in many cognitive tasks: 'intelligence', though in certain technical circles it is referred to as 'g'.

We may then take various courses. We can ask what 'g' is; we can analyse the sorts of things 'g' enables us to do, such as seeing relations, or finding an appropriate item to fill a gap, when we understand the relational system in which the gap is; or we can construct tests which we think will bring out this ability and so spread people that we can say who has more or less of it than the average for their age.

All these lines of investigation and many more have been pursued About the nature of intelligence we need only say that the question: 'What *is* intelligence?' is a misleading one, because it implies that intelligence is a thing like the liver or the pineal gland. As Sir Cyril Burt has put it: 'It is essentially a "dispositional property", not a substantial "entity".' Like all such properties, it implies a certain 'if-then' proposition, not a certain 'here-is-a . . . proposition'.[1]

About the analysis of the cognitive activities which involve 'intelligence' we need say nothing.

Tests have been constructed of three main kinds. Verbal paper-and-pencil tests, non-verbal paper-and-pencil tests, where the tasks are presented by means of picture and diagrams, and performance tests which require the manipulation of objects. Some, such as the Binet test and the performance tests, are given to subjects separately; most

---

[1] Burt, Sir C. 'Trend of National Intelligence.' *British J. Sociology*, 1950, 1, p. 164.

verbal and non-verbal tests can be done by a group of subjects writing at the same time.

The subjects are told to do their tasks within a certain time, their results are marked, and the result of each is compared with a scale indicating what may be expected of children of the same age: i.e. what marks are expected of the relatively few bright ones, what marks are to be expected of the few dull ones, and what marks are expected of the bulk of the population with whom the comparison is being made. This 'calibration' of the test has been made beforehand and we are not concerned with the methods employed. One thing, however, we have to notice, and that is that the assessment of the intelligence of any subject is essentially a comparative affair.

The results of assessment are expressed in various ways, the most familiar being in terms of what is called the Intelligence Quotient. For our purposes we need not consider how this has been devised, it is enough to say that an I.Q. round about 100 is 'average', while more than 105 or less than 95 are above or below the average respectively.

Now since the assessment of intelligence is a comparative matter we must be sure that the scale with which we are comparing our subject provides a 'valid' or 'fair' comparison. It is here that some of the difficulties, which interest us, begin. Any test performed involves at least three factors: the intention to do one's best, the knowledge required for understanding what you have to do, and the intellectual ability to do it. The first two must be held equal for all who are being compared, if any comparison in terms of intelligence is to be made. In school populations in our culture these assumptions can be made with fair plausibility, and the value of intelligence testing has been proved up to the hilt. Its value lies, of course, in its providing a satisfactory basis for prediction. No one is in the least interested in the marks little Basil gets on his test, what we are interested in is whether we can infer from his mark on the test that Basil will do better or worse than other children of his age at other tasks which we think require 'general intelligence'. On the whole such inference can be made with a certain degree of confidence, but only if Basil can be assumed to have had the same attitude towards the test as the others with whom he is being compared, and only if he was not penalized by lack of relevant information which they possessed.

It is precisely here that the trouble begins when we use our tests for people from different cultures. If, as happens among the Dakota

Indians,[1] it is indelicate to answer a question if you think there is someone present who does not know the answer already, this means that a
Dakota child's test result is not comparable with the results of children
brought up in a less sensitive environment. Porteus found difficulty
among the Australian aborigines. They were brought up to believe
that all problems had to be discussed in the group, and they thought it
very eccentric to be expected to solve one by oneself.[2]

Supposing, however, a satisfactory attitude towards the test can be
assumed, what about equality in relevant knowledge? In a society
where children play with bricks, performance tests involving the
manipulation of little cubes presents an easier problem than it would
in a society where such toys were unknown. Bartlett[3] reports that a
group of East African natives were unable to arrange coloured pegs in
an alternating series, but they planted trees according to the same plan
in everyday life.

Then there is the story of the little boy in Kentucky[4] who was asked
a test question: 'If you went to a store and bought 6 cents worth of
candy and gave the clerk 10 cents what change would you receive?'
The boy replied: 'I never had 10 cents and if I had I wouldn't spend it
on candy and anyway candy is what mother makes.' The tester re-
formulated the question: 'If you had taken ten cows to pasture for your
father and six of them strayed away, how many would you have left
to drive home?' The boy replied: 'We don't have ten cows, but if we
did and I lost six I wouldn't dare go home.' Undeterred the tester
pressed his question: 'If there were ten children in your school and six
of them were out with the measles how many would there be in
school?' The answer came: 'None, because the rest would be afraid of
catching it too.'

This story raises the question of town versus country. In many
researches it has been found that the country population do not get
such high scores as the town population of comparable ages. May this
not be partly due to the incomparability of the two groups? Certainly
something of the sort accounts for Gordon's[5] canal-boat children.
He found that they gave normal results up to the age of six, but then
seemed to regress so that at nine their average I.Q. was only 69.

---

[1] Klineberg, O. *Race Differences*. Harper, 1935, p. 155.
[2] Porteus, S. D. *The Psychology of a Primitive People*. Longman, No. 7, 1931, p. 308.
[3] Bartlett, Sir F. C. *Psychological Methods and Anthropological Problems*. Africa, 1937, 10.
[4] Quoted by Klineberg, O. *Social Psychology*, p. 253.
[5] Gordon, H. 'Mental and Scholastic Tests Among Retarded Children.' Board of
Educ. Educational Pamphlets, 1923, No. 44.

When tested with performance tests, where their lack of schooling was less likely to be a handicap, the average I.Q. mounted to 83.

Thus all intercultural comparisons of intelligence are vitiated by the lack of true comparability, and any generalizations about 'racial' difference in intellectual competence which do not take account of this, are worthless. So are many comparisons which have been made between children of different social classes.

So far we have been dealing with the inadequacy of intelligence tests when used for the purpose of comparing groups drawn from cultures so different that you cannot assume similarity of attitude or equality in relevant knowledge. We now have to consider a rather different problem. Supposing you have two children of the same age and you give them a test at which they both try to do their best, and which requires no 'specialist' knowledge that one may chance to have and the other not. Suppose the performances are different, and one gets a high score, the other a low one. You say that one is more intelligent than the other, and, let us further suppose, your judgment is justified by later events. The question may now be asked: is this difference due to 'innate' endowment, or is it due to the fact that one comes from a brighter home than the other, with the implication that if the one from the less bright home had been more fortunate the results would have been different? You cannot get 'pure' intelligence to measure; the very notion is idiotic. The capacity to do any test is a product of experience operating upon an initial equipment. The difficulty, however, is to gauge how much of the product is due to innate ability and how much to the particular sorts of experience any subject has had. Put in another way we may say that innate ability must be there, and it must have experience for it to manifest itself, but how can we tell whether the experiences with which it has been presented have allowed it to develop to its fullest capacity? You can't make a silk purse out of a sow's ear, but can you be certain that any given piece of material came from the ear of a sow?

The evidence for the innateness of intelligence is of various kinds. The correlation between the I.Q.s of identical twins has been found to be as high as .90 or .86. The average difference between their I.Q.s has been found to be 5 points in the case of identical twins reared together, but the range of the difference may be from 0 to 20 points.[1] In spite of

---

[1] Klineberg, O. *Social Psychol.*, p. 238. Newman, H. H., Freeman, F. N. and Holzinger, K. J. *Twins: A Study of Heredity and Environment.* University of Chicago Press, 1937, p. 369.

the cases in which there is disparity between identical twins, their measurements when reared together are closer than is the case with fraternal twins for whom the I.Q. correlation lies in the region of .70, while for siblings the I.Q. correlation averages .50. Between parent and child, and between cousins the correlation is about .30.[1]

Another piece of evidence comes from such material as is presented by F. Roberts. Out of 3,400 children of school age he investigated the siblings of the brightest 4 per cent. and the dullest 4 per cent. He found that 62.3 per cent. of the siblings of the brightest were bright and 6.6 per cent. were dull, whereas of the dullest 3.7 per cent. of their siblings were bright and 56.3 per cent. were dull.[2]

Again it was found that in an orphanage sixty-seven children, whose mothers were estimated to have a low I.Q. but whose fathers were estimated to have a high one, had an average I.Q. of 103.2. On the other hand 105 children whose fathers and mothers had low I.Q.s only averaged 88.6.[3]

Finally children brought up in residential institutions, where they are supposed to have much the same environment have different I.Q.s, while children who are brought up by foster parents resemble their own brothers and sisters more than they do the children of the foster parents.

All this kind of evidence provides ammunition for those who emphasize the importance of innate endowment, and to it one might add the general studies, made by Galton and others, of families noted for their high quota of intelligent members or, as in the case of the deplorable Jukes family, their dismal record of defectives and degenerates.

We do not know the way in which we must conceive intelligence to be inherited, and we do not know what significant changes may occur *in utero*, but the evidence for *some* difference in innate endowment is overwhelming and would not be denied by the sturdiest champion of the environmental factors. The question still is: how much is the contribution of each factor?

That changes in environment can bring about changes in capacity to do intelligence tests is perfectly clear. The evidence, as might be supposed, consists chiefly of comparisons between the I.Q.s of children who have been brought up away from one another.

Studies of twins reared apart cannot by the nature of circumstances

[1] cf. Murphy, Murphy and Newcomb. op. cit., pp. 32 f.
[2] Roberts, J. A. F. An Introduction to Medical Genetics. Oxford, 1940, p. 237.
[3] Burt, Sir C. 'Ability and Income.' *B. J. Ed. Psych.*, 19, 13, p. 91.

be frequent, but they have been made. In some cases[1] it has been found that the average difference in I.Q. after they had been separated was 7.7 points, but ranging from 0 to 17 which is not very different from the findings of twins reared together. This fits in with Burt's estimate that 'Even when the twins have been reared separately from early years the correlation is still .77'.[2] However, in a rather more detailed study of twenty cases of separated identical twins Newman[3] found that in four cases in which one twin had better education advantages than the other a marked difference of ability was demonstrated by their performance on a variety of different tests.

Wellman[4] compared the performance of children who had had nursery school training with that of children who had not and she declares that, 'A permanent change in intellectual standing can be effected in one to one-and-one-half years that will last four to eight years'.

W. C. Bagley[5] has insisted on the overwhelming potential influence of schooling with such force as to make teachers almost uncomfortable about their inadequacies when faced with dull children—and they are many—from 'good' homes.

In the University of Iowa, Dr. Stoddard and his colleagues have taken the same line.[6]

More general researches have been made by Otto Klineberg[7] on the effect of urban life on Negroes. Klineberg has accumulated a considerable amount of evidence in rebuttal of the crude hypothesis of racial superiority in intellectual ability. We are more concerned with a special aspect of his work. He found that Negroes in cities get higher scores than those who live in the country. This is in line, as we have already mentioned, with the results of a great many other inquiries with white population. The results, however, are by no means uniform. In New Jersey the scores of migrants were lower than those of the non-migrants,[8] and Dr. E. O. Lewis found in this country that

---

[1] Klineberg, O. op. cit., p. 237.

[2] 'Intelligence and Fertility.' Occasional Papers on Eugenics, No. 2, 1946, p. 37.

[3] Newman, H. H. *Multiple Human Births.* Doubleday, Dunn and Co., N.Y., 1940. cf. *Readings in Soc. Psychol.*, p. 1.

[4] Wellman, B. L. 'Growth in Intelligence under Differing School Environments.' *J. Exp. Educ.*, 1934, 3, p. 59.

[5] Bagley, W. C. *Determinism in Education: Paper on the Relative Influence of Inherited and Acquired Traits in Determining Intelligence*, 1925.

[6] Burt, Sir C. *Occup. Psych.*, 1945, 19.

[7] Klineberg, O. *Negro Intelligence and Selection Migration*, Columbia, U. P., 1935. *Race Differences.* Harpers, 1935.

[8] Klineberg, O. *Soc. Psychology*, p. 257.

'The level of intelligence in some villages, judged by the results obtained with group tests given to the schoolchildren, compared very
favourably with that of urban population.'[1] This disposes of the
hypothesis that *all* migrants are more intelligent than the stay-at-
homes, and that therefore the superiority of urban scores is due to
selection. Clearly, sometimes it is the go-ahead who migrate, sometimes those who are unsuccessful, and sometimes migration is due to
factors which affect bright and dull alike such as a famine or the arrival
of the boll weevil.

However, to return to the urban Negroes, it was not only found
that on the average the urban scores were higher than the rural ones,
but that they increased with length of residence in the city. The general
result of this piece of research is in agreement with the result of an
investigation, also carried out by Klineberg, on ethnic sub-groups in
Europe. One result was that no uniform superiority was found for
either of the three sub-groups: Nordics, Alpines and Mediterranean,
the German Nordics coming top, and the French Nordics one from
the bottom, thus disposing of 'racial theories'. Another result was that
the city boys from Paris, Rome and Berlin were all better than the
country ones. It is interesting to note that when the intelligence test
scores of American army recruits were analysed there was a high correlation (+ .72) between the scores of recruits and the efficiency of
education in the State from which they came.[2]

The last type of evidence brought forward in this connection is
drawn from foster homes.

Freeman, Holzinger and Mitchell[3] investigated some 401 foster
children in and about Chicago. They found that there was a difference
between the I.Q.s of the ones brought up in poorer homes and those
brought up in better ones. When seventy-four of them were retested
after they had been four years in their foster homes the ones who went
to the 'better' homes had gained 5.3 points while those in the poorer
ones had gained 0.1. The effect of the environment is greater the
younger they were adopted, and when they were adopted into different
kinds of homes the correlation between their I.Q.s was reduced to .19,
which contrasts with the average correlation of siblings brought up
together which is about .50. They go so far as to say that the 'maximal

---

[1] Papers of the Royal Commission on Population. Vol. V, p. 48.
[2] Blackburn, J. *The Framework of Human Behaviour.* Kegan Paul, 1947, p. 84.
[3] Freeman, F. N., Holzinger, K. J. and Mitchell, B. C. 'The Influence of Environment
on the Intelligence, School Achievement and Conduct of Foster Children.' *Twenty-
seventh Year Book. Nat. Soc. Stud. Educ.*, 1928.

effect of the best home environment raises the I.Q. 20 points.' Indeed
it was found that when the average I.Q.s were classified in accordance
with the occupation of the foster father, the order in which they were
lined up from highest to lowest corresponded to the order found in all
the studies relating the intelligence of children to the economic status
of their parents. This piece of evidence is slightly weakened by the
possibility that the foster parents of the professional class may have
chosen the brightest children for adoption, but there is no evidence
that they made any determined effort to do so.

Burks[1] compared 214 foster children with 105 children living with
their parents. She found in the first place that the correlation of test
scores between foster-child and foster-father was .07, between foster-
child and foster-mother .19, which are lower than those found by Freeman and his colleagues (.37 with foster-father and .28 with foster-
mother), and that the correlation between children and their parents in
the control group was .45 for child-father, and .46 for child-mother.
This might be taken to indicate the operation of inheritance. The correlation between the I.Q. of the foster children and the quality of the
home was .42, which is like Freeman's estimate of .48. The correlation
of I.Q. and measurable home environment was subjected to further
analysis and as a result Burks arrived at the estimate of the relative
weights of home and innate factors: about 17 per cent. for the home,
about 33 per cent. for parental intelligence, while 'the total contribution
of innate and heritable factors is probably not far from 75 or 80 per
cent.'[2]

This celebrated estimate is quoted with approval by Sir Cyril Burt,[3]
but it is not universally accepted. One of the difficulties is that Burks
had to calculate her correlations on 'measurable' features of home
environment, and that does not provide an entirely satisfactory basis
for so definite an estimate; in any case, what about school, friends,
neighbours and so on? Burt himself, in the same paper, gives a rather
more restrained estimate of 'one-half *at the very least* attributable
to 'nature' as distinct from 'nurture'.[4]

Leahy[5] conducted an investigation very similar to that of Burks on
194 adopted children each matched with a child living with its own
parents. The correlation between various characteristics of the children

---

[1] Burks, B. S. 'The Relative Influence of Nature and Nurture upon Mental Development.' *Twenty-seventh Year Book. Nat. Soc. Stud. Educ.*, 1928, Part I.
[2] ibid., p. 309.   [3] *Intelligence and Fertility*, p. 43.   [4] ibid., p. 37. Burt's italics.
[5] Leahy, A. M. 'Nature-nurture and Intelligence.' *Genet. Psychol. Monog.*, 1935, 17,
p. 235.

and their own parents was always higher than that between the adopted children and their foster-parents.

Children in institutions have also been investigated. One of the most important studies is that of Lawrence[1] in London. She found that children removed from their parents when they were less than a year old showed differences in intellectual ability which correlated with the occupation of their parents, and this was higher in the case of other children who were admitted after they were three years old.

Crissey[2] in America found that the intelligence of newcomers is affected by the general level of intelligence in the institution; the bright lose a little by being put among the dull, those below the general level on admission will remain so or are slightly improved.

To produce, as evidence of the inheritable element in intellectual ability, the numerous studies carried out in the British Isles and America on the relation between the intelligence of children and the occupational level of their parents is to beg the question. There is no doubt about the evidence itself.[3] In all cases a small positive correlation has been found between the average I.Q. of children and the occupational class of their parents. The interpretation of the evidence, however, is by no means easy. In the first place the overlap is very great[4] and this means that many children from the homes of people in 'higher occupations' are not particularly bright while a very large number of children coming from the 'lower occupations' are brilliant. Of course the best test performance must come from the 'high occupations' in order to put their average at the top, but even so one cannot say with any confidence that their good performance is due to superior inheritance. Further difficulties of interpretation present themselves when we contemplate the dullards from 'good' homes. Are their homes not as 'good' as we thought, or are their parents not so intelligent as we assume, or is the inheritable factor for father and mother more complex than we have yet realized? At the back of our minds, when discussing this question, lurks the whole problem of social mobility. Do people achieve positions in the 'high' occupational ranks through competitive skill in the open market, as certainly has happened to a great extent in

[1] Lawrence, E. M. 'An Investigation into the Relation between Intelligence and Inheritance.' *B. J. Psychol. Monog. Suppl.*, 1931, 16.

[2] Crissey, O. L. 'Mental Development as related to Institutional Residence and Education Achievement.' Univ. of Iowa. *Studies in Child Welfare*, 1937, 13.

[3] cf. Burt, Sir C. 'Ability and Income.' *B. J. Educ. Psych.*, 19, 13, p. 83. Fleming, C. M., ibid., p. 74. Klineberg, O. *Soc. Psychology*, p. 239.

[4] Gray, J. L. *The Nation's Intelligence*. Watts, 1936.

America,[1] or is mobility less easy so that a relatively stupid man can get a good job if he comes from the higher income group? The weight given to these considerations will, of course, vary with the general assumptions, and the political affiliation of the theorist.

The relation between intelligence and occupation of parent taken in conjunction with the differential birth-rate has obvious sociological implications into which we need not enter. One curiosity which has recently come into prominence, however, has a social-psychological aspect, and that is the inverse relationship between intelligence and size of family. This has been found in numerous researches[2] to be in the neighbourhood of $- .25$. One inference, of course, is that the more intelligent parents limit the size of their families, but that this is not the whole story is shown by Thomson's inquiry into cases when the father has died in circumstances which make it impossible to foresee whether they would have had more children if they had lived. In such cases, too, he found a negative correlation between intelligence and size of family.[3] According to Burt social factors are not of great importance. 'The conclusion to be stressed,' he says[4], 'is not so much that the smaller well-to-do or professional classes are producing few children, but that among the far more numerous working classes it is still the intelligent families who contribute fewest to the next generation', and accordingly he predicts a fall in the general level of intelligence, a prophecy with which the results of the recent Scottish inquiry are not entirely in accord.

Blackburn[5] who champions the environmentalist position shows that in some inquiries it is only among the poorer classes that the negative correlation is significant. He takes the line that in the poorer homes the congestion, lack of means, and defective parental attention are responsible for some of the children showing up badly in intelligence tests, a view in flat contradiction with that of O'Hanlon[6] to the effect that 'intelligence is little if at all affected by congestion in the home' and Sir Godfrey Thomson does not think 'that environment and social inheritance explain more than a fraction, at most half, of the negative correlation'.[7]

[1] cf. Sorokin, P. A. *Social Mobility,* 1927.
[2] cf. Burt, Sir C. *Intelligence and Fertility.* Thomson, G. *The Trend of Natural Intelligence.* Occasional Paper on Eugenics. Hamish Hamilton, 1947.
[3] Papers of the Royal Commission on Population, Vol. V, p. 38.   [4] op. cit., p. 17.
[5] Blackburn, J. 'Family Size, Intelligence Score and Social Class.' *Population Studies,* 1947, I, p. 165.
[6] O'Hanlon, G. S. A. 'The Relation between Fertility and Intelligence.' *B. J. Ed. Psychol.,* 1940, 10, p. 211.
[7] Paper Royal of Commission on Population, Vol. V, p. 35.

Another possible factor is life in a large family in modern times. The correlation of $-.25$ is small and it means that there are substantial numbers of bright children coming from large families and dull children coming from small ones. It may be that on the whole, though being a member of a large family is not as such disastrous, the chances of whatever attention is necessary to enable intelligence to develop may be slightly less forthcoming when there are several children than when there are few. At any rate it is clear that both the innate contribution and the environmental one have to be taken into account and that the weight which must be given to each is not necessarily uniform for all cases.

From all this conflicting evidence it is obvious that no clear conclusion can be drawn as to the effects of social environment on intellectual ability. A methodological principle, however, must be insisted on. We know that environment influences test performance, we know nothing whatever about innate intellectual equipment. This means that we must first try to explain intellectual difference in term of environment (save in cases of pathological defect) and, only when this fails, have recourse to the 'residual category' of innate endowment.

CHAPTER IX

CULTURE AND THE DEVELOPMENT OF PERSONALITY

SINCE there is, to say the least of it, a strong argument for saying that we only exist as persons because of our social interactions, it may readily be accepted that the sort of persons we become will be largely determined by the culture in which we are brought up. It is, as has been said before, a mistake to think of the 'person' as a pre-fabricated structure waiting at birth to be erected, well or ill, by the adults in charge of it. Prior to an infant's earliest contacts with other human beings it simply does not exist as a 'person' at all.

The way in which our personalities are shaped by the cultures in which we participate is, however, extremely complicated, and to deal with it we require two models. In the first place we can think of the culture as a fixed system of accepted behaviour to which the new-comer has to adjust himself, and to play his part in which the child has to be trained. Though the culture of course is continually changing, sometimes very slowly, and sometimes very fast, we may picture it as a relatively static structure, confronting the new member of the society, and we speak of him or her as 'adjusting' himself or herself to it. We have to analyse the concept of culture, and thus make our model more precise, we have to see the sorts of characteristics which must be acquired, and we have to find out how the training is accomplished.

The culture itself, however, is an abstraction from actual social intercourse. We must therefore make use of another model which presents the actors of the culture in dynamic relation with one another. This really involves a further analysis of the culture itself.

The purpose of this may be seen if we take an example. Supposing it is culturally acceptable for parents to treat their children with great solicitude, to give them food whenever they cry for it, not to force them to discipline themselves more than is appropriate to their capacity to control themselves, and, in general, to support them in such a way that the sense of insecurity is reduced to a minimum. It is argued that the resulting personality will be different from what it would be if they were given less attention. This argument is based partly on clinical studies of maladjusted persons in our own culture, and partly on general psychological considerations which are more or less confirmed by observations in everyday life.

The clinical observation of psycho-analysts has made it almost certain that what happens in infancy has a profound effect on later life. What this adds to common sense observation is the point that we must not think of infants as mere bundles registering but little; we must rather think of them in terms which we all agree to be appropriate to children and adults. Children and adults feel secure when they can count on their needs being satisfied. They feel a sense of worth, a sense that other people appreciate them and so forth. If, on the other hand, they are systematically denied attention, thwarted in the satisfying of their desires, and continually meet with rebuff, they resent it. They may 'show temper', they may be cowed, they may become sly, they may adopt a policy of evasion, or they may just become apathetic. This is surely common experience, and 'common sense'. Now all that is said of children, who can overtly display their sense of security or their resentment and anxiety, seems to be true of infants who cannot express themselves. If this is the case, and there seems very strong evidence to support it, then if a certain method of child care is fairly uniform in a society one may expect it to have its repercussions in the sort of person regarded as 'natural' or 'normal' in that society.

This hypothesis has far-reaching implications. The children (as distinct from the infants), the adolescents, the adults, and the old men and women are the actors of the culture. The culture *is* nothing but such of their conduct as has social approval, and is recognized as the 'done thing'. Of course they do enormous numbers of things which are culturally neutral, though what is culturally neutral will vary from one society to another. When they behave in accordance with what is generally expected of any member of the society in their position, they are tracing, or acting out, a fragment of the 'culture pattern'. If, therefore, treatment in infancy partially determines the out-look on life of the adult, does it not mean that the sort of culture these adults will act out will be partially determined by the methods of child-training in vogue in that culture? The suggestion is that there is a certain psychological coherence in culture-patterns. Given the general treatment of infants and children, *other* cultural features become intelligible. Or, to put it in another and rather more accurate way: if the upbringing of children is such and such then certain cultural features are extremely unlikely. If the infants in a culture, such as that of the Mundugomor,[1] have been treated with some hostility by their mothers, and have been allowed and expected to react with hostility, so that only by fighting have they gained their ends, you cannot expect them to grow up into peaceful co-operating adults. Their experience is all against it. Their own technique, and what they expect of others will be likely to lead them to precipitate a culture-pattern, which bears some intelligible relationship to what they have been through.

This type of inquiry is relatively new and some of the theories which have been put forward will be discussed in the next chapter. In this one we will use the other model—the cultural structure which confronts the new member who has to be trained to play his part in it.

'Cultures,' said Linton,[2] 'are, in the last analysis, nothing more than the organized repetitive responses of a society's members.' It is obvious that this is a highly abstract construct. Socially expected configurations of behaviour are actually executed in as many different ways as there are executants. No man takes off his hat to a lady in exactly the same way as another, or as he does himself on the next occasion. No dedicated priest performs precisely the same ritual acts. No shop assistant sells his goods in exactly the same way that another shop assistant does, even if they both deal in the same wares. Yet we can think of 'taking off one's hat to a lady' as being the culturally expected behaviour of men in one culture, certain action as the 'right' thing for priests to do in certain contexts, and certain conduct as appropriate to shop assistants. To cope with this contrast between actual varieties of performance, and the underlying similarity of pattern, Linton[3] proposes the term 'real culture' and 'culture construct'. 'The real culture of any society consists of the actual behaviour and so on of its members. This, in any culturally defined situation, will constitute a range of conduct within which what is done is acceptable, outside which it is reprehensible or inefficacious or both. The 'culture construct' is the 'ideal type' of conduct which the scientist invents by a process of abstraction from the 'real culture'. It is a rather indefinite norm; indefinite because no one has any clear image of it, and a 'norm' because there is an 'ought' attached to it.

A culture-pattern, then, is no strait-jacket imposing identity of behaviour on all members of the society. Each plays out his part in his

[1] Mead, M. *Sex and Temperament in Three Primitive Societies*, 1935.
[2] Linton, R. *Cultural Background of Personality*. Kegan Paul, 1947, p. 4.
[3] ibid., p. 28.

own particular style. This brings us to the problem of individual differences. 'Every man is in certain respects (*a*) like all other men (*b*) like some other men (*c*) like no other man.'[1] This is obvious enough. Every infant is 'like no other infant', and immediately he is born he is in contact with men and women who are like no other men and women. Differences between persons are catered for, but a difficulty presents itself. Consider the simple case of an infant and its mother. Since she is different from all other mothers, she will manipulate her child in her own unique way—indeed, that is part of what we mean by saying that she is different from all other mothers. If she bears identical twins she will behave uniquely to each so that they start off with *different* treatment. Thus much of the difference between people is due to the different treatment they have had from their mother, and now we may add their father and, indeed, anyone else with whom they come in contact. Can we therefore say that they all start alike, but receive different treatment? Not at all. First, this would leave the difference between the adults ultimately unaccounted for, and second, there is evidence that certain psychological characteristics are partially innately determined. The latter evidence is, of course, strongest in the case of intellectual ability, but even then, as we have seen, it is quite impossible to assign the proportion of any performance due to innate constitution, and that due to experience or training.

It is, however, abundantly clear that a man's abilities and his temperament have been influenced by his social contacts, in the sense that if these contacts had been different his abilities and his temperament would probably have been different too. The *range* of variation, if one envisages all possible social environments, would appear to be fixed by his initial constitution. What that range is we have at present no means of discovering. His 'initial constitution' is therefore a residual category. It must be conceived of as an indefinite potentiality, wherein all infants differ, with the possible exception of identical twins (and even here interuterine life may be a differentiating factor). It is a residual category because what we say in effect is: all the differences between children which we cannot trace to their social environment must be there from the start. We do not begin with a knowledge of the initial constitution and then watch the play of social environment on it; we begin with the infant in social relationship, and have recourse to the initial constitution when we cannot tell any other more plausible story.

[1] Kluckhohn, C. (ed.) *Personality*, p. 35.

Thus the infant with its unique but unknown potentialities is born and immediately meets adults and children, each with his or her unique individuality, which is due in turn to their unique experience, springing out of the meeting of *their* unique constitution with *their* unique social environment.

So much for the new-born child. Confronting him is the 'culture pattern'. To bring some formal order into this, Linton and other writers make use of the following concepts: *status, role,* and *basic personality pattern*. What we actually *have* is people behaving overtly and covertly (i.e. in ways for which we use body language and in ways for which we use mind language). What we are interested in is such ranges of actual behaviour as are culturally acceptable. This behaviour is centred round certain positions in the society. There is appropriate behaviour for children, appropriate behaviour for adult men, appropriate behaviour for adult women, and so forth. These positions have been called '*statuses*', and the appropriate conduct to each status is the '*role*'. Statuses, however, are not all of the same order, and Linton[1] distinguishes between *ascribed statuses* and *achieved statuses*. The former 'are assigned to individuals without reference to their innate difference or abilities'. Everyone is an infant at some stage of his career, and if he survives he reaches the statuses of 'child', and, in due course, of adulthood and old age. Nearly everyone is male or female, husband or wife, father or mother and so forth. To each of these statuses a certain role is ascribed by every culture to the persons occupying them.

The 'achieved statuses' are those which are not reached by some natural process; they are specialisms which 'are left open to be filled through competition and individual effort'. There are certain statuses which in all societies are what Linton calls 'ascribed'. The 'achieved' statuses, on the other hand, will clearly vary from society to society; in the first place the jobs which have to be done by specialists will vary from group to group, and in the second place, if *all* the males of a certain family were brought up to be priests, the status would be 'ascribed' to them, whereas if priests were selected because they are deemed to have certain characteristics, then this status would be 'achieved' by them.

There are, then, statuses ascribed on a biological basis, and statuses achieved by effort. In a society with class differences these will further define the ascribed statuses, and may determine to a large extent the accessibility to statuses which are achieved. Thus an 'upper-class' child

[1] *The Study of Man.* Appleton. Century, 1936, p. 115.

will have a status and its role to play which is different from that of a 'lower-class' child in many respects. He will also be more likely to achieve the status of Judge or Archbishop, should he desire it, than the boy from a 'lower-class' level in the hierarchy.

A few more points remain to be noted. Clearly any given individual can occupy several statuses at once, and in succession. How far one says that he is playing a multiple role, or a single one at any given moment, will depend upon the purpose of one's inquiry. A bank manager in action is carrying out the roles of adult, of middle-class male, and of bank manager in so far as he learnt them. One can lump all the roles together and call them one, or one can separate them out, as one would if one wanted to say that he was performing the bank manager role adequately at any moment but that he displayed certain traits of speech or manner which were not accepted as characteristic of middle-class male adults. The succession of roles presents no difficulty. When he leaves his office the businessman may play the roles of a 'sport' at the club, a father in the house, and a mason in the lodge throughout the course of an evening. In doing so he will be influenced by something we have not yet mentioned.

The roles in any society are, as we have seen, abstract patterns of conduct to which the *actual* conduct of people occupying the relevant statuses approximates. The members of a society, however, often formulate in their minds and in conversation verbalized versions of 'ideal roles', which are patterns of conduct which 'ought' to go with certain statuses. In the case of statuses involving specialized skills the roles which we, as observers, abstract from the behaviour we witness may be extremely like that behaviour; that is to say, the range of variation in doing whatever it is may be small. Furthermore, if we were to ask for a verbal account of the 'ideal' performance, it might not be very different from the role we have abstracted or from the actual performance we have witnessed. In roles of a more general order, such as those of father or mother, son or daughter, this does not always hold. We watch fathers behaving as such and they all behave differently; there is, however, a certain general pattern of conduct which seems expected of fathers; this is the 'role' we construct from observation. It may be, however, that the *'ideal'* father of whom they talk is nowhere to be seen. Nevertheless, the 'ideal' role is not by any means without its influence. Fathers may be restrained from certain courses of action by thinking of the 'ideal' father they 'ought 'to be. The 'ideal' roles may give rise to feelings of guilt in those who depart from them too far. But what the social psychologist has to bear in mind is that he must check his concepts of 'roles' by observations of actual behaviour, and not rely on the verbalized version which may be far from the facts.

Finally it must be observed that statuses are reciprocal in the sense that the role of any status calls forth in response the role of some other status. The role of child elicits appropriate responses which are the roles of 'other children of the same age', 'older child', 'younger child', 'father', 'mother', 'adult' and so on. The role of employee has its reciprocal in the roles of employer, fellow-employee, student of industrial psychology, etc. This knowledge of what to do and what to expect is what makes for smooth social living. It is, in fact, a version of the 'frame of reference', which we have met before.

One of the features of our own time is the indeterminacy and rapid changing of roles. Of children, of employees, and of public servants, one constantly hears the indignant cry: 'One does not know what they will do next,' followed by: 'One can't say anything to them.' To many people this is a distressing situation.

We come now to the third concept: *basic personality*.

We have so far given a formal analysis of culture, passing from actual conduct with its recurrent patterns to the positions from which these patterns radiate in the reciprocal interaction of roles. The 'basic personality' is a rather more abstract model; it corresponds roughly with what one is trying to indicate by such expressions as 'a typical Frenchman' or 'a "good" Comanche'. Every Frenchman is different from every other, so is every Comanche Indian, but there is some rather indefinite type of personality which is taken to be 'normal', 'right' and 'proper' among the Comanche which is very different from any notion we might form of the 'typical' Frenchman. '*Basic personality* structure,' for Linton,[1] 'represents the constellation of personality characteristics which would appear to be congenial with the total range of institutions comprised within a given culture.'

The concept was first used by Kardiner and Linton, and in their hands it is a tool for the analysis of cultures in the way which was indicated at the beginning of this chapter and which will be discussed later on. In addition to the 'basic personality type', characteristic of a culture, we may also borrow from Linton the notion of 'status personality' which is a kind of consolidation of the status/role concept. The doctor occupies a status and has a role to play, but we expect him

[1] In Kardiner A. *The Individual and his Society*. Columbia. Univ. Press 1939, p. vi.

to be something more than a mere performer of the motions. We expect him to have a certain attitude towards his work and his patients and certain standards of professional conduct; such a complex makes up the 'status personality' of the status of doctor.

The infant is faced with a system of *statuses*, some of which he must learn to occupy, and a '*basic personality*' type, in terms of which his education will unconsciously conspire to mould him. Before him lie certain *status personalities* which he must learn to accept.

So far we have shrunk from a definition of personality. We can accept the one given by Allport in his *Personality*[1] to the effect that: 'Personality is the dynamic organization within the individual of those psycho-physical systems that determine his unique adjustments to his environment.' The merit of this definition is that it combines inclusiveness with the feature of organization. For our purpose it is convenient to distinguish, however roughly, between those adjustments that are relatively specific to certain situations, and those which are more general and 'come out' on all sorts of occasions. The appropriate adjustment to the demands of a skilled occupation, for example, or to those of an 'unskilled' one, for a matter of that, are more specific than such general adjustments as go by the description of 'aggressive', 'sly', 'anxious', 'suspicious' and so on. The former are a matter of explicit training, the latter are the resultants of more complex factors. In so far as one thinks of a man's skills—manual, linguistic, athletic, etc.—as ingredients in his personality, it is quite clear that different cultures will produce different results in personality because they involve different sets of skills. But it is plausible to say that these skills, which may require innate abilities, such as intelligence and manual aptitudes, are relatively superficial to the 'real' personality of their possessors. It is perfectly true that many 'status personalities' involve general attitudes and ways of thought besides the specific performances their roles entail, but the distinction between the specific skills and general attitudes can be appreciated when we remember that not all civil servants are 'typical' civil servants, while many people, not in the Civil Service, are.

The method adopted by societies for the training in special skills will vary from one culture to another, and it will partly depend upon the nature of the skills involved, and whether they are sacred or secret, or open to anyone to acquire. The subject will not be pursued here because we are more interested in the general attitudes and ways of thinking, as features of the personality which social intercourse in-

[1] Holt, 1937, p. 48.

fluences. Two observations, however, must be made. If any skills are held to be sacred and if only a few are allowed to learn them, these facts and the method of imparting them, are likely to have an effect on the 'general' personality of the initiates. They may be treated with reverence or avoidance, and they may feel themselves to have a power which others have not. Furthermore, as we shall see, the achievement of the status to which these skills belong may serve as an outlet for social deviates who have not been able to acquire the accepted set of general personality traits.

The second point is this. Some simple skills, which may be all that are required for the majority of persons to live a normal life in a community, may be gradually taught to children as they become capable of carrying them out. Where this is the case there is no need for the status of 'educator', at any rate for such skills. More important is the fact that the child can be given a place in the work of its family or kin. This may well induce a sense of responsibility which may be absent in children whose activities have nothing whatever to do with the serious work of the community. Not all primitive peoples seem to expect their children to undertake serious work at an early age, even when they can, but the imposition of such responsibilities can still be observed in remoter corners of our own urbanized society. Children of small farmers are often brought up to participate in the work of the farm. They are relied on to do such small but essential jobs as lie within their competence. One result of this is that they are treated seriously, and casual observation would seem to show that they do not suffer so much from those upheavals which used to be thought 'natural' to the period of adolescence.

When, on the other hand, the sorts of things that adults do and the sorts of things they are expected to know are such that specialized training is required, the child is taken from its house for various periods, it enters a new and specially structured society for hours, almost every day or for months at a time, and thus social situations present themselves which cannot but make a difference to its personality. The things the children do in such a culture are different from the things the adults do, and this contributes to the gulf between them. The way this tension manifests itself will, of course, vary with circumstances. The boy may be taught more up-to-date things than father knows. Father may be disgusted at his son's lack of progress. Pride, disappointment, encouragement, envy and nostalgia may colour the relation between children and parents in ways which are not likely to be found when the child passes slowly from a little inept grubbing to being entrusted with larger and larger tools, without having to leave the family hearth.

Thus the acquisition of a skill as such may not make a deep impression on a personality, but the circumstances in which it is acquired may be of significance.

Infant Training. Turning now to the training of infants with respect to more general traits we are faced with such a variety of cultures, basic personalities, and status personalities, and such an array of different family structures, kinship structures, statuses, expectations and assumptions, that it would require a great many volumes to bring together all the different ways of life that human beings have produced. All we can do here is to consider certain very general principles which seem to emerge, indicating the sort of ways in which different set-ups are likely to be significant. This is not only a matter of 'academic' interest; it is of practical significance. If we consider some of the social 'experiments' which humanity has unintentionally tried out, we may be better equipped for a study of our own 'experiment' as it stands at present, and we may perhaps be tempted to experiment further, not by leaving the unintentional drift to follow its course, but with an intention to produce certain effects.

Now if you are moulding a piece of plasticine, the material is passive to your touch. When you are 'moulding' a human infant this is by no means the case. You have to exploit its dynamic potentialities. Let us reduce them to the simplest statement: (1) There are bodily states of tension which demand release. The process of release gives pleasure; the consistent experience of release gives security. (2) There is a need for what may be called 'social recognition'. This may be derived from the association of the attentiveness of other people with the release of primary tensions. Whether this need is derived or not, it is of major importance as an educational lever. (3) Certain bodily experiences are painful, the persistence of tension is unpleasing and the denial of good-will is distressing. The infant may be calculated to make some response to such situations. Avoidance or aggression are possible responses, and there are certain round-about techniques, such as finding some substitute method of satisfying a need, or displacing a tendency from a disallowed objective to an allowed one, or developing a system of beliefs in which the unsatisfied tendencies are 'projected' on to fictitious entities. The 'entities' in this third technique may be stereotypes derived from real life or purely imaginary beings.

It is not suggested that the responses to pain or non-satisfaction which have been mentioned are an exhaustive list. They are merely examples of possible responses, all of which have an importance in this context.

It will be seen that if we put the tension-release system and the need for social recognition together, they provide a basis for reward-value, while the pains and non-satisfactions make some situations disrewarding. This word which has been coined for this purpose must be excused. The word 'unrewarding' which is the contradictory of 'rewarding' does not carry with it the implication of positive painfulness. The word 'punishing' carries with it moral implication. The word 'disrewarding' is intended to convey the notion of 'off-putting'.

From this a simple scheme emerges: situations, courses of action, persons, and things which are 'rewarding' will tend to be sought, while those which have been found to be disrewarding will tend to be avoided, and other courses of action may be taken. With these simple concepts, when the general principles of learning are added, a considerable amount of human behaviour can be explained. Whether all human conduct can be reduced to such simple terms is very doubtful. The technique of reduction is as follows: take any objective sought by any human being and see whether, as you trace its origin, you require nothing more than the concepts mentioned above. Can you, that is to say, trace it back to certain primary tension-release systems together with the need for social recognition, and account for its specific character by means of the principles of learning, plus the mechanisms which are brought into action under circumstances of dis-reward? The alternative, of course, is that you must introduce some other dynamic principle, such, for instance, as what is sometimes called 'Moral Sense'. For example, suppose a man devotes himself to, say, the relief of the suffering of lepers or the improvement of the lot of criminal lunatics, is it *ever* the case that his conduct cannot be accounted for, without residue, in terms perhaps of his happy home-life, which has made him friendly disposed to other people, or his unhappy home-life, which has engendered such hatred that he has to behave with exaggerated solicitude in order to hide from himself and other people the raging storm that lies within? Or do you *ever* have to introduce some flash of moral awareness to account for it?

No decision upon the subject can be arrived at without a great deal of research. The point of mentioning it is that psychologists often ignore moral problems altogether and assume that because a very large range of human conduct can be explained with the simple scheme outlined above, moral decisions, when they get round to them, will prove equally amenable. This may, indeed, not be the case.

We now have to consider some of the situations which seem to be significant in the shaping of the personality. Again, not all the significant situations can be mentioned, but it is hoped that a selection may indicate some of the ways in which a culture exerts its first pressures.[1]

To begin with the new-born infant has to be tended, and this is done with varying degrees of solicitude, from one culture to another. 'The Mundugamor women,' Margaret Mead[2] tells us, 'actively dislike child-bearing, and they dislike children.... Mothers nurse their children standing up, pushing them away as soon as they are the least bit satisfied.' The Alorese mothers, as described by Dr. Du Bois, leave their children after about fourteen days and go and work in the fields. Their tensions are intermittently relieved by anyone who happens to be at hand and can no longer stand the noise of the child crying. In the former case, though treated with hostility, the Mundugamor child can develop an aggressive snatching technique to get what it wants; in the latter it is, so Kardiner[3] suggests, so overwhelmed by its tensions, and the intermittent and uncalculable nature of such release as it gets, that it cannot form 'effective action systems'. The foundations are laid by the Mundugamors for an aggressive personality. The Alorese, however, who have no continuous emotional contact, grow up 'anxious, suspicious, mistrustful, lacking in confidence [and] with no interest in the outer world'. If this interpretation be correct it would appear that some coherent emotional treatment is a prerequisite for the development of responsiveness, leaving aside the nature—aggressive or otherwise—of the responses.

Affectionate and solicitous treatment would appear to pave the way for co-operation and a sense of security and personal value. There is, however, a possible danger. If dependency and passivity are overstressed the male may not be able to put up an effective struggle against his neighbours if they are aggressive. This is what is said to happen among the peaceable Arapesh.[4] The women are prepared for their role of motherhood by the way they were cherished as children. The men are not so well placed; the active sexual role does not come easy to them, and they are at a disadvantage in their social and geographical environment.

[1] For a list of key situations cf. Kardiner *et al. Psychological Frontiers of Society*, p. 26.
[2] Mead, M. *Male and Female.* Gollancz, 1949, p. 69.
[3] *Psychological Functions of Society*, p. 169.
[4] Mead, M. ibid, p. 67.

Another factor, which some writers believe to be significant, is the degree of freedom of movement allowed. We are used to infants lying in their cots or prams, kicking their legs and waving their arms. Many American Indians, many Italians and Yugoslavs, are denied this freedom. They are, in various ways, swaddled. The evidence about the effect of swaddling is ambiguous. Much has to be taken into consideration:[1] the degree of freedom allowed, the attitude of the swaddlers, and the amount of liberty from swaddling. Recently Geoffrey Gorer[2] has attempted to deduce certain characteristics which are familiar to the reader of Russian works from the prevalence of swaddling in that country. The hypothesis is that the swaddling impedes movement, this gives rise to aggressive responses which are inhibited, and the nursing of such aggressiveness in the breast gives rise to a sense of guilt. Furthermore the alternation of freedom and unfreedom, when the child is undone and done up again, plays its part—so it is suggested—in building a somewhat explosive character.

Clearly the influence of swaddling, as with methods of feeding, must be taken in conjunction with other factors, and more research is required into, for example, the personal qualities of Russians who have not been swaddled, before we are able to assess its influence.

Another element in child care, and this time one about which we have considerable clinical evidence, is the training it receives in the control of its sphincters. Proficiency in this control is expected at different ages in different societies, and the attitude towards the processes of urination and defecation also vary. In our culture, or, rather, in many of our sub-cultures, the topic is one which arouses strong feelings of disgust and it prompts all sorts of avoidance-reactions. Such attitudes make cleanliness discipline a matter of importance in the relationship between parent and child, which transcends the social importance of the control itself. So far as the latter is concerned, sphincter control is one of the child's first essays in social responsibility. The pleasures which it gets from its bodily functions have to be restricted to certain times and places, and the child is the only person who can do this. Here is an act for which he can be blamed. It is obvious, therefore, that if he is expected to achieve self-control at a very early age, and if his lapses are followed by severe treatment, a diminution of self-confidence is likely to result.

[1] cf. Greenacre, P. 'Infant Reaction to Restraint.' *Am. J. of Orthopsychiatry*, 14, 1949. Abridged Version in *Personality*. (Ed.) Kluckhohn, C., p. 390.
[2] Gorer, G. *The People of Great Russia*. Cresset Press, 1949.

All this is made the more significant when the whole subject is approached in a heightened emotional atmosphere. On the one hand the child may be besought to produce, and its performance is often referred to as its 'duty'. On the other hand its productions are regarded with agitation and disgust, particularly when they appear in the wrong place. Now if we accept the hypothesis that the reactions of the infant are to be thought of in adult terms, it is obvious that the situation is full of possibilities. The response may be one of obstinate refusal to give what is demanded; it may be that an exaggerated regard for cleanliness, tidiness, accuracy is generated as a kind of countermeasure to the primary interest in the abominated thing; it may be that the child, dimly apprehending the sensibilities of adults, realizes that in untimely urination it has a weapon which it can use against them. Now the psycho-analysts[1] hold that these responses tend to become generalized and form permanent components of the personality. If this is so, then the way in which a culture handles the problem of sphincter control is relevant to the type of personality which is produced by it.

Before proceeding to other, and rather more obvious, ways in which 'culture' shapes 'personality', a possible source of misunderstanding must be removed. Each infant is influenced in its subsequent development by the particular treatment he has received from his particular parents. His feeding, his freedom or lack of it, and his training in control of his natural functions are specific to him and have worked upon his own peculiar constitution. All that is meant by saying that 'cultural influences' are at work is: (1) that the treatment he has received is very wide-spread among the members of the society to which his own parents belong, and (2) that such treatment is deemed by such persons to be within the range of treatments which they regard as acceptable. This is evidenced by verbal expressions of disapproval at treatment which lies outside the accepted range, and expression of approval, or the mere taking-for-granted, of treatment within it. There is no thing called 'culture' which constitutes an additional force.

Childhood. The next social influence to be noted is the range of social relations open to the child as it grows up and becomes mobile. This, again, varies enormously, and we can only consider the sort of effect which such variety may have.

To begin with, in our cultures the infant is usually brought up by

---

[1] cf. Freud, S. 'Character and Anal Eroticism.' *Collected Papers XI.* Jones, E. 'Anal-Erotic Character Traits.' *Papers in Psycho Analysis.* Baillière, Tindall, 1923, p. 630.

two people, its mother and father, and these are almost the only adults from whom the satisfaction of its needs can come. Now the Samoan children enjoy a much less restricted range of adult attention. It is true that there are more people to order them about, but if they are uncomfortable with one set of adults they can go to another. 'Few children,' says Margaret Mead,[1] 'live continuously in one household, but are always testing out other possible residences.' So that: 'No Samoan child, except the *taupo* (a girl destined to be a ceremonial hostess), or the thoroughly delinquent, ever has to deal with a feeling of being trapped. There are always relations to whom one can flee.'

Among the Marquesans, as described by Linton,[2] and analysed by Kardiner, there is a shortage of women. The result is that a household is liable to consist of a head and his wife and a group of 'secondary husbands' whom she has brought with her. The children are not welcomed by the women because they interfere with their sexual lives. It is the group of 'fathers' who keep an eye on them. They seem to know who their actual fathers are, but this matters very little; they are dependent indiscriminately on all their mother's 'husbands'. This, again, as with the Samoan, gives rise to a diffuse dependency. If one 'father' does not do what you want, you try another. Interestingly enough, the same course of action is applied to the ancestor-gods. If your offerings have not had the desired effect, it is not because you are wicked, but because the God is inefficient;[3] you go elsewhere with your presents.

In both cases, Samoan and Marquesan, the disciplinary technique of demanding a sacrifice as the price of love and protection is excluded. This device, the establishment of the principle 'If I do this, Mother (or Father) will (or will not) love me', requires a more intense and concentrated emotional relationship than is found in either of these cultures, or in any culture in which the father and mother have not got the monopoly of protection and care, with which to force compliance.

Thus, the range and nature of adult contacts is a matter of importance in personality development. So, too, is position in the family, though the significance of this will vary, in turn, with the general accessibility of companions outside the circle of siblings. Every child, in a household of legitimate children of the same parents (the possible situations which can arise if we include illegitimate children, and chil-

---

[1] *Coming of Age in Samoa.* Penguin Books, 1943, p. 32.
[2] Kardiner, A. *The Individual and His Society.* Columbia Un. Press, 1939, p. 137 f.
[3] ibid., p. 211.

dren of different spouses are here ignored for the sake of brevity and not because they are unimportant), is either the only child, the eldest of a number, the youngest of a number or an intermediate if the number is more than two. And every child is separated by a certain distance in age from his older or younger siblings if he has any. All these possible positions must make a difference. 'There is probably no position in the family circle which does not involve as a consequence of its own peculiar nature certain problems of adjustment.'[1] The positions of an only child, eldest, or youngest are different, and the kind of treatment and range of contacts which apply in each of these positions are different.

The nature of the difference, however, must depend on the culture. In the first place there is a well-known difference in the value placed upon children in terms of their sex. If girl children are socially ill-esteemed, the treatment of a first-born girl child is likely to be different from that given to a girl who follows a series of boys. Again, among the Marquesan, 'the eldest child of either sex, or the child who was adopted to take the position of the eldest, becomes the official head of the household from the moment of birth or arrival'.[2] This situation places all younger children in a markedly subordinate position *vis-à-vis* the eldest sibling. Thus no supra-cultural generalization about birth-order can be made. In America a considerable volume of work has been done on the influence of birth-order upon social behaviour. Much of it is conveniently summarized by Murphy, Murphy and Newcomb.[3] The 'Individual Psychologists', followers of Adler, have exploited the possibilities of inferiority which a family circle consisting of more than one child presents.[4] The results of investigation are often inconclusive and the results of one investigation frequently conflict with the results of others. This does not mean that birth-order is a negligible factor, it means that its effects are not uniform for every position. In the life of the *individual* they may be of vital importance.

As an example of the way in which cultural factors may operate in this matter, we may consider an unpublished piece of research by J. P. Lees on the subsequent careers of fifty miners who attended Nottingham University College for two days a week. When the data are

[1] Goodenough, F. L. and Leahy, A. M. 'The Effect of Certain Family Relationships upon the Development of Personality.' *J. of Genet. Psych.*, 34, p. 45.
[2] *Individual and His Society*, p. 154.
[3] op. cit., p. 348.
[4] cf. Wexberg, E. *Individual Psychology.* Allen and Unwin, 1930, p. 185.

analysed in terms of birth-order, it appears that an unexpectedly high proportion of those who availed themselves of the opportunity were eldests. Of them, some did conspicuously well afterwards, others returned to the pit. The remarkable thing is that the siblings of those who did well had almost all got out of the typical occupation of miners' families—mining for the boys and domestic duties for the girls— while in the case of those who returned to the pit this was not the case. There is no reason to suppose that family intelligence accounts for this, and Lees offers a social-psychological explanation. Mining, at the time when the men were offered their two day a week course, was an ill-thought-of occupation. The eldests, finding their position of importance jeopardized by the arrival of siblings, compensated by going 'to college'; that is why there were so many of them. Those whose siblings had remained in the ill-thought-of occupation did not have to do anything more than this; their superiority was unchallenged; they had been 'to college', and they could go back to the mine. The others had to do something better. Going 'to college' was not enough; they had to put forward an even greater effort to ensure their need for independent superiority.

The 'intermediates', on the other hand were in a different case. They had enjoyed the importance of the youngest and the relative unimportance of an intermediate position. Their very unimportance in the family made them look outside for backing, and a high proportion of them did achieve some improvement in their status through distinguishing themselves in group activities such as Local Government and Trade Unionism.[1]

The numbers in this inquiry are small, but it illustrates the factors which have to be taken into account in future research. The conduct of the eldest in this context is determined by: (1) the status and role of 'eldest' in a mining family, and (2) the fact that mining and domestic occupations were, at a certain time, considered of low value. If either of these were otherwise, the situation would be radically changed. The same is true of the intermediates. From a formal point of view all 'intermediates' have, by definition, been youngests and then displaced. Their status must, of course, be culturally determined and may vary from one culture to another. The interesting question remains: in our culture do they all tend to find solace in hanging on to a person or a group of persons outside the family circle? The intermediate position

---

[1] I am indebted to Mr. J. P. Lees, Lecturer in Social Philosophy at Nottingham University for permission to quote from his research.

has been neglected by investigators, and only further research will throw light on this not unimportant problem.

As time goes on the infant grows into a mobile child and comes into active relationship with other children. The opportunities of such contact will vary from one community to another, and, in large-scale societies, from one class to another. Sometimes they live a comparatively care-free life, sometimes, as in Samoa, some of them—the little girls—have duties put upon them of looking after children younger than themselves. As usual the range of possibilities is enormous, and it is difficult to see in detail how different systems of inter-child relationship make their specific contributions to the personalities in process of creation. Certain formal changes, however, would seem to be brought about in this context.

The infant in a restricted home circle, or surrounded by a number of potentially helpful adults, is dependent. He makes his claims, he succeeds or suffers rebuffs, he develops techniques of holding out his arms, or howling, or snatching to get what he wants, but the relationship between him and others is unequal. Among siblings too the relationship is unequal, and depends upon the position of each. It is when he meets children of his own age, who can make no demands on him and on whom he makes no demands, that he experiences the full blast of equality, with its independence and its responsibilities.

Piaget,[1] indeed, traces a sense of moral responsibility to the development of children's relations with one another. His main data came from the study of a group of Swiss children playing a game. The attitude towards the rules seems to change as the child grows out of its readiness to accept them as sacrosanct, and reaches a stage at which the rules are regarded as necessary conveniences for the playing of the game, but alterable and 'breakable' if it would on occasion be 'fair' to do so. This notion of 'fair' presupposes an appreciation of another person's position. It may, of course, be learnt in the family circle, but it is fairly obvious that it is sharpened in a group of children each fending for him or herself, and yet learning that regard must be paid to the interests of others if one's own interests are to be regarded. In fact the child becomes aware of 'other people', and in so doing it is hardly too much to say that he participates in the child sub-culture of his society, with its standards, its approval, its disapproval, its prestiges and its heroes.

In the family circle in which, particularly if a restricted one, a child

[1] Piaget, J. *Moral Judgment of the Child.* Kegan Paul, 1932.

has to renounce much that he would like to do in order to get the goodwill of its parents, restrictive mechanisms are incorporated. It is sometimes suggested that these restrictive mechanisms, implanted at an early age, are almost the only ones of any importance. This is clearly not so. Whether these mechanisms are formulated in the dramatic language of a forbidding 'super-ego', or whether they are thought of as an acquired and habitualized set of inhibitions, they are continually undergoing modification and addition. The earliest are surprisingly persistent and cover a very much wider range of activities than was 'rationally' intended, sometimes making *all* pleasure or *anything* that comes to be associated with sex a matter of anxiety. But the safeguards of goodwill which one learns and makes part of oneself in one's effort to stand well with one's co-equals in age, and, even more with those a little older, add their quota to the inhibitive system.

It is for this reason that more attention should be paid to differences in the sub-cultures of children in different social classes in our own community. One would suppose that children who meet in the street to play would be likely to develop a different system of social manipulation and restraints from that which would be developed in a world of arranged parties supervised by adults. This only concerns what we might call the informal and spontaneous social relations between children. When one considers the formal educational system with the opportunities which it affords for inter-child relationships there can be no doubt about the part they play in personality making. Indeed, many aspects of our educational system are deliberately designed to make a mark on the personality of the children subjected to it. There is segregation of the sexes, or deliberate non-segregation; there are 'purity', 'honour', and 'sportsmanship'; there are the 'prefect system', the 'house system', and the 'morning assembly', with or without an 'act of worship'. All these are devised as techniques of moulding personality. The difficulty is that we know very little about how they work; we know very little about the boy-culture or girl-culture that is precipitated by these 'systems' and 'ideals'. Casual conversation would lead one to suppose that the little pitchers are not always shaped quite as the potter intends, and we have next to no knowledge about the working of different systems in other cultures, with the possible exception of the 'dating' system in America.

In this matter, then, of the effect of inter-child relationships on the differential shaping of personality we have to confess deep ignorance.

There is, however, a point of interest raised by Ruth Benedict.[1] She points out that in some primitive societies a child is regarded as having the same kind of responsibility as the adult only not being able to do so much. They are expected to do things like shut doors if asked without anyone going to their aid, though they will not do it as quickly as someone older. Again, in some societies children are expected to joke and tease certain adults on an equality and with the freedom expected of grown up people, while submission is positively disapproved of by many American Indians. The point of this is that at a very early age they are practising what they will be doing when they are grown up and a sense of responsibility is inculcated very early. This contrasts with our methods, with the possible exception of remote rural areas, as has been suggested above. With us the child normally participates but little in the life of adults and therefore has responsibility thrust upon him unprepared. We train children to respectful dependence on elders, which means the playing of a role that has to be unlearnt when they grow up. It is not surprising that some people find the change-over more than they can manage.

The same is true of our culture-patterning of sex. In infancy, in childhood, and in adolescence it is 'dirty', in young-man-hood and young-woman-hood it is regrettable, in marriage it suddenly becomes a 'joy'. It is not surprising that when the time for enjoyment comes, many of the partners are ill-conditioned for it: they find it difficult to unlearn all they have been taught.

Disciplinary Methods. In all this process of social-interchange by means of which a child's personality is slowly created in a form more or less congenial to the statuses he will fill and the institutional patterns in which he will participate, some of his spontaneous impulses will have proved disrewarding. When this happens he either has to give them up or 'inhibit' them, or he has to find round-about ways of satisfying them, or he has to run the risk of the disreward if he allows them free rein. In point of fact somehow or other almost all members of societies manage to establish within them a method of control which seems to work automatically.

Looked at from the point of view of the society, it may be said to 'discipline' its children through the parents and other relatives who have disciplinary responsibility. The question is: how is this done?

[1] 'Continuities and Discontinuities in Cultural Conditioning.' *Psychiatry*, Vol. I, 1938, p. 161 also in Kluckhohn, C. (ed.) *Personality*, p. 414.

We are familiar with a theory that we 'introject' our version of our parents and that this, in the shape of the 'super-ego' keeps watch over the impulses which surge up from our instinctual nature. Either (1) the super-ego holds such an impulse at bay in which case we are completely unaware *in every respect* of its existence, or (2) a disapproved impulse comes through, is executed, and we feel specific guilt for what we have done, or (3) the conflict is such that, although we remain unaware of the nature of the impulse, we feel anxious and guilty either in a diffused and unattached form or attached to something other than the peccant impulse. This is a very simplified form of the hypothesis, and no account is taken of various manoeuvres to avoid anxiety or otherwise get out of the difficulty. Nor is account taken of the range of items which come under the ban of the super-ego—a range which clinical research has shown to be unexpectedly large. What interests us here is '*guilt*', and the terms which go with it: '*right*' and '*wrong*'. The importance of this lies in the fact that some cultural anthropologists and others tell us that our method of discipline is only one of many, and a deficient one at that.

Thus Kardiner[1] writes of the Kwakiutl: 'Although sense of shame is inordinately sensitive, sense of guilt seems to be lacking,' and then observes that the Marquesan 'had a horror of being laughed at, an aversion which was a powerful factor in maintaining the *mores* of the society, for the nonconformist was certain to be subjected to ridicule'.[2]

Erikson,[3] who compares two American Indian tribes with contemporary America says: 'Children are largely educated by older children, and are kept in check by fear of tangible ridicule rather than by the vague discomfort of guilt feelings. They are encouraged to be virtuous by the promise of concrete and universal prestige points. On the plains, at least, no threat of violence or abandonment estranges parent and child, no talk of sinfulness, body, and self.'[4] Similarly, the Henrys report that 'Among the Pilagá (Indians) there is no strong sense of guilt and no institutionalized support for guilty feelings. This does not mean that they do not experience guilt feelings, but rather that those feelings are different in some respects from what is experienced in our culture. . . . *Self-punishment and self-accusation do not occur in any of the Pilagá material.*'[5]

---

[1] *Individual and His Society*, p. 119.   [2] ibid., p. 177.
[3] Erikson, E. H. in Kluckhohn, C. (ed.) *Personality*, Chapter 14.
[4] ibid., p. 195.   [5] ibid, p. 238 (author's italics).

It is, however, Margaret Mead who has explored this question most carefully. In two chapters[1] of Kluckhohn's *Personality*, from which some of the above material has been taken, she contrasts other methods of disciplining with our own. The Samoan baby is simply removed from the scene by its child-nurse, and therefore learns: 'If I am to be let alone and allowed to stay where I like, I must keep quiet, sit still, and conform to the rules,' which is just what the ceremony-loving Samoan does. 'Obviously,' says Dr. Mead, 'in such a setting there is no room for guilt.' The Balinese baby is continually put through the right motions, quietly pulled from places in which it should not be, and occasionally, if very naughty, terrified by its guardian with simulated fear on her part. 'From all this the child learns that a pleasant mood and cultural conformity to fixed patterns occur together, and meets any possibility of deviation from that pattern with vague, uncertain distrust.' Finally the vigorous Iatmuls who expect their children to be as wilful as they are, learn: 'If I do not assert myself, I will get nothing; and if I anger other people I will get slapped; and if I temporarily escape from being slapped, hunger and mosquitoes will drive me back again within range of retribution.'

How different, Dr. Mead's point is, from us. 'Our own super-ego system of character-formation appears as a special and rather complicated development,' and, again, 'Comparative studies . . . demonstrate that this type of character—in which the individual is reared to ask first, not 'Do I want it?' 'Am I afraid?' or 'Is it the custom?', but 'Is this right or wrong?'—is a very special development, characteristic of our own culture, and of a very few other societies. It is dependent upon the parents personally administering the culture in moral terms, standing to the children as a responsible representative of right choices, and punishing or rewarding the child in the name of the *right*.'

The special utility of the incorporation of the parental image is recognized by Mead and by Kardiner.[2] Both agree that it functions when nobody is about.

The importance of this whole matter can hardly be overestimated. We can see it from two points of view. Mead suggests that the establishment of what we can call the 'super-ego', modelled upon the infantile notion of the parents, will work well enough in a very slowly changing society, because there is very little conflict between the parental ideals incorporated by the infants and the sort of life which they and their generation will live. If, however, the standards and skills

---

[1] Chapters 36 and 37.   [2] *Psychological Frontiers of Society*, p. 153.

of the younger generation differ markedly from those of the older one (and of course this is more likely to be the case with immigrants in America, as we have so frequently been told) then a conflict may arise between what they have absorbed from their parents, and what their own age-group approves of. The disciplinary sanction of guilt conflicts in its incidence with the age-group sanction of social shame. We may, in our society, assume that young people have acquired the 'guilt' mechanism, while in fact this has been partially supplanted. If this were the case, it would have an obvious bearing on the treatment of delinquents.

The other point of view is that of Erich Fromm. In his *Man for Himself*[1] Fromm takes the line that the 'guilt' control, springing as it does from an authoritarian régime, is bad and stands in the way of the creation of a many-sided and satisfied personality.

This brings us to the verge of ethical theory and this is not the place to make an excursion therein. One thing, however, must be said, and that is that whatever theory eventually emerges we must allow for what may be called 'second order' moral judgments. We may, for instance, have a first-order moral judgment to the effect that pre-marital sexual intercourse is 'wrong'. Contemplating this, however, we may judge it 'a good thing' or 'a bad thing' that people should make that judgment. The problem for the student of ethics and, for a matter of that, the student of social psychology is: how do we come to make such 'second-order' judgments, and any final theory must account for the indubitable fact that we do?

Here we shall confine ourselves to 'first-order' judgment.

Before attempting to disentangle the problem of alternative sanctions, there is one point which does not receive enough attention. We tend to concentrate on 'temptation', the impulse or desire to do something against which we have acquired a rejecting attitude, but it is surely true that many of the actions which a society deprecates may be as it were excluded from the purview of many of its members by the course of approved action which they have incorporated. Cowardice might be strongly disapproved of by the Indian 'brave'. This does not necessarily mean (though occasionally it may) that he is constantly fighting against a temptation to behave in a cowardly way. Save under dire stress, when his controls may come into play, cowardice is simply ruled out by his positive fighting spirit. Temptation to embezzle may occasionally present itself to a clerk, and then fear, shame or guilt may

[1] Kegan Paul, 1949.

or may not play their part, but for the most part the clerkly role excludes the 'temptation' altogether. Thus much not-doing of that which is forbidden is excluded by the very doing of that which is permitted.

However, that of course does not dispose of the question. Broadly speaking it will be agreed that social discipline is effected by rewards and disrewards. The primary rewards are release of tension, pleasant stimulation, and enhancement of self-feeling, the primary disrewards are continuance of tension, painful stimulation and diminution of self-feeling. The child develops techniques for ensuring rewards, techniques which may include the acceptance of certain disrewards; it also develops techniques for safeguarding itself against disrewards. Among these techniques are a registration of the signs of reward and of the warnings of disreward. Here we must distinguish between the nature of the rewards and disrewards, and the interpretation put upon the conduct rewarded or disrewarded.

Supposing you have a society in which the disreward took the form of pain or threats of spirits who would cause pain, then that which brings pain will be regarded in future with apprehension, and such acts and their associated accompaniments, whatever they may be, will be avoided as we avoid a live wire or a hot surface. They are not wicked, but dangerous.

The nature of the disreward is pain, but the problem about which we know all too little is the interpretation put upon the *type* of thing which is now thought of as dangerous. If pain or threats are widely used we can easily see that a generally apprehensive attitude may develop—as seems to be the case with the Balinese. At the same time there may be a certain amount of selection as, for example, in some of our own sub-cultures. When mother says: 'If you do *that* the cops will get you,' the '*that*' made dangerous by the threat gets linked with other '*thats*' similarly charged with danger in actual experience, and also, presumably by hearing other people talking with bated breath, with other '*thats*' which have not been experienced. Exactly how this generalizing and spreading of the dangerous is accomplished we do not know.

It would be possible to establish—indeed, it is done—a system of controls based upon fear, without 'guilt' coming in at all. The weakness of such a system would be that if the pain did not always follow the act which is to be eliminated, or if the pain did not outweigh the reward, then the subject would be liable to be prepared from time to time to take the risk.

Much the same may be said of ridicule. This makes use of the need for a sense of worth as its lever. The effective jeer is deflatory and not mere merry laughter. In this case, however, the attitude of other people is more important; they are not mere sources of danger, but potential sources of goodwill. What will be important, therefore, is the range of persons whose jeers are important—jeers, *as such*, need have no effect. In a relatively small society, and this seems to be the case with many primitive communities, ridicule may be a satisfactory method. The difficulties of accounting for generalization remain with us, but at the same time ridicule would appear to have this advantage over pain: the subject shares, as it were, in the ridicule he receives. Having met with jeers as a response, he 'takes on the attitude of the other', and becomes capable of jeering at himself, so that he can be a fool in his own eyes. This clearly extends the range of conduct over which ridicule may operate. At the same time the puzzling problem of generalization, to which reference has been made, is a matter worthy of further research, not only into its mechanism, but into its scope. The question is: are fear and ridicule more specific in their incidence than the other methods to which we must turn? If, for instance, a child is laughed at for masturbating and laughed at for his preliminary sexual play with the opposite sex, does this mean that all sex is made ridiculous, and therefore something to be shunned? One would guess not, but there is very little evidence either way.

In our society we use ridicule, pain and threats, and the extent to which these devices are used varies from one part of our culture to another. We do, however, make use of another method. In the first place with us the child is solely dependent upon the mother and father in most cases. Sometimes the mother is the cherisher, the father the disciplinarian, sometimes both are both. Now a simple account of the story is that when the mother, forcibly or by withholding her rewards, frustrates her child's enjoyment, the child responds with antagonism. This is tantamount to a death-wish and therefore conflicts with the child's love and with its needs. The death-wish is repressed and when it arises again to the surface is responded to by a sense of guilt. The sense of guilt, which subsequently gets tacked on to other things, is primarily a specific feeling caused by the hostility to the mother.

This theory is hardly acceptable, because one cannot understand why this specific feeling should be generated under circumstances in which fear of retaliation would be the 'natural' response. However, the theory does pose the question: why *guilt*? Some may reply that the feeling of guilt is the 'natural' response to a recognition that what we have done is *really* wrong. This, however, is unsatisfactory, too, because there is no general agreement about the wrongness of all the acts or thoughts or desires about which people feel guilty.

Some light may be shed upon the matter by the following reflection. Suppose a child does that which it should not or refuses to do that which it should, and its mother gives it a sharp box on the ears or smack on the bottom. A wail may be set up, but it is likely to refrain from doing what it is not supposed to do, and possibly, with reluctant and rebellious gesture, it may do what is being demanded. Let us assume that on the whole the mother feeds, comforts, and generally provides rewards, then the episode may be what is called 'a lesson', and it may have the desired after-affects. The question of an aftermath of 'repressed' hostility we will leave aside. What is important for our purpose is that the child notes the angry face, the raised voice, the uplifted hand as danger signals. They portend a sharp pain, but not *necessarily* anything so portentous as loss of love.

Now we all know that this is not the only thing that happens by any means. Very often the mother puts on a special expression, evincing shockedness, amazement at such conduct, disapproval, sorrow, and conveying a sense of withdrawal from contamination. At the same time and in a special voice she says things like: 'That's naughty' or 'That's wrong'—'Mummy won't love you if you do things like that.' All this solemnity makes the offence not merely dangerous but enormous. Now in a situation in which 'Mummy' and 'Daddy' are the only protectors, this is a serious matter. We have all experienced or witnessed it. We all know the heavily charged atmosphere when Father has taken a misdemeanour *seriously*, rather than merely *irritably*. Angry, of course he is, but not merely angry, as with a child he 'cops' making finger-marks on the newly painted door and just cuffs in a rage, but scandalized at such things being possible in his children; in fact, he looks 'grave'.

The suggestion put forward is that this special demeanour on the part of adults is what makes the difference between the risky and the shaming on the one hand and the 'wicked' or 'wrong' or 'naughty' on the other.

Just as the child takes the jeering audience into himself and thus can shame himself, so he takes the sinister figures of his morally outraged parents into himself and is horrified at his own wickedness. There is no conflict between what is said here and the psychoanalytic doctrine of the super-ego, with its unconscious threats, and its excessive hostility, partly derived from the child's own hostility and its misconception of the parents' 'real' attitude. What is being suggested is that this formulation applies in its fullness to situations in which (1) the child is completely dependent upon a small number of adults, and (2) is addressed in this peculiarly portentous way. What is left unexplained, it must be admitted, is the origin of this special attitude to the infringement of rules. It is not wholly impossible that it might be traced back to a primitive response to the 'sacred' as distinct from the 'profane', in fact to that specific awe-ful response to anything apprehended as charged with magic from which religion may have its source. Once the original response is made and attached to forbidden conduct, it can be passed on from one generation to another in the way suggested above.

There remains the important question of *what* is learnt to be so forbiddingly forbidden. The conduct itself, no doubt, and conduct like it. But how is the conduct presented, besides being presented as bad? Or, rather, what general aspect of the conduct stands out? Two aspects are often picked upon: pleasure and/or obedience, though this does not exhaust the list. We have to bear in mind the obvious fact that the infant learns only by actual here and now checking in a specific social situation, and we do not know how either of these two aspects (particularly the first) is singled out from the total configuration. Somehow or other pleasure is sometimes selected, and all that is pleasurable is tarnished with doubtfulness, and has to be paid for with pain, because the sequence pleasure-pain has been followed by the rehabilitation of 'forgiveness'. The 'obedience' factor is, perhaps, easier to account for because it is verbalized: 'This is wrong, because I told you not to.' It is obvious that stress on obedience will vary from one society to another as is illustrated by the contrasting structure of the Marquesan and the Tanala; in the latter the obedience of the younger sons is essential to the economy.

We may say then, by way of summarizing this rather lengthy discussion that as the infant grows up, it becomes 'socialized' by acquiring a set of controls which aim at preventing its doing what the adults and its contemporaries dislike. It may learn that such conduct is dangerous, or ridiculous or wicked. The stress varies from culture to culture, and within any large-scale culture from one sub-culture to another. Some rely on danger, all use ridicule to some extent, we use both, and 'sin' in addition. Cultures also vary in the content of the forbidden, though all conduct which prejudices social living is likely to be banned by all societies. Furthermore, when a plurality of disciplinary techniques are employed, some conduct is controlled by fear, some by ridicule and some by 'guilt'. Variation in the incidence of these techniques is of great importance for the understanding of delinquency.

Whatever be the technique adopted by a society the majority of its members will acquire its restraints and seek after the rewards it provides for doing what it encourages and not doing what it penalizes. General forms of behaviour which are acceptable or the reverse will vary, but all socialization involves some measure of renunciation.

Frustration. This brings us to the important matter of the response to such frustration. The simple answer to this is that frustration causes aggression and *per contra*, that all aggression is caused by frustration. This hypothesis has been worked out by J. Dollard and his collaborators in *Frustration and Aggression*[1] in which they bring together a considerable amount of evidence to support their principle. The matter is, unfortunately, not as simple as it appears, but the principle is one of great heuristic and practical value. Certainly, where frustration occurs aggression is likely to follow in some form or another, and where hostility is manifest we do well to look for a frustrating situation as its basis. This implies that hostility may be reduced if frustration is curtailed.

We must, however, first consider what is meant by 'aggression'. All creatures in pursuit of their ends tend forcibly to manipulate the means that will lead to them. This necessarily involves a certain expenditure of effort, a certain display of force, and, on occasion, a certain amount of destruction. A dog crunching a bone or a man 'attacking' his dinner are destructive and forceful but they are not necessarily behaving in a hostile fashion. Children, too, in their exploration pull things to pieces, so do puppies and parrots. Again, this may be 'aggressive' in one sense, but not in another. Furthermore people of a vigorous constitution will be likely to be more forceful in their efforts to achieve their ends and this may well be accompanied by what can plausibly be called 'violence', but not necessarily 'hostility'. The point is that forceful manipulation need not imply anger and resentment and therefore many acts that might be called 'aggressive' spring from a lively pursuit of ends and not from the desire to work off aggression. We should, perhaps, go even further, and exclude from 'hostility' such 'aggressive' acts as children snatching what they want from other people. The 'attack' may be hostile as well, but it may be mere determination.

[1] Eng. Edit. Kegan Paul, 1944.

It is worth noting that the minute records of child behaviour, referred to by Murphy, Murphy and Newcomb, show that 'children who had the highest and most stable scores for sympathetic behaviour on the playground were unsympathetic or distinctively aggressive when their ego was threatened, when they were teased or misunderstood or put into inferior positions'.[1] In fact a great deal of forceful inter-child behaviour is part of the process of developing social awareness, in which the child becomes sensible of other children as fellow-sufferers, play-mates, competitors, and obstacles. It is not denied that aggressive acts are performed, but one must recognize their functions as fleeting social responses which play their part in the process of social adjustment.[2] E. H. Green[3] who studied friendships and quarrelling among young children, reports that it was the friends who quarrelled most, not the less friendly.

Aggression, then, in the sense in which it interests us as a response to frustration is not mere forceful manipulation. It is, as Dollard and his collaborators say, 'an act whose goal response is injury to an organism or organism surrogate'. To this we may add the undercurrent of hostility which marks it out from other violent behaviour.

Ordinary everyday experience is enough to show that hostile aggression is an extremely common response to frustration. If nothing else serves, you kick a stone or the offending mechanical object, and you may even 'kick yourself'. In experimental studies the same kind of thing is observed. In the 'authoritarian' régimes of Lewin, Lippit and White's experiment,[4] some of the boys responded with overt aggression, others displayed aggression when they changed over to democracy. In the experiment of Barker, Dembo and Lewin, which is described below, aggression was one of the responses to the frustrating situation. Sears, Havland and Miller[5] subjected six subjects to twenty-four hours' sleep deprivation and during that time they were frustrated in all sorts of ways. They were not allowed to smoke, the games were 'forgotten', and food which was promised did not arrive. The subjects, as might be expected, got 'nasty'. Overt aggression by violence was inhibited by their training, but their remarks showed well enough their

[1] op. cit., p. 539.
[2] cf. Murphy, L. B. *Social Behaviour and Child Personality.* Columbia Univ. Press, 1937.
[3] 'Friendship and Quarrels among Pre-school Children.' *Child Development*, 4, p. 237. Quoted: Kimball Young. *Personality and Problems of Adjustment.* Kegan Paul, 1947, p. 117.
[4] p. 79 above.
[5] Sears, Robert R., Havland, Carl I. and Miller, Neal E. 'Minor Studies of Aggression.' *J. of Psychology*, 1940, IX, 277. cf. *Readings in Social Psychology*, p. 261.

state of mind. One of them drew a page full of pictures depicting a man being hanged, a torso spilling entrails, and a head and shoulders dripping blood. When asked what these atrocities represented, he replied: 'Psychologists.'

More evidence of displaced aggression comes from an experiment of Miller and Bugelski[1] who promised thirty-one young men in a camp that they should go to the theatre, and then cancelled the engagement. In this mood of frustration the subjects were asked to rate Japanese and Mexicans (this was before the war). They had already done so before the 'frustrating' experience, and the score of unfavourable characteristics showed a notable increase.

The experimental evidence, besides generally confirming our expectation, contains one or two items of interest, which are not so obvious. The experiment of Barker, Dembo and Lewin[2] has been mentioned above. In it a group of children were given play material which could either be used constructively or just fiddled with. From their methods of handling a scale of constructiveness was devised. In the frustrating situation a partition in the room was then removed, disclosing the play material mixed up with a mass of fascinating toys which the children proceeded to explore. They were encouraged to do this until they became absorbed in their play and then the experimenter picked up the original play material, whisked the children off to the other part of the room, and down came a wire grille fastened by a padlock, shutting them out from paradise.

Not unnaturally some of them displayed aggression when they were invited to go on with their dull old 'constructive play'. Their play became very much less constructive; that was one result. When the experiment was repeated with pairs of children by Wright,[3] another point emerged. The pairs of children who were strong friends did not suffer so much in loss of construction, and were more emboldened than the 'weak' friends to take such hostile action against the experimenter as was taken. It may be that the fact that they could 'let off steam' enabled them to go on with their co-operative play.

[1] Miller, Neal E. and Bugelski, Richard.' Minor Studies of Aggression.' *J.of Psychology*, 1948, 25, p. 437.

[2] Barker, R. G., Dembo, T., Lewin, K. 'Frustration and Aggression.' Univ. of Iowa. *Studies in Child Welfare*, 1941, XVIII, No. 1.

[3] Wright, M. E. 'Constructiveness of Play as Affected by Group Organization and Frustration.' *Character and Personality*, 1942, XI, p. 40, and 'The Influence of Frustration upon the Social Relations of Young Children.' ibid, 1943, XII, p. 111. cf. also Combined account by Barker, Dembo, Lewin and Wright. *Readings in Social Psychology*, p. 283.

The same kind of effect was noticed in French's experiment with organized and unorganized groups, to which reference has already been made.[1] They were asked to solve problems which could not be solved in the time allotted. The 'organized' groups, who were friends already, let off steam by blaming one another, and this they were able to do without risk, simply because they were friends. It has also been found by other experimenters that overt aggression is often accompanied by superior performance.[2]

Finally we must refer to an experiment by Rosenzweig[3] in which he gave a difficult intelligence test to two groups of adults. One group was invited to co-operate in a piece of research and it was impressed on them that their performance would in no way redound to their discredit, while the others were given the opposite impression. The frustrating element was their inability to complete the test, but the response of each group was different. The first group exhibited a persistent need to finish the task, the second were what he called 'ego-defensive'. Significantly enough, when asked afterwards to remember what they had done, the former remembered more of the unfinished tasks, the latter more of the finished ones.

Rosenzweig[4] has made a further contribution to the subject by noting the objectives against which aggression is directed.

He classifies people in three groups: 'extra-punitive', 'intro-punitive' and 'impunitive'. In the first case the frustration is 'blamed on to' external persons or things. If it is uninhibited a direct attack by violence or criticism may be made; if it is inhibited the response may find expression by the roundabout means of projection, whereby some, possibly innocent, agent is accused as the aggressor. The 'intro-punitive' response is directed inwards, and the subject blames himself for his failure to achieve his end, and therefore tends to express guilt or remorse. The third alternative is a conciliatory attitude; defeat is accepted and glossed over. Such responses are by no means 'pathological' in nature; they are only pathological if misdirected. A man may justly blame the careless motorist who has run into him; he may justly blame himself for his foolishness, and he doubtless should accept some slings and arrows 'philosophically'. What, however, happens is

[1] p. 52.
[2] Himmelweit, Hilda. 'Frustration and Aggression' in *Psychological Factors of Peace and War.* Ed. T. H. Pea. Hutchinson, 1940, p. 177.
[3] Rosenzweig, S. 'An Experimental Study of Repression.' *J. Exp. Psych.,* 1943, XXXII, 64.
[4] Rosenzweig, S. 'Types of Reaction to Frustration.' *Journal of Abnormal and Social Psychology,* 1934, 29, p. 293-300.

that some people put the blame for all misfortune on to external
agencies—it is never their fault. Other people always blame themselves for everything that happens to them, while still others carry
indifference too far.

The problem is: are these differences, when they are built into the
personality structure, due to constitutional pre-disposition, or are they
due to training in infancy? Obviously we should expect that training
will have left its mark. Rosenzweig suggests that the extra-punitive
response is the most infantile one, that intro-punitive responses come
later and the impunitive attitude last of all. This sounds plausible
enough, but the question of great importance for the explanation of
some forms of delinquency is: are there cases in which, because of some
constitutional defect, the passage from the first stage to the second
cannot be made with success? To that there is so far no answer.

It will be noted that other responses besides aggression in violent or
verbal form may be made in a frustrating situation. The children in
Barker's experiment 'regressed' to a less constructive level. Another
possible response, found in the same experiment, is simply to give up,
and accept defeat. Yet another, noticed by Allport, Bruner and
Jandorf[1] is apathy. They studied the accounts of ninety German refugees who had suffered under the Nazi régime. 'Besides aggressive
responses, direct or displaced,' they say, 'we find defeat and resignation,
regression, conformity, adoption of temporary frames of security,
changes in standard of evaluation, lowering of levels of aspiration,
heightened in-group feeling, increased fantasy and insulation, and,
above all, increased planning and problem solving.'

Furthermore, according to Maier,[2] frustration may give rise to a
response, which is non-purposive—a mere exasperated gesture, and
which gets 'fixated' and is repeated in the frustrating situation over and
over again, irrespective of its uselessness.

The above list, which rings true to life, reminds us of the limitations
which attend the experimental method in this field. The kind of
frustration possible in a laboratory can only be a pale imitation of the
frustration of real life. This does not mean that experimentation is
useless; on the contrary, it makes us look for features in real life which
we might otherwise miss, and suggests hypotheses which we can then
proceed to test. It does mean, however, that we must expect the responses to frustration in real life to be more complicated than those

---

[1] 'Personality under Social Catastrophe' in *Personality*. Ed. Kluckhohn, C. Chapter 25.
[2] *Frustration*. McGraw-Hill, 1949.

elicited under experimental conditions. As Dr. Himmelweit observes, the laboratory experiments 'touch the fringe only of the frustration experience considered important by Freud'.[1]

We therefore have to supplement the evidence of everyday experience and that of experiments by adding that of clinical study. In psycho-analytic theory the theme of aggression has for some time displaced that of sex. In the first place many neurotic symptoms and dreams, together with the ideas associated with them, can be made intelligible if we interpret them as signs of hostility. In the second place the anxiety and guilt, which are so prominent in the experience of neurotic patients and others, become intelligible if we think of it in terms of aggression directed inwards. The following scheme emerges: the infant responds to the frustration of its parents with aggression; this must be repressed for security reasons; a control is established on the model of parents and charged with the hostility attributed to them; this control inhibits (a) the kinds of aims which have been frustrated, and (b) the aggression which this frustration has engendered.

Such a schematic account does scant justice to the dramatic insight and ingenuity of the psycho-analysts. The point of it is to serve as a reminder of the enormous amount of aggression, repressive and repressed, which lurks within us, if their hypothesis be accepted. They have certainly shown abundant evidence that besides the anger aroused by obstacles of which we are conscious there is a mass of undischarged aggression trying to discharge itself if it gets a chance. So much, indeed, that Freud thought that it could not all be accounted for in terms of a response to frustration and accordingly postulated an innate destructive tendency, which represented in us the Death principle in the universe.

We need not follow him into these fanciful realms. If we accept the view, that the infantile response must be thought of in adult terms, and if we add that the infant cannot understand the conduct of its parents and therefore responds blindly, there may well be enough frustration to account for the aggressive tendencies revealed by analysis.

To sum up this somewhat bewildering mass of data we may say that aggression in some form or another, immediate or delayed, overt or disguised, and directed against the frustrating agency or against a surrogate (including the self), is a common result of frustration. To this we must add: (1) a situation may be frustrating to one person and not to another; (2) this will depend partly on the way in which the

[1] op. cit., p. 168.

situation is faced (cf. Rosenzweig) and partly on the 'unconscious' aggression in the subject; (3) an overt expression of aggression relieves tension and may enable the subject to act more efficiently; (4) the circumstances under which this is the case are related to the subject's confidence that his aggressive act will have no untoward repercussion; (5) aggression, overt or 'repressed' may be directed 'outwards' or 'inwards': if the latter is a persistent tendency and if there is considerable tension we may expect a psycho-neurotic constellation, while if the former we should expect a criminal one.

It is clear enough that the problem of aggression is one of importance when we are considering the induction of a child into his culture. In so far as he responds aggressively to frustration his aggressive conduct is a function of the amount of frustration his culture provides, heightened or reduced by the version of it he meets with in the specific adults who act as mediators. He will be further influenced by the amount of aggression allowed by his culture and its mediators. He will be influenced by the degree to which he is encouraged to act out his aggression on external things or persons, and the degree to which he is encouraged to blame himself. Finally, if a culture is characterized by a fairly uniform system of infantile frustration (e.g. the Mundugamor feeding system) we may expect aggressive personalities to emerge as typical of that society, and if a culture imposes strict non-aggressiveness (e.g. among the Saulteaux)[1] we may expect signs of disguised hostility in the form of fantasy or beliefs in sorcery.

We have seen that there are other responses to frustration: defeatism, regression, fixation of a useless gesture, or a persistent pursuit of the frustrated act, rather in the manner of Dr. Levy's puppies, who, when their sucking needs were left unsatisfied, 'sucked each other, their own paws, objects, and later on, after eating, licked the plate interminably'.[2]

A question of greater importance is : can frustration be accepted or rendered acceptable?

We have seen that what is frustrating to one person is not frustrating to another, in terms of the way in which it is presented. This is common knowledge and has obvious practical implications. But common experience, backed by experimental evidence, teaches us that as we grow older our 'frustration tolerance', improves. It is significant that in experimental situations younger children and neurotics, who may

---

[1] Hallowell, A. Irving. 'Aggression in Saulteaux Society' in *Personality*. Ed. Kluckholn, C. Chapter 15.
[2] Levy, David M. 'The Hostile Act.' *Readings in Social Psychology*, p. 264.

be assumed to have a high aggressive tension, stand frustration less well than older children and non-neurotics. Indeed, maturity positively *is* an increased capacity to stand frustration.

This, however, is not the heart of the matter. The infant starts *ex hypothesi* immature. He is frustrated in the course of his social training. One hypothesis is that because of the *inevitable* hostility this engenders he *must* go through life with a load of hatred proportionate to the frustrations he has experienced. Hence the discontents of civilization.[1] Now there is a danger here of theorizing too much. It is one thing to say that the overt hostility we observe is traceable to unexpected sources of frustration, and that a great deal of conduct, much of which looks exactly the reverse, is really hostility in disguise; it is quite another thing to say that because the situations responsible for these manifestations are common to everyone, there must be a considerable amount of hostility lurking in them *even though it does not show itself.* Granted, we must prepare for surprises. The mildest of men may suddenly go 'hay-wire' and the theorists will say: 'Ah, we told you so.' But we have no business to say that there is unconscious hostility present until we require that hypothesis to explain a piece of conduct.

As we look about us, with our eyes opened by the psycho-analysts, we see more signs of hostility than we bargained for, but it sometimes crosses the mind that there is not nearly as much as might be expected, considering the renunciations we all have to make. A good point is made by Maslow,[2] who calls attention to 'an important distinction between deprivation and threats to personality'. Deprivation we may learn to stand, and may even welcome it if it be deemed a means of grace; a threat to our sense of worth, of being loved, is what really matters to us. This is, indeed, in line with Kardiner's concept of a satisfaction-frustration balance.[3] 'Where the rewards of impulse suppression cannot be realized by the individual, the super-ego loses its tonicity,' which means that the restraint is not accepted but resented. There will no doubt be immediate overt aggression in the early stages of socialization, but if the rewards of renunciation are great and if the method of training is not taken to be a threat to the worthiness of the personality, then it would seem that a system of controls can be established without an undue measure of internal tension.

We may agree, therefore, with Miller and Dollard, who have

[1] cf. *Civilization and Its Discontents.* S. Freud.
[2] 'Deprivation, Threat and Frustration.' *Psychological Review*, 1941, XLVIII, p. 364 and *Readings in Social Psychology*, p. 281.
[3] *Individual and His Society*, p. 130.

modified the original frustration-aggression hypothesis as stated in *Frustration and Aggression*, that 'the position aggression will occupy in the initial hierarchy of responses to any situation is largely a product of learning'.[1]

So far we have considered aggression as a response to frustration. The question must now be raised: if the response to frustration is aggression, is the aggressiveness a measure of the degree to which the subject is frustrated? Or can aggressive conduct appear independently of frustration? Ruth Benedict in her article on *Continuities and Discontinuities in Cultural Conditioning* to which we have already referred,[2] quotes Prince Maxmilian von Wied as reporting the instance of a Crow Indian father boasting about his young son's intractability even when it was the father himself who was flouted: 'He will be a man,' his father said. She mentions another case of a disobedient urchin striking its father. When the mother, who was a white woman, protested, the father said: 'But why? He is little. He cannot possibly injure me.'[3]

In these cases one may assume that the aggressive conduct was precipitated by frustration, but so far from the tantrums being deprecated, they are praised. The conduct after all has two aspects: it relieves tension, and it is itself—a clenching of fists, a stamping of feet, a pummelling of Dad. As a relief of tension it is tied to the tension it relieves, but as a piece of conduct it may acquire reward-value if it is greeted with admiration. Thus, it would appear, aggressive conduct may be trained as a quasi-independent type of behaviour which may even acquire such autonomy as to be pursued for its own sake. Similarly gestures of sympathy, kindness and affection may be reduced in frequency if they are not encouraged or if they are actively discouraged, and may, as Kimball Young[4] has it, become 'reduced by lack of practice'. The relative frequency of such gestures marks one of the great differences between the middle- and working-class cultures in this country.

Childhood Continued. We must now return to the problem of social induction. The infant has passed through a certain initial handling which varies from culture to culture. Whatever this may be, it established certain expectancies and techniques which will echo down

---

[1] *Social Learning and Imitation.* Kegan Paul, 1945, p. 534, n. 3.
[2] p. 168.   [3] In *Personality.* Ed. Kluckholn, C., p. 419.
[4] *Handbook of Social Psychology*, p. 73.

its life. As a boy or a girl its roles become more differentiated. It is either tied emotionally to a few adults or else its emotional attachments are diffuse. It is encouraged and rewarded for doing and saying some sorts of things, and discouraged and disrewarded for doing others, and from such experiences a control system is established, which repeats within a threat of what lies in store outside, to such an extent that some untoward impulses may be blocked at source. If the tension is too great alternative round-about methods must be used. More or less responsibility is thrust upon him or her, varying from culture to culture and from class to class in the same culture.

Armed with a certain wariness, the boy and girl look round. In a slowly changing society they are aware of a consistent chorus of admiration and deprecation directed by adults towards other adults. The recipients of praise are their models and bit by bit what has been conveniently called an 'ego-ideal' is elaborated. In a complex and swiftly changing society the situation is different. In such a society praise and blame are not so consistent. Even in the home father may have one view and mother may differ, while auntie is a pacifist and uncle a Free Thinker. Outside the home circle it is worse. Not only do adults differ, but the company of youth may be arrayed against them. This is particularly true of Americans, where so many of the younger generation who want to be good Americans are bound to be critical of their parents if they persist in following the culture of their country of origin. No wonder the cry goes up that we must, in such large-scale societies, 'educate for choice'.[1]

However, even in large-scale societies, models present themselves. The main difference is that, on account of the hostility which frequently develops between adult standards and the standards of the young, the choice of models may be complicated by a desire to choose certain models just because the adults—in particular the parents—disapprove of them. It is *à propos* of this that Margaret Mead's[2] analysis of the different disciplinary methods is of importance. She points out that there may be a conflict between the conscience-backed standards of the elders and the ridicule-backed standards of the young. This, she suggests, may lead to a sense of guilt which might be assuaged by devotion to a father-substitute—religious or secular.

At any rate, there the models are, and the child, awed or otherwise

[1] cf. Mead, M. *Coming of Age in Samoa*. Penguin, 1943, p. 137. Linton, *Study of Man*, p. 285.
[2] Mead, M. *Social Change and Cultural Surrogate in Personality*. Ed. Kluckhohn, C., p. 518.

by the spectacle, sees the kind of thing in store for it. Infantile treatment, emotional relation to parents, happiness or otherwise in the home do not automatically turn the child into a good American, a good Japanese or a good Arapesh; the living representatives are required as patterns. What childhood's experience does is to make the copying of them easy or difficult.

Adolescence. As time passes the important changes of puberty occur. In our society this has long been thought of as a period of stress, due to the physiological disturbances which accompany sexual maturation. This view was elaborated by G. Stanley Hall.[1] Since his day, however, it has become obvious that the troubles of adolescents are culturally determined; and that the problem is handled in many different ways.[2] Among the Samoans for instance the tempo of development is slow and the adolescent passes into his or her status by easy stages. For the girl 'adolescence becomes not the most difficult, most stressful period of life, but perhaps the pleasantest time the Samoan girl will ever know'.[3] Among them menstruation is taken lightly.[4] The boy has his boy friend who helps him in his courting and in his more clandestine adventures, sometimes varying monotony with alternative intimacies. They are circumcized together and at seventeen join the Aumaga, 'the society of young men and the older men without titles'—the 'strength of the village' as it is called.[5] He indulges in all sorts of affairs, but at the same time makes himself proficient at some skill or other, which will bring him prestige if he is good at it, and may provide an entry into superior circles.

For the young Manus boy the position is very different. Sex is abhorrent and in the old days his only chances were with outsiders on whom he wreaked his vengeance and his pleasure. However, the young men were left pretty free to enjoy themselves. Nowadays they have to go away to work when they are sixteen or seventeen. Even so they do not have much responsibility. It is when they get home, or, in the past, when they had to marry that a new role confronts them. They must change from insubordinate, irresponsible fellows, into humble, hard-working sycophants, toiling to pay their uncles for the price these have paid for a bride the young men do not want, and struggling to achieve some measure of independence. No wonder they

---

[1] *Adolescence.* Appleton, 1905.
[2] Mead, M. 'Adolescence in Primitive and in Modern Society.' *Readings in Social Psychology*, p. 6.
[3] ibid., p. 8.   [4] *Coming of Age in Samoa*, p. 53.   [5] ibid., p. 27.

hang about the villages—'meek, abashed, sulky, skulking about the back doors of their rich relations' houses'.[1]   And all this, according to Mead, is brought about through the leverage of shame.   Sulking though they may be, however, no 'period of emotional stress' is apparent with the onset of sexual potency.

From the evidence of cross-cultural research it would appear that puberty *as such* need have no overwhelming effects. The effects which it will have depend rather upon the attitude towards sex which has been inculcated. When it is not regarded as shameful in any way—as with the Marquesans, described by Linton[2]—the boy and girl now find themselves capable of new enjoyments. They naturally experiment with the opposite sex and with one another.[3] When, however, sexual gratification is treated as a shameful thing, the onset of puberty may lead to violent forms of indulgence, as with the Manus, or to guilt, as with ourselves. The difference may be due to the terms in which the 'tabu' is phrased. If guilt is the response to the new impulses, then the upheaval of puberty is likely to be the greater, though even so, sex is by no means the only factor operating in such disturbed states as are popularly associated with adolescence in our culture.

When the new capacity for enjoyment is not so hag-ridden by guilt that no experimentation is possible at all, experiments will be made. The absence of companions of the opposite sex, certain emotional experiences in childhood, and possibly in some cases a constitutional bias (though this is by no means certain) may, any or all of them, lead to sexual intimacies between members of the same sex. This may be temporary, intermittent, or a manifestation of a persistent preference. The social view of such conduct varies from society to society, and from class to class.

In some simple societies it is thought extremely comical. In others no notice seems to be taken. In yet others it is institutionalized; either those showing a persistent preference for their own sex are given a special position, or such relationships are an established part of the culture, whether or not other modes of sexual behaviour are indulged in. Ruth Benedict, for instance, tells us that: 'The life-cycle of the Keraki Indian includes in succession, passive homosexuality, active homosexuality and heterosexuality.'[4] A man is not made unless these phases are gone through.

[1] Mead, M. *Growing up in New Guinea.* Penguin edit., 1942, p. 121.
[2] *Individual and his Society.*   [3] ibid., p. 218.
[4] Benedict. R. 'Continuities and Discontinuities in Cultural Conditioning.' *Psychiatry*, 1, 1938, p. 161, cf. Kluckhohn, C. (ed.) *Personality*, p. 422.

In our culture, however, for reasons which are very difficult to determine, such conduct arouses strong reactions of disapproval. This may possibly be traced to the assimilation of elements of the Jewish culture-pattern through religion, but that cannot be the whole story, because other peoples who have come into contact with the same elements do not appear to feel so strongly. It is doubtless connected with the general disapprobation of sex, which is likely to be more intense when intercourse does not carry with it those responsibilities of parenthood, which might restrict other forms of indulgence.

Disapproval is very strongly expressed by unmarried men who do not seek heterosexual satisfaction, and this may possibly be interpreted as a sign that they themselves are inhibiting the inclinations they condemn. If this is the source of their disapproval, one would look to emotional relations in the family circle as responsible for the syndrome from which they are suffering: repressed homosexuality plus overt preoccupation with the subject and condemnation of it. Thus it may be that intimate family relationships, characteristic of our society, are responsible for this curious attitude.

Culture contact on a religious basis is not a satisfactory explanation, for unless there are emotional grounds of acceptance, an attitude which reason condemns has no chance of being assimilated. A great deal of further research is needed to discover the causes of our anomalous pattern. Meanwhile our attitude towards homosexuality affords an instructive example of the resistance of a culture-pattern to change; judges and even doctors are caught up in it and lend their prestige to its perpetuation.

To return to the adolescent; the physiological changes of puberty also include changes in size, musculature, and the secondary sexual characteristics. These may place the adolescent at a disadvantage in societies in which much attention is paid to physical appearance. In the case of girls there is an additional factor: menstruation. This is handled by some societies with great precaution. The girls may be segregated and their freedom limited by numbers of taboos, which serve to underline the specialized role of the female in such societies.

More important, however, than sexual development is the social status of the adolescent. This has two aspects: the young man is on the threshold of participation in that part of the total culture that is mainly responsible for its preservation, and he is being received as a newcomer by the adults already in possession. In many simple societies a ceremony of initiation marks the passage from one status to another. The convenience of this is that fairly definite roles are established—before and after. The ceremonies differ widely, some of them symbolizing rebirth, some of them involving tests of endurance, and some of them including such striking opportunities for cruelty on the part of the initiators that we cannot help wondering whether they are not outlets for the resentment of the adults towards their future dispossessors.

In our society, save in those interesting cases of 'initiation ceremonial', when a young man goes to work for the first time, we have no clear-cut roles. This, as is often said, is the cause of most of the disturbance associated with adolescence. 'In our society,' says Kingsley Davis,[1] speaking of America, 'even apart from the family, the adolescent finds an absence of definitely recognized, consistent patterns of authority. Because of the compartmentalization of the culture he is defined at times as an adult, at other times as a child.'

The same point is made by L. J. Barnes in his *Youth Service in an English County*.[2] À propos of the view that the obstreperousness of youth is a sign of insufficient discipline he says: 'It would be nearer the mark to say that he is suffering from chronic overdoses of it already. The capacity for responsibility is like any other human capacity; it arrives at health and strength through exercise. If modern youth is irresponsible, a main reason is that the adult world accords it few chances of shouldering responsibility.' While Linton[3] writes: 'In societies which recognize adolescents as a distinct category and ascribe to them activities suited to their conditions, the period passes with little or no stress.' As for us, 'We alternately demand from them the obedience and submission of childhood and the initiative and acceptance of personal responsibilities which go with adult status.'

The social position is obviously difficult. In the country 'Youth' does not seem to be a problem; they already know what to do. In the towns this is not the case. In the first place they are not as skilled as the adults and in the second place they are faced with opportunities of enjoyment which they find it difficult to handle with restraint. The nagging frustration of their dependency tends to exacerbate their desire to show their age.[4]

The hostility towards the older generation can easily be exaggerated. In our own society it would be improper to say that 'Youth' really does not present much of a problem, because there is a 'Movement', and

[1] Quoted: Sherif, M. *Outline of Social Psychology*, p. 320.
[2] *King George's Jubilee Trust*, 1945, p. 20.
[3] *Culture Background of Personality*, p. 44.
[4] cf. Fleming, C. M. *Adolescence*. Kegan Paul, 1948, p. 22.

where there is a Movement there must be something for it to 'move' about. To the casual observer, however, the crisis is not as apparent as it is to those of more refined sensibilities. Elsewhere, on the other hand, youth has become a cult. In America the desire which the parents have to see their children flourish in popularity and sweep on to success has led them to cultivate Youth, to place their hopes in the Young, and to accept them as having rights which past generations would not have tolerated. Doubtless the anxiety to shed the vestiges of another culture and become adept at the 'American way of life' is an important factor.

On the Continent at the turn of the century 'German Youth of Karl Fischer's day loathed and hated the world of their elders'.[1] Spontaneous groups, often attached to a leader, were the forerunners of an organization, fired with the ambition to undo the mistakes of the old men of Weimar.

It is interesting to note that in Germany particular emphasis has been laid on the 'community of male youth', whereas in America 'a much stronger emphasis has been placed on the cross-sex relationship'. One of the results of this is that in America youth culture has had much less political significance than elsewhere.[2]

Where change comes about through culture contact, the young often adopt the new ways with avidity and parade their up-to-date fashions with defiance. Thus we are told of Egyptian town boys denouncing their fathers as 'reprobates' and even 'robbers' while the girls outrage their elders by adopting Hollywood styles.[3]

The German example illustrates in a somewhat extreme form another feature of adolescence, at any rate in cultures when the home circle is restricted. This is the tendency to seek companionship. It is a period of what Hollingworth has called: 'psychological weaning'.[4] An untying of the apron strings and a reaching out for other circles in which to satisfy the need for social acceptance.

The experience of home life, of acceptance, rejection, displacement or dependence, will determine the kind of group life which will be sought, and the role to be played—cringer, follower, bosser, comic, or just 'one of the boys'. It may be, of course, that experience has contra-indicated companionship of large numbers, and the 'isolate' keeps himself to himself. Such complexes of experience, in the home and in adolescence do much to determine the attitude of men and women in

[1] Becker, Howard. *German Youth.* Kegan Paul, 1946, p. 73.
[2] Parsons, Talcott. *Essays in Sociological Theory.* Free Press, 1949, p. 230.
[3] Hindus, M. Quoted by Sherif. op. cit., p. 328.
[4] Hollingworth, H. L. *Psychology of Adolescence.* Appleton, 1928.

adult years. They may feel themselves to be unworthy of companion-ship, or they may withdraw into themselves, or they may take to blaming others for their own unacceptability. They may become hail-fellow-well-met, uncomfortable unless with the gang, or suspicious or shy or prickly or prepared to do anything to raise a laugh; the list is endless.

The period of adolescence is, as we have said, conventionally a period of stress. We have examined the causes of this. We should not, how-ever, forget its joys, not so much the romantic joys of Youth—we are scarcely allowed to forget *them*—as the insidious joy of jolly com-panionship, often with people rather younger than oneself, which are sometimes so enthralling that adulthood is not achieved. The chrono-logical age mounts up and the hair falls out, but the shorts and the open shirt are kept on, and the elderly adolescent bikes off with knap-sack and gadgets, never so happy as when he is with the boys—*primus inter pares*.

Having passed through the key experiences of infancy, childhood and adolescence, of which some of the more important have been discussed, a personality has emerged with at least three features: (1) a set of tech-niques for satisfying basic needs. This set includes techniques for handling other people, e.g. by obedience, by badgering, by bullying, by whining, by clamouring, etc., and also attitudes of dependency, demandingness, assumptions of service being forthcoming and so forth. (2) A set of controls which prescribes certain actions and proscribes others in terms of shame, fear, and/or sin. (3) A set of atti-tudes towards other people resulting from the treatment which the need for social acceptance has received. This may colour a whole cul-ture, but it is also of importance in large-scale communities, within which smaller groups work or play together in face-to-face relation-ship.

These three 'features' are, of course, not the only acquisitions by any manner of means. 'Functionally autonomous' interest systems will have been established, intellectual ability will have developed as far as innate capacity and environmental opportunity have allowed, and a host of other characteristics will have been acquired. The three features selected above are of major interest to the social psychologist.

Now the significant varieties of social situations, which are respons-ible for the creation of different personalities, are of interest to the social psychologist from two points of view. In the first place they are im-portant as social factors which play a part in producing different personalities within the *same* culture. Here the interest of the social psychologist overlaps with the interest of the 'individual' psychologist. In the second place, however, where differences in these key situations enable us to contrast *groups* of people, as, for example, the Arapesh and the Mundugomor, or the upper class and lower class in the same culture, they may throw a light on some of the general characteristics of the different groups. This is partly due to the fact that the effects are, as it were, cumulative.

Supposing it were true that the children of the 'middle' class are brought up to be more responsible than is the case with children of the 'lower' classes,[1] then that sense of responsibility is likely to be reinforced by mutual expectation among nearly all 'middle'-class people who consort together. The same would be true *mutatis mutandis* of the 'lower' class. If, again, a child of either class were brought up by the methods characteristic of the other class one might expect a sense of responsibility or the lack of it to develop, but he would present an entirely different social-psychological problem. We could not regard him as illustrating the prevailing culture, for he would not do so, we should be interested in his fate as an oddity and possibly as a mis-fit.

These two different points of view alternate when we consider the future that opens up to the young men and young women, whose moulding agencies we have been discussing. Ever since they were able to take note of the people about them and understand what is said in praise or criticism, they have been forming stereotypes of the statuses with which they have come in contact, directly or at second-hand, through conversation, through reading, or on the films. They know what is expected of a man and a woman in their culture, and also what is expected of a husband, a wife, a father or a mother. They learn not only what such roles involve to the player, but also what responses are expected towards the player. Besides the 'ascribed' roles, there are others: occupational roles, dignity roles, sporting roles, and so forth.

It is important to recognize that each individual only sees a very small part of the whole society, and that our model of a culture with its status/role system is a construct. The son of a miner, for instance, in a remote mining village sees intimately the playing of the miner's role, less intimately the playing of the shopkeeper's role, and very one-sidedly the playing of the role of teacher, doctor, and clergyman. The son of the landed gentry may have a notion of the roles of doctor,

[1] cf. Davis, A. and Havinghurst, R. J. *Social Class and Colour Difference in Child Rearing*. Kluckhohn, C. (Ed.) *Personality*, p. 252.

lawyer, clergyman and landed gentleman which might prepare him for undertaking any of them, but he would be likely to have only a remote notion of the roles of engine-driver, dustman, or shopkeeper. Both boys may well construct stereotypes of all the occupations mentioned, but they will vary in content, accuracy, and clarity. In a very simple society, in which the number of statuses is small, and most 'status-personalities' available for inspection, the young men and young women can make but few choices. As we have already seen, they may be slowly trained for adult life, or, as with the Manus, it comes as a nasty shock. Their destiny, however, is more or less fixed, and the only problem is whether their up-bringing has been such as to make all the adult roles available congenial. The point of interest here is as to whether on the whole there is, in simpler societies at any rate, a general coherence between the prevailing methods of dealing with the key situations in infancy, childhood and adolescence, and the major adult roles which confront the boy or girl when they have grown up.

In our complex societies there is an enormous variety of statuses to choose from, though of course economic circumstances, lack of information, and availability of jobs, materially limit the choice. Furthermore every role requires certain qualities for its effective performance and involves conduct which many people would find unpalatable. In so far as choice is possible, some statuses are excluded because the stereotype, which may be a sketchy and mistaken affair, is not attractive. On the other hand choices may be made which prove unsatisfying. To meet this the twin sciences of vocational guidance and vocational selection have become established.

We have been thinking in terms of the individual choosing, in so far as he can, the status he wants to, in Linton's sense, 'achieve'. A problem of interest arises when we think of groups of persons. Supposing, as we did above, that one can speak sensibly of 'class subcultures', with their prevailing methods of up-bringing and prevailing standards of culture, and supposing occupation-statuses which were once confined to one class now become open to another. Will the newcomers acclimatize themselves to the roles as previously 'defined', or will the roles themselves gradually alter? There is very little evidence upon which to base an opinion, but the subject is one to which research in the future will doubtless be directed.

The need to learn 'achieved' roles is obvious enough, but nowadays in some societies there is growing up a notion that 'ascribed' roles have to be explicitly taught. Of course we have already seen that in some sense *all* roles have to be learnt, but for biological roles this is done largely by the ordinary methods of praise, blame, imitation and the like, rather than by lectures. However, there are so many different notions of the role of young man, young woman, husband and wife, that a good deal of confusion arises. Side by side with vocational guidance we are presented with the astonishing spectacle of marriage guidance and lectures upon the subject at our universities.

There would appear to be two views about this predicament; on the one hand we are urged to 'educate for choice', on the other hand efforts are made to limit the choices made to such few as the propagandist approves of. Which you prefer, will depend, presumably, on whether you think that people's needs are so varied that they must learn to choose the best way of satisfying them, compatible with the least amount of human suffering, or whether you think that people cannot be trusted to do this and must be persuaded to conform to a pattern on the grounds that less human suffering will be caused that way.

Adulthood.   Of the cultural shaping—or, rather, creating—of personality there is little more to be said. Certain general personality traits are largely determined by early experience. The roles of adult life—'ascribed' and 'achieved'—will make their mark on top of them. The doctor, the lawyer, the shop assistant and the clerk will be alike in certain respects—as, say, Englishmen or Frenchmen. They will be unlike in certain respects in regard to which the doctor and lawyer may resemble one another more than either resembles the shop assistant and the clerk. Each will be more like others of his occupational group in some respects than he is like a member of the other occupational groups. But here the multiplicity of statuses a man may occupy from time to time must not be forgotten. Thus, the lawyer may be different from the doctor when considered as exercising his professional role, but he may be like him as a father or as a member of the 'professional class'.

All the same, since the personality operates as a whole and not as a mere collection of roles, the fact that one person plays the role of doctor another that of lawyer, another that of shop assistant and the fourth that of clerk, is likely to make them behave slightly differently as father, as husband, and even as sportsman, though the influence of the 'status-personality' associated with an occupation on other roles will vary from person to person, from occupation to occupation, and from one situation to another. The civil servant may carry his meticulousness into all his dealings. The doctor may 'drop' his professional manner readily. The lawyer may seal his lips almost automatically in all situations.

Combined with the concept of personality we have to take the 'situational approach' into consideration. The question as to how far 'achieved' status shapes personality depends upon (*a*) how far the conduct appropriate to the achieved status becomes habitual and (*b*) how far other situations elicit it. For instance the meticulousness appropriate to the civil servant may become so habitual that it becomes part of the personality structure and any situation may elicit it because orderliness is applicable to almost all situations. The respect of confidences which is part of the lawyer's role may become habitualized, but only a restricted number of situations may be relevant.

A lawyer might be prepared to reveal to his wife his opponent's score at golf, even if it were superior to his own, but he might not be prepared to reveal that old Pinkerton had claimed to go round in less than Bogey—or he might. It depends upon habitualization and the 'definition' which the lawyer makes of golf. If as a golfer he is playing an entirely different role, then his role of lawyer may be irrelevant. If his lawyer-role makes him 'define' his golfing-role as that of 'a responsible-man-playing-golf', his training as a lawyer is relevant and gossip about the boastfulness of his potential clients may be out of order. In the case of roles which are highly technical but involve no general traits of conduct, one would expect the status to make but little difference to conduct in other situations.

Old Age. After adult life comes old age. Here the personality changes are a function of the way in which the status of old man or old woman is 'defined'. This, in turn, will depend in part on the need the community has for their skill and wisdom. Among the Comanche, for example, 'the good old man abandoned his medicines and dropped back into a condition of innocuous dependence upon the younger generation. The attitude of such old men toward their sons who supported them was one of almost pathetic gratitude.'[1] Here we have the Oedipus situation in reverse. Those who could not bear this subservience kept to their medicine and tried to sustain their prestige by fear. In such a situation the skill in hunting and fighting is gone, and the old are not the repositories of any special lore, save that of magic, which is more of a liability to the community than an asset.

Elsewhere, however, respect is paid to the aged because their ex-

[1] Linton, R. in *Psychological Frontiers of Society*. Kardiner *et al.*, p. 79.

perience is considered valuable, and because the system of authoritarian up-bringing has taken hold of the young. They are expected to be dignified and learned, and the role is one which obviously has its attraction, and will be carefully safeguarded.

In our society, as so often happens with biological statuses, the status of 'old person' is ambiguous. On the one hand they are in theory wise and venerable, on the other hand they are out of date and in the way. This results, in many cases, in a tinge of resentment colouring their personalities, and an idiosyncratic response to a sense of being abandoned. Of course it is absurd to suggest that all old men and old women are alike. In our complex society there is enormous variety. There is, however, this common predicament: their skills and wisdom are not as highly regarded as in times past, and they do not normally live with their children. These are social conditions, and each adult faces these conditions in terms of his or her adult personality as it has been shaped by past social relationships. The point of interest to the social psychologist is not so much the variety of responses as the changing social situations of the old, to which these responses are made.

CHAPTER X

CULTURAL ANALYSIS AND NATIONAL CHARACTER

IT will be remembered that when embarking on the subject of the cultural influence on personality, it was said that there are two possible approaches. One can picture the child confronted by the structure to which he has to adapt himself, or one can make an attempt to render parts at least of the culture itself psychologically intelligible. It is to the second of these projects that we must now turn.

Let us take two cultures, described by Linton and analysed by Kardiner in *The Individual and His Society*, the Tanala and the Betsileo,[1] both of whom inhabit the island of Madagascar. Only a few features will be selected for our purpose and the reader is referred to the original work for a fuller account.

The Tanala live by dry rice cultivation. This involves the co-operation of large numbers of men who have to clear the forest. The head of the family is in supreme control over his sons and their families, his place being taken, when he dies, by the eldest. He, too, having prestige and the property in cattle and money that goes towards enhancing it, lords it over his brothers unless they manage to get together enough property, which is very difficult, to set up for themselves. Thus there is the familiar pattern of dominant fathers and privileged eldest sons having effective control over the majority who are younger sons. Elaborate rules govern attitudes of respect to the father, and though there are strict rules of inheritance by which the eldest son benefits, he can give presents to the younger sons if he pleases. Thus submission and ingratiation are their only chance. Their situation is mitigated by the fact that their labour is required and also by the general disapproval of display. They can, too, enter into blood-brotherhood relation with friends who will help them, and men of initiative can become warriors or magicians (*ombiasies*), a status to which we must refer again later. Another important mitigating factor is that subsistence and prestige do not go together. The man of property, who owns cattle and money, makes no use of his wealth save as insignia of prestige. So far as food

[1] cf. Digest from the original in *Readings in Social Psychology*, p. 46.

and shelter go everyone fares much alike. All the same, there is considerable hostility generated by the struggle for favour.

Now among the Tanala the following points are also noted: (1) the anal training is severe and a child is expected to be continent at the age of six months;[1] (2) 'All worship is directed to the management and placation of an ancestral ghost,'[2] to whom sacrifices have to be made, and there is also a belief in an 'impersonal fate or destiny'; (3) there is a certain amount of malevolent magic.

The Betsileo live nearby. They cultivate rice by the wet method and there is reason to think that they may originally have lived the same sort of life as their neighbours, the Tanala. Their life as described by Linton is, however, quite different. Wet rice cultivation does not involve nearly so much co-operation, and a system more like private property is possible. The Betsileo have a structure of King, nobility, commoners and slaves. Land is allotted by the King, who owns it all, and in return a rent in rice is paid. The nobility sub-let to tenant farmers, so that a kind of feudal structure is established. This places the commoners in a much worse position than any of the Tanala, because prestige and subsistence-security go together.

Significant differences are found: (1) The ancestral ghost becomes more like a god. He arranges everything and causes illness if he is displeased; (2) there is much more malevolent magic—'Much more general apprehension exists in Betsileo than Tanala, as is shown by the increase in belief in omens, dreams, and superstition.'[3] (3) 'There is also considerable increase in crime, stealing in particular, but also murder';[4] (4) the King is much more powerful than the family head in Tanala; (5) —a small point—the levirate (marriage of brother's widow), which the Tanala allow, is forbidden because a man who married his sister-in-law would be suspected of having made away with his brother; and (6) the successful view their success with trepidation.

Now the first thing which occurs to us is that the principal determinants of these differences are the different methods of production and distribution. This is obviously in line with the principles of economic materialism. These principles are, of course, psychological in nature; they are based upon man's basic needs, the methods he has worked out for their satisfaction, and his tendency to hang on to any favourable position in which he finds himself in the general struggle for existence.

This is not disputed by Linton and Kardiner. What they have

[1] op. cit., p. 262.   [2] ibid., p. 268.   [3] ibid., p. 289.   [4] ibid., p. 290.

attempted is to fill in the picture. Dry rice cultivation demands co-operation, but co-operation may be based upon various psychological configurations. There is nothing in co-operation, for instance, to ensure privileged positions to the father and the eldest sons, who appear to be exempt from the severer forms of toil. How that came about we cannot tell, but once established, together with the father's complete control over resources, then a certain attitude is to be expected from the younger sons—an attitude of resentful ingratiation. There is nothing in all this to ensure any particular form of anal training. In fact it comes early and there are severe penalties for any errors of judgment. Assuming the hypothesis that such early training can be used to induce obedience, then it will pave the way for that orderly respectfulness towards the father which we find in this culture. They learn: 'If I obey I will not be punished; if I obey I will be fed.'[1] This is, in fact, borne out by later experience and therefore re-inforced.

Their position is, however, hedged in with frustration. The technique of ingratiation may bring its rewards, but more often than not there is disappointment and jealousy, and there is always the favoured elder brother in the way. In their hour of need they may call upon an ancestral ghost, modelled, significantly enough, upon the father whose goodwill must be bought by sacrifice. The dissatisfactions, however, are such that considerable hostility must be generated. Hence, says Kardiner, the fear of magic, the elaborate legal system, and a peculiar kind of neurosis called *tromba* for those whose aggressiveness overwhelms them.

Among the Betsileo, so like and yet so different, there is a system of access to rice fields limited to those who can pay rent, leaving a large number of people with no assured subsistence. There is class structure rendered possible by the wet rice form of cultivation. No one seems to know exactly how this structure of King, nobility, commoners and slaves grew up, but if, as Linton suggests, it sprang out of a way of life like that of the Tanala—and there is a legend among the Betsileo that once the land was free to all—then an authoritarian régime is the one most likely to develop. At any rate we have to take it as we find it, but we also find characteristics which, on psychological grounds, we might expect.

According to Kardiner,[2] inflated prestige is based upon a relationship of extreme dependency. The more dependent you are, i.e. the less the source of supply is prepared to grant requests, the greater the

[1] ibid., p. 294.   [2] ibid., p. 342.

prestige with which you endow him. Thus the king among the Betsileo is regarded as a magic being of great potency. More obvious, perhaps, and more intelligible, is the enormous increase in signs of hostility among the Betsileo when compared with the Tanala. The increase in crime and malevolent magic, and the fear of attack if you succeed, all give evidence of heightened aggressiveness and its accompanying anxiety.

The Betsileo culture confirms the analysis of the Tanala culture in the sense that when the pressures are intensified, the alleged effects are intensified, and this can be shown to occur in more features than we have room to describe.

We must now turn to the magicians mentioned above, the *ombiasies*. 'The only way in which a young man could acquire individual wealth from the outside was by cattle-raiding or by becoming an *ombiasy*.'[1] Their main tasks are to 'determine the workings of destiny' and to 'make and teach the use of charms'. The point about them is that they are independent persons. If, as one may suppose, it is the more energetic of the younger sons, and it is they who become *ombiasies*, who undertake the training necessary for this status, then in fact it provides a convenient way to side-track potential disturbers of the peace.

This phenomenon, in itself a mere anthropological curiosity, may assume greater significance if we consider societies from another point of view. Every society, if it is to continue in existence, must develop what Kardiner calls a 'security system' which will safeguard it from external danger and from internal disruption. This means that internal hostilities, based upon frustration, must be kept in check. This is done by training and by what we might call policing. Societies differ in the pressure they put upon their members, and at some risk one can consider certain social institutions as devices for reduction of internal tensions; 'at some risk' because this way of looking at the matter carries the quite false implication that such 'devices' have been consciously established. With appropriate safeguards, however, we might think of the *ombiasy* status of the Tanala, the institution of blood-brotherhood, and the deprecation of the display of wealth as 'devices' adopted by the society to reduce tension by providing an avenue of escape, by providing a method of getting support, and by avoiding at least one source of jealousy.

The advantage of this formulation is that it helps to focus attention

[1] ibid., p. 257.

on the main problem which confronts all societies—the disposal of inter-member hostility. Somehow or other this is managed by all societies that do hold together. This is not to say that the enjoyment of participation is of no importance. On the contrary, it is of vital importance, but the need for effective participation cannot be satisfied if the hostilities engendered by the social pressure are uncontrolled. It may be argued that it is precisely the need for social participation, in whatever form it has been experienced, that leads to the preservation of that form even among those who are least favoured by it. Even so the pressure may become so severe that the structure cracks and the society re-forms itself on a different pattern.

It may be that there is very little cause for hostility to develop. Among the matrilineal and matrilocal Zuni, for instance, there seems to be complete security in childhood, followed by mutual dependency in adulthood so that the opportunities for envy and jealousy are absent, and, says Kardiner, 'they need not have recourse to other means of supplementing the prevailing security, as for example, by wealth or prestige.'[1] The only thing that worries them is drought, and religious ceremonial is mainly concerned with rain.

Now the Zuni are well-known from the description of them by Ruth Benedict in her *Patterns of Culture* to have strong rules against aggression. This seems to imply that there is a certain amount of hostility, but since we hear of no outlet we must assume that it is sufficiently small to be contained and that the rewards of conformity enable this to be done with ease. The Salteaux, on the other hand, are also renowned for their amiability, but according to Hallowell[2] this is not the whole of the story. Gossip, sorcery and magic are rampant, and 'the belief system of the Saulteaux fosters fantasy situations in which aggressive impulses become easily entangled with interpersonal relations in ways that may engender deep and irrational consequences'.

This brings us back to Kardiner's method of analysis. In the first place there are what he calls 'primary institutions', such as 'family organizations, in-group formation, basic disciplines, feeding, weaning, institutionalized care or neglect of children, anal training and sexual taboos including aim, object or both, subsistence technique, etc.'[3] These are the starting point, and to these are added in *Psychological*

---

[1] ibid., p. 115.
[2] 'Aggression in Saulteaux Society,' in *Personality*. (Ed.) Kluckhohn, C., p. 204.
[3] op. cit., p. 471.

Frontiers of Society,[1] various rational techniques of control, and scientific hypotheses. The infants born into the society and subjected to the pressure of its primary institutions project 'secondary institutions' which 'satisfy the needs and tension created by the primary or fixed ones'. These are such elements as taboo systems, religion, rituals, folk tales and techniques of thinking. It is noteworthy—and of doubtful plausibility—that he includes the status of *ombiasy* among the secondary institutions of the Tanala.

This interpretative technique may be further illustrated from the analysis of the Marquesan culture. Among the 'primary institutions' are an unusual sex ratio in which the men predominate, and food scarcity. The sex ratio is met by a form of polyandry in which a man marries a woman who brings her other lovers with her into the household. These supernumerary 'husbands' have rights of access to their 'wife' and are required for co-operative labour. The women, since they are in scarce supply, have a distinct advantage. They dominate in sexual intercourse, which is promiscuous and frequent. They dislike having children and nurse them badly. The result is a certain hostility against them which is responsible for the 'secondary institution' of a belief in dangerous female spirits. The shortage of food creates a food anxiety and canalizes their thought along eating channels. The result is that anxiety is phrased in terms of being eaten up, and folk tales are shaped accordingly.

In their second work two more simple societies are analysed by Linton and Kardiner according to the same general principles. The Comanche Indians present but few new problems. They used, it seems, to live on the Plateau, struggling for existence and respecting the old men whose skill and knowledge were of value to them. Down on the Plain among the herds of buffalo they were transformed into a competitive society of hunters and warriors; the young men came into their own; the old men were expected to retire. So, again, the type of life changes with a change in the economy. On the Plains there is, on the face of it, considerable basis for mutual hostility. Between father and son the relations are almost the opposite to those to which we are used. The son admires his father's prowess as a warrior or a huntsman, the father lavishes praise on the son whenever he shows signs of marksmanship, and takes great care to be on good terms with him because when he gets old it is he that will be the dependant.

It is rather between the 'bloods' that enmity might be expected.

[1] p. 30.

Once more the mitigating circumstances are noted. Fraternal wife-lending reduces sexual jealousy. The warrior only has prestige while he is objectively successful so that any given person only captures the limelight for a limited period, and while he stands supreme he is expected to show his confidence in his magic by a display of generosity. For some, life is too strenuous, and our attention is called to a curious institution: the 'contrary man'. He is a kind of accepted comic and his role is to do the opposite of what he says he will do. Is this, as Kardiner suggests, another of those methods of institutionalizing the mis-fits, like the '*berdache*',[1] also found among the Comanche, who wore women's clothes, and were expected to be rather better than women at women's work?

The Alorese raise an interesting problem. The babies receive but little care and attention. Their mothers leave them after, at most, two weeks because they have to work in the fields. The infants are looked after in a slap-dash kind of way by the men and old women, who silence them by stuffing their mouths with pre-masticated food. No help is given them in learning to walk, and they are plagued with per-petual teasing. In fact there is no one towards whom they can form a satisfactory, reliable, emotional relationship. The result is that no effectively co-ordinated system of conduct develops. They are des-cribed as 'anxious, suspicious, lacking in confidence, devoid of enter-prise', and an *independent* check by submitting individual Alorese to a Rorschach test seemed to bear out the inferences drawn from the cul-ture by Kardiner. The argument is that from the culture pattern Kardiner inferred a certain personality type, and this was remarkably confirmed by the tests. We are told also that they have a great fear of any loss of control as manifested in drunkenness or mania. This Kar-diner puts down to their having established no firm mechanism for the control of their own aggressiveness, so that they are therefore terrified of its breaking out.

Now side by side with this rather dingy picture we are presented with another almost equally dingy. The Alorese men, as in several other simple cultures, devote their time to elaborate deals in pigs—a concern which is quite divorced from the problem of subsistence, but wherein prestige is gained. Their whole lives seem to be engaged in this useless marketing activity. It seems odd, but our surprise, if not our ridicule, may be moderated if we ask ourselves whether the buying and selling of shares in our own culture has a more essential connection with

[1] Linton. *Study of Man*, p. 480.

the production and consumption of commodities, than the pig marketing among the Alorese has with their economic system.

However this may be, the facts about the pig deals are not what we
would expect from so apathetic a people. The anxiety and suspicion are
there but not the lack of enterprise. Kardiner himself interprets
the prestige-giving value of the pig marketing as a method of com-
pensating for the sense of unworthiness which the scurvy treatment
they have received has produced.

Whatever the truth in this matter may be, the interesting question
poses itself: can a form of child-rearing be such as to render complicated cultural elaboration impossible, or at any rate very ineffectual?
Only further research will enable us to answer the question, but mean-
time an attempt must be made to assess the contribution made by the
method of analysis which we have been considering. No attempt has
been made to give a full acount of Kardiner's theories, many of which
are highly controversial; the above account is merely intended to
convey a general idea of his approach.

In making our assessment of the Kardiner-Linton approach, however, we are confronted with a difficulty. No account of the shaping
of cultures is possible without some mention of the theories of Marx
and Engels, who have undoubtedly thrown more light on the subject
than anyone else. At the same time it is impossible in a book of this
kind to do proper justice to their contributions without overweighting
the argument with controversial discussion. We will therefore content
ourselves with one quotation from Marx's Preface to the *Critique of
Political Economy*:[1] 'The mode of production of the material means
of existence conditions the whole process of social, political, and intellectual life.' This sentence is followed by the celebrated statement:
'It is not the consciousness of men that determines their existence,
but, on the contrary, it is their social existence that determines their
consciousness.' In the first quotation the important word is *conditions*
(*bedingt*). This does not mean anything so ridiculous as that every
detail of social structure, every detail of political history, and every
product of thought is determined by the 'mode of production of the
material means of existence', but rather that no social structure, no
phase of political history and no system of thought is intelligible without reference to the mode of production of material means, their
ownership, and the way they are distributed.

---

[1] Marx, Engels. *Selected Works.* Moscow, Vol. I, p. 239.

This was clearly the view of Engels. In a letter to J. Bloch[1] he remarks: 'According to the materialist conception of history, the *ultimately* determining element in history is the production and reproduction of real life. More than this neither Marx nor I have ever asserted. Hence if somebody twists this into saying that the economic element is the *only* determining one, he'd transform that proposition into a meaningless, abstract, senseless phrase.'

In any physical environment two things must happen if a tribe is to survive: they must exploit the resources of the neighbourhood to provide themselves with food, and they must rear their successors. In any case of a primitive community there must be established a method of gaining a livelihood and a method of rearing children. How such methods got established we cannot say. The ingenuity of individual men and the acceptance of their techniques by their followers must have played their part, and sometimes tradition bears witness to a past which we can dimly reconstruct.

We shall find in all societies two things: (1) a certain method of production and (2) advantages and disadvantages accruing to the members of the society from such methods of production and distribution as are in force. The methods of production will be in part determined by the natural environment, in part by the technical knowledge of the inhabitants, and in part by the genius of individual men who think of new techniques. Every new technique, once it has 'caught on' is likely to provide new opportunities for individual enrichment, and these will be exploited, in so far as the existing structure of society with its beliefs and traditions do not stand in the way. The resistance to change will be in inverse ratio to the advantages foreseen from the new methods, and in direct ratio to the power of the vested interests, if any, which they threaten.

Every change is therefore likely to be accompanied by conflict, but when the prizes are very large, and where those who expect to benefit are already powerful, or where those who expect to benefit can combine forces, the supporters of the ancient régime are fighting a losing battle. The point to be noticed is that the circumstances of the battle will vary from one situation to another. The overthrow of the aristocracy in Europe by the bourgeoisie was quite a different story from that of the infiltration of the aristocracy by the bourgeoisie in Japan.

Some of the changes in technique as Marx and Engels pointed out,

[1] Marx, Engels. *Selected Works.* Moscow, 1949, Vol. II, p. 443.

had significant effects in improving the position of some members of a
society as compared with others.

Either, as in the case of the Betsileo, where the new methods of rice-
cultivation did not require the co-operation of many persons, those
who, as it were, get possession first can manage without their fellows,
with the result that their fellows are reduced to dependency, or—
the more significant case—the new methods involve capital equipment so complicated that only a few are in a position to exploit it.
In either case, the many are dependent upon the relatively few. Practically everyone has *some* rewards, true, but now a situation arises in
which the policy of those in possession of the means of production may
run counter to the interests of those who are dependent upon them for
their livelihood.

There are therefore two possible sources of conflict: the introduction
and establishment of new forms of production which threaten the
position of the people in control of the old ones, and the divergence of
interest between the owners of the means of production and the people
who work for them. It is essential to know the alignment of forces on
these issues at any moment of history in any society if one is to understand what happened.

Now in every society, except in revolutionary situations, there is a
general acceptance of the *status quo*, otherwise the social pattern could
not continue to exist. This means that there will be theories, beliefs,
traditions, slogans and moral principles which justify, explain and
legitimize the set-up. If conditions are quite intolerable for a significant number of people they may rebel in blind fury at their plight.
Peasants and slaves have done this from time to time, but the equipment
and accepted legitimacy of their enemies have almost always been such
that these rebellions have ended in defeat of the rebels.

Normally, however, conditions of life have been sufficiently bearable—and what is bearable will vary with the prevailing knowledge of
what is possible—to the majority of the people so that they have
accepted whatever moral justification for their circumstances happens
to be current in the community. Such justifications are naturally supported wholeheartedly by people in the society who gain most from
the established economic methods, and they will view with alarm any
dangerous thoughts which threaten their position. So delicate is their
sense of which side their bread is buttered that they are frequently quite
unaware of the real motives which are operating in the formation of
their judgments. The privileged are for the most part honestly doing

what they believe to be their best for the community, they are for the most part not hypocrites, but their frame of reference is so determined by their own interests that what they believe to be for the best nearly always turns out in fact to be to their own advantage. This is the primary sense in which the 'social, political, and intellectual life' is economically conditioned.

We must now introduce what might be called the 'innovators'. By 'innovators' are meant the people who invent new techniques of production and social organization and new moral and philosophical ideas. At any particular juncture there are actual methods of production and distribution, kept going by habit, and justified by accepted doctrine. They operate within a physical environment whose laws they must respect. They operate according to a 'logic' which determines much of what happens. This 'logic' is part of the subject-matter of economics and concerns such principles as: 'you can't get two pints out of a one pint jar', and 'if in a money economy people have very little money they will not be able to buy the goods they produce', and so forth. These are all hypothetical propositions and their application depends on the relevant circumstances being present at any given time. Thus what happens is secondarily conditioned by economic 'logic'.

However, from time to time, within the limits set by the prevailing conditions, individual men do have ideas which are not determined by the economic structure, in the sense that, if you knew what that was, you could not infer the new ideas. Someone must have had the idea of harnessing power to machinery in a large building, others must individually have followed his example. The advantages of small factories must have suggested to individual persons the advantages of large ones, and so on. The point is that there are no mysterious 'economic forces' which 'make' people take to building factories, an element of what one can only call 'creative ingenuity' is at work.

Of course the successive stages of technological development and its social repercussions, viewed *ex post facto*, look obvious enough and one is tempted to look upon them as following inevitably in sequence, pushed forward by some underlying evolutionary process. There is nothing inevitable about it. Some future developments might be, of course, predictable, but predictable, be it noticed, by people who share the creative ingenuity of those about whom their predictions are made. Given small-scale factories, an onlooker interested in the game might say: 'Large factories would be more profitable and would drive small-scale competitors off the field; I bet someone will do this because it is

so obvious.' When that prediction was made, true enough entre-
preneurs did have the same idea. Given a 'profit-making ethic', it
might be so obvious that it was 'inescapable'. At the same time you
did have to have the entrepreneur with the wits—modest though they
may be—to see the advantages, and there is nothing in small-scale
method and production *as such* to ensure this. Moreover generalizations about large-scale production proved to be risky because it appears
that it is only profitable for certain processes, and besides this, the
bureaucratic developments of large-scale production were not foreseen,
so that the general prediction that the economic world would be
divided between a small number of capitalists and a vast array of
proletarians was falsified in the event by the rise of the 'new middle
class'. As Stalin observed: 'We have no right to expect of the Classical
Marxist writers, separated as they were from our day by a period of
forty-five or fifty-five years, that they should have foreseen each
and every zigzag of history in the distant future in every separate
country.'

Besides the unpredictable innovation in technique and in governmental administration, there are innovations in the world of ideas.
Ideas are conditioned by an economic structure in the sense that they
are influenced by the interests of the persons concerned in it, and also
in the sense that many of them are 'about' it. Marxists have never
taken ideas as mere epi-phenomena, they have always accepted the
reaction of ideas on the economic processes out of which they were
formed. This is, indeed, a field of 'dialectic' operation. Many of the
systems of ideas in any community are, as has been said above, justi-
ficatory of the structure, which has been built upon the economic
basis. It is concerning the range and function of these that Marxist
analysis is most illuminating.

Some ideas, however, are not justifications but, on the contrary,
criticism. If they sprang from the oppressed classes, and were uniformly
rejected by the oppressors, and by everyone who benefits from the
economic system, one could say that they were verbal formulations of
the interests of the workers, just as other ideas express the interests of
the privileged and their entourage. This, however, is not the case.
Almost all 'revolutionary' ideas spring from members of the classes
against which they are directed, and the first people to be attracted to
the new moral insight are members of the bourgeoisie. Very naturally
they are welcomed by members of the working classes, when they
come to hear of them, but even here their conditioning has been such

that it takes some time before the new possibilities are accepted. The acceptability of a doctrine, which favours the interests of those sections of the community which are in the least advantageous positions, is a function of their level of education and of the degree to which they are discontented.

Broadly speaking, Marxism includes a social-psychological theory about the structure and changes of social patterns, a moral doctrine, and a programme of action. It is not concerned with non-human 'economic forces', because there are no such things; it is concerned with human relationships, human conduct, and human thought with respect to the basic problem of production, distribution and consumption. It interprets human behaviour in terms of economic interests and it attempts to predict behaviour on the *assumption of certain general psychological tendencies*.

As a moral doctrine it may be regarded as a symptom of that heightened concern with fairness which is characteristic of our age. Not unnaturally and in accordance with the principles of economic conditioning, those whose unfair advantages are attacked are resentful, but it becomes increasingly hard for them to justify their claims.

With programmes of action we are not concerned. They depend upon what results are desired, the existing conditions, and the relevant rules. Whether the programme of action proposed by Marx and his followers is to be adopted is a practical issue, which can only be decided in each case after an analysis of the relevant conditions, an estimate of the validity of the social-psychological principles to be applied, and of the probable effects of their application.

In the theory of economic conditioning outlined above, an attempt has been made to give due weight to economic interests as primary factors in the analysis of culture. It is a social psychological matter because, as has been insisted, it deals with human intentions, human relations, human decisions, and human thought. In considering any culture at any moment of its history attention must be paid first and foremost to the interrelation of the members of the society in the pursuit of their basic economic needs. Then we have to consider the current system of thought, the accepted moral code, in the widest sense of that expression, including *all* standards of conduct, and the existing structure of institutions, class hierarchy and traditions. Every man, woman and child is influenced, in his or her conduct, by all of them.

Where, then, does the kind of analysis which Kardiner and Linton have elaborated fit in? The answer is: everywhere. This does not mean that the specific psychological thesis of Kardiner need be accepted. The point is, rather, that the method of child-training is bound to condition what one might call the specific *quality* of the society. And, *per contra*, the economically conditioned factors will clearly influence the methods of child-training. There is, in fact, a complex interaction throughout. One cannot say that capitalism causes children to be brought up in a certain way, but one can say that the way in which they have traditionally been brought up will condition the 'quality' of the capitalism, while the individualistic ethic of capitalism may have its effect in stressing competition as an instrument of training.

Again, adult life puts certain pressures on individual adults and these are largely determined by psycho-economic factors. The method of child-training puts certain pressures on the children. The 'quality' of the culture will be in part a resultant of these two sources of pressure. To take a simple example, Comanche babies are tenderly cared for. This means that resentment and anxiety are reduced. It would be quite ridiculous to suggest that this 'causes' them to take to hunting buffalo because, in any case, they got their living in other ways when they lived in other surroundings. What one can say—assuming the description to be correct—is that if their training had been different as infants, the buffalo hunting would have put different pressure upon them and that this would have been revealed in their culture. We might even say that certain methods of child-training might have stood in the way of their becoming competent hunters altogether.

Again, the cleanliness of the Tanala, to which reference has already been made, is alleged to have had an effect in inducing an attitude of obedience. It does not appear to have led to an elaborate drainage system, as it has in the Anglo-American culture, for the obvious reason that the requisite techniques were not developed. In our own culture cleanliness-training may have played its part in the history of plumbing, but obviously other factors, such as a desire to prevent disease, were also operative. It may be that obedience and a sense of responsibility are first learnt with the inculcation of control over bodily functions, but these traits play a different part in England, from the part they play in America. If we accept the evidence that the middle-classes in Chicago are stricter with their children in these matters than are the working classes,[1] we should hesitate to say that to this factor alone is

[1] Davis, A. and Havinghurst, R. J. 'Social Class and Colour Differences in Child Rearing in Kluckhohn, C. (ed.) *Personality*, p. 252.

due the alleged greater sense of responsibility in the former when compared with the latter.

The point is that all these psychological elements—economic interests, standards of conduct, methods of child training and so on—form a unique configuration at any point in history. They form the 'apperceptive mass', which receives new material, and the matrix out of which changes emerge.

In simple societies the 'basic personality structure' for a society may remain much the same for a very long time. In modern national communities what we call 'national character' is constantly changing, because of changes in the factors which are responsible for it. In the U.S.S.R., where the changes have been very drastic, an alteration in the standards and outlook of new generations is certainly to be expected. This element of change must always be remembered when dealing with the difficult subject of 'national character' to which we must now turn.

National Character. The study of 'national character' is carried out on two levels. There is the noting of characteristic traits, and there is the attempt to 'explain' them. The latter aim is obviously the more significant if it can be done. It is the latter aim that prompted Gorer's definition of national character as 'an attempt to isolate and describe the motives shared by the members of a society who manifest the same shared habits or culture.'[1] The material, out of which this concept of national character is constructed, includes institutions, public policy, ways of thought, and cultural products, as well as traits of personality.

These last, however, are a starting point, and it is here that the major difficulties present themselves. In the first place, as we have seen above, the members of any nation tend to form stereotypes of other nationals. Thus, to take one example, Katz and Braly[2] found a great deal of agreement in the adjectives chosen as characteristic of various nationalities. This is only one of a number of such inquiries and it is referred to here because Eysenck and Crown[3] conducted a similar inquiry with an adult, middle-class, non-student population. Their results were in line with those of the previous experiment: the Germans were thought

[1] Gorer, G. 'The Concept of National Character.' *Science News* 18. Penguin Books, 1950, p. 109.
[2] 'Stereotypes of One Hundred College Students.' *J. of Abs. in Soc. Psych.*, XXVIII 1933, p. 280.
[3] Eysenck, H. J. 'War and Aggression,' in *Psychological Factors in Peace and War*. Ed. T. H. Pear. Hutchinson, 1950, p. 82.

scientifically minded, industrious, arrogant, aggressive, and over-nationalistic, while the Japanese were thought cruel, fanatic, treacherous, imitative and industrious.

Now in the Eysenck-Crown study the subjects were invited to write about their assessments and about half of them made it clear that they did not hold to these descriptions very seriously. On these grounds Eysenck argues that the evidence on stereotypes ought to be supplemented by more detailed methods of investigation, and that much of the talk about stereotypes is vitiated by the fact that the unfortunate subjects have been forced by the experimental procedure into making a reply which does not do justice to their real views.

This may well be the case, and if cross-questioned people might be quite prepared to say that they really did not know what Negroes or Italians are like. All the same, the two collections of adjectives given above as examples are not at all surprising, and it is arguable that what people say without reflecting is itself evidence of their spontaneous attitude. At any rate, this can be said: in so far as stereotypes do operate—and Eysenck agrees that they do—they will influence the perception of other nationals, by providing a frame of reference in terms of which what agrees with the stereotype will stand out.

It may be said, however, that the observer can with an effort discount the stereotyped version of typical characteristics, and view the scene with an innocent eye. We can accept this, with the proviso that in time of crisis—war and revolution—no man is quite as innocent of prejudice as he would like to be. We now come to a second difficulty. No observer is able to observe every member of the nation he is studying. That is obvious enough, but there is a risk that observers will meet and mix with people of one class more than with people of another, and devote their attention to one area from which they will proceed to generalize to the whole country.

It is clear enough that Tartarin could only have lived in Tarascon, and that the atmosphere of Normandy is very different from that of Provence. Similarly, Prussians are different from Bavarians, and he would be a rash man who attributed to the Scots certain traits he might notice among the English. Class differences and regional differences abound and any assertion that certain traits are prevalent in a nation must be backed up by a clear account of the evidence upon which such statements are made.

Popular estimates of the traits prevalent in a nation are, therefore, often misleading, and at least one writer has questioned the validity of the concept of national character altogether.[1] This seems to be going too far in the direction opposite to that taken by the club bore who talks about: 'Your Frenchman', 'Your Arab', and 'Your Jap'. Common observation, and convergent assessments by many people, do bear witness to a differential distribution of human qualities; the difficulty is to pin down those which are of significance for the understanding of other peoples, and to see whether, behind all the variety of behaviour which a national group presents, there are any recurrent themes, which throw a light, not only on the social conduct of everyday life, but also on their institutions and their ways of thought.

We now pass on to the second method of tackling 'national character', the attempt to 'isolate and describe the motives shared by the members of the society'. Here, as we have seen, we must take into consideration the institutions, the historical circumstances, the class structure, the economic relations, and the cultural products of the nation, whose 'character' we are trying to construct. Together with these we have to consider the effects of the methods of child-training which are prevalent. All these are in a relationship of 'reciprocal interaction rather than of causality'.[2]

To start with we return to the noting of traits by several observers. This might be done by making a collection of characteristics noticed by people who are not members of the nation we are studying, as has been done by H. S. Commager in *America in Perspective: The United States through Foreign Eyes*,[3] or one may study what nationals have thought of themselves.[4] Another starting point is a description of salient features of the ethos or standards of a community, either at first hand, as in Margaret Mead's *American Character*,[5] or from interviews with 'displaced' nationals, and a study of literary sources, as in Benedict's study of the Japanese Character.[6] Obviously these sources can be combined, and it will also be noticed that the selection of salient features necessarily depends upon preliminary hypotheses about what is likely to be important.

The task of interpretation, the construction of a model of interacting

---

[1] Fyfe, Hamilton. *The Illusion of National Character*, 1940.
[2] Ginsberg, M. *Reason and Unreason in Society*. Longman, 1947, p. 136.
[3] New York, 1947. For other examples cf. Klineberg, 'Tension Affecting International Understanding.' Soc. Series. Research Council, No. 62, 1950, p. 12f.
[4] Ginsberg, M. *Reason and Unreason*, Chapter VIII, 'German View of German Mentality.'
[5] Penguin Book, 1944 (an English version of *And Keep Your Powder Dry*, published in America in 1942).
[6] *The Chrysanthemum and the Sword*.

forces, may be approached from various angles, which may be complementary or conflicting. Let us take one or two instances to illustrate
different methods of interpretation. What follows is not intended as
final description of the 'character' of the nations referred to, but rather
as an illustration of methods.

Ginsberg,[1] in the course of a closely argued discussion about the
concept of national character, compares the views that have been put
forward about the English and the Germans. 'With regard to two
qualities of the English mentality,' he says, 'there is universal consensus
among observers both English and foreign, namely its empiricism and
individualism.'[2] This is evidenced, not only in individual conduct,
but also in English law and English politics, as well as in the English
philosophical tradition. This is the data. Pursuing it further we find
that a feature in which both traits play their part is the 'capacity for
spontaneous organization', and a good-humoured readiness to agree
to differ, or to collaborate with opponents. What has led to these
recurrent themes?

Ginsberg refers with approval to Kantorowicz and Bardoux who
look to historico-geographical conditions. He calls attention to: 'The
peculiarities of the English class structure which has put the conduct of
foreign affairs in the hands of a class with special codes of behaviour,
and the feeling of security and confidence generated by the absence of
the fear of war and the fear of revolution which has formed the background of Continental diplomacy.'[3] The general implication is that our
ad hoc method of conducting affairs, and our respect for other people,
are rendered possible by the security which we have enjoyed for a long
time, and which has enabled us to mature quietly, while the historical
development of our class structure has played its part in the establishment of decent standards. To this we may add the absence of a dominating central government, which has favoured the development of
political individualism.

The themes which recur among the Germans, according to themselves and other observers include: depth of feeling unhampered by a
desire for precision, individualism, and docility. The first is exhibited
in their philosophical products, in their devotion to vague and often
grandiose ideals. The second is illustrated by their lack of political
capacity, and, in combination with emotional intensity, by their
identification with parties and condemnation of those who do not

---

[1] *Reason and Unreason in Society*, Chapter VII, 'National Character.' cf. also Chapter
VIII.   [2] ibid., p. 139.   [3] ibid., p. 153.

agree with them. Their docility is, of course, exhibited in their love of rules and submission to order.

Here we have a somewhat contradictory list, and a German writer, Muller-Freienfels,[1] to whom Ginsberg refers, interprets it in terms of compensatory devices. The underlying instability and the rampant individualism require a check. They are potentially disruptive and actually disturbing, so that external rules are clung to as the only means of keeping the self stable. The love of order is, in fact, a 'reaction formation'.

'A far more promising approach to the study of German character', says Ginsberg,[2] 'is to be found in the analysis of the structure of German society.' First, he suggests, there is the recent unification of the country under Prussia, which has not been given time to mature. The unification brought together forcibly a larger number of feudal states, which had been able to establish themselves because of the weakness of the Emperor. The people never had any help against the feudal nobility, and the bourgeoisie were never powerful enough to check their pretensions. Thus the classes were separated from one another and the general atmosphere was pervaded with the principle of authority. The docility and submission 'cease to be so surprising when it is remembered that for many generations Germans were accustomed to the rule of feudal lords,'[3] while 'the lack of balance or poise . . . is no doubt connected with the absence of a steady or continuous tradition.' The Lutheran tradition, too, is interwoven into the interpretation. The stress on faith within, and obedience without, is reinforced by the fact that Lutheran preachers often came from families accustomed to obedience, while 'many of the bureaucracy came from clerical homes.'

This account does not include all the points in Ginsberg's interpretation, and it should be said further that he does not suggest that the factors he mentions are the only significant ones. However, it may give some idea of the kind of model which can be constructed on an historico-political basis.

Very different is the analysis given by H. V. Dicks.[4] His evidence is the study of German prisoners of World War II. 'Our typical German,' he says, 'is earnest, industrious, meticulous, over-respectful to authority, docile and kow-towing, tense and over-polite,'[5] but a little martinet and unpleasantly ferocious in his dealings with those he can

---

[1] *Psychologie des Deutschen Menchen*, 1937.   [2] op. cit., p. 164.
[3] op. cit., p. 167.
[4] In *Psychological Factors of Peace and War*. Ed. T. H. Pear. Chapter IX.
[5] op. cit., p. 199.

dominate. To which list of traits he adds: 'His queer sentimental far-away romanticism.'

The description fits the characteristics selected above. The explanation, however, is in psychological terms. The German child is brought up in a home in which the father is dominant and harsh, while the mother backs him up. She, on the contrary, is tender and meek, and the boy learns to despise her though he secretly idealizes her. This leads to a resentful acceptance of the father as a model and the longing for the mother, whose love he has never been able to enjoy. This, in turn, leads to an overt dominating, manly attitude, combined with obedience and subservience to those *in loco patris*.

The combination of domineering and subservient behaviour is explained as being due to the relationship of the boy to his father; the emotional instability and the longing for a promised land is attributed to the relations between the boy and his mother. Upon this basis the love of hierarchy, 'knowing one's place', and insistence on rank and title, are intelligible. Hostility, too, is aroused by the paternal dominance, hostility which is not soothed by maternal comforting, and this comes out in the familiar forms of displacement and projection, whereby 'out-groups' are made a target and credited with hostile intentions which really have their source in the minds of the Germans themselves. The 'gift for painstaking organizations', too, springs from the same basic situation; it is 'a defence against the deeper inner anarchy and division.'[1]

This hypothesis finds some verification in the analysis of a group of German prisoners of war, who were divided into five sub-groups ranging from 'fanatical Nazis' to 'active convinced anti-Nazis'. The pro-Nazis were found to have 'an undue acceptance of paternal authority' and other characteristics which go with it, while among the anti-Nazis these features were not marked. For them—the anti-Nazis—tender relationships were possible and they were able to develop anti-father attitudes towards authority.[2]

Here we have two interpretations of the same data. Which is the more acceptable? Such a question may be misplaced. Dicks himself points out that he has given a psychological account of the present generation. 'How the pattern originated and grew must be left for the social historian to determine.'[3] The two stories do not, in fact, conflict, and the two together must be supplemented by some account of

[1] ibid., p. 206.   [2] ibid., p. 212.   [3] ibid., p. 200.

the economic interests involved, which might make for variants of the basic-personality structure along class lines.

It may be that historical circumstances have allowed the development of the strong-father ideology. When this is established and encouraged by other events, such as the domination of Prussia, where the ideology was highly developed, and by a vulnerable geographical position, then certain psychological resultants may be expected on the lines of Dicks's analysis. Furthermore when economic crisis and defeat in war are present, this may well intensify any uneasiness which family relations may have engendered. The 'strong man' will find his opportunity for dominance, and the instability which lies behind the façade will find comfort in following him. According to Dicks the Nazi 'harbours in concentrated form some of the most distorted characteristics of the basic "political" personality of Germany.'[1] The inter-war crisis impinged upon a certain personality structure, and, as it were, 'selected' the more extreme cases for promotion.

We have taken two different methods of analysing national characters and seen how they may be combined. Ruth Benedict in her *Chrysanthemum and the Sword*[2] uses both at once, in the sense that child-training, character formation, and social structure are inter-related. Japan emerged into the modern world with a long history of carefully protected and elaborated feudalism, in which the functions, mode of life, standard of conduct, and hierarchical position were fixed for everyone. This is the historical background, and 'taking one's proper station' with its duties is the principal basis, according to Benedict, of the Japanese national character. The duties are debts which must be paid, and their irksomeness is lessened by the implication of benefits received.

In fact it would appear that Japanese life is lived in a structure of indebtedness. There are the great and unpayable debts to the Emperor and to one's parents, and there are debts one owes to anyone who has benefited one; these must be repaid in full. A further binding obligation is the obligation 'to one's name', which means that insults must be avenged, no failure admitted, and all the proprieties must be kept.

Life is divided into circles of relationship. There is the circle of public life involving the paramount indebtedness, there is the circle of home life with its obligation to parents, to wife, and to children, and there is a free circle of private life in which uninhibited enjoyment is permitted, provided that it does not interfere with the duties of the more serious circles. In the home there is a formalized structure of

[1] ibid., p. 213.   [2] Secker and Warburg, 1947.

father-dominance and mother-subservience, but, unlike the Germans, it seems, this is so much part of the formality of life that the father does not have to preserve his position by domineering behaviour, and the wife is not despised as a woman, but rather looked up to for 'keeping her place' with dignity and devotion. The dominant theme is duty, with a place reserved for holidays. The training which leads up to this adult acceptance of such an unquestioned system of burdens is unexpected. The children up to the age of six or seven are allowed complete freedom of action. They must, of course, show appropriate respect for their fathers, but they are allowed the greatest freedom in their behaviour to their mothers. They have, as the Japanese say, 'no shame'. And yet a life in which avoidance of shame is a key to conduct lies before them. Benedict calls attention to the difference between American and Japanese methods. In America a man in the prime of life is given a wide freedom of choice: 'The Japanese rely on maximizing the restraint upon him.'[1]

How is this done? Even during their care-free period, children are subjected to a good deal of teasing by their parents, so they are conditioned in early life to fear ridicule. Then there is strict anal training upon which Gorer[2] lays emphasis as being responsible for their tidiness and perfectionism. Two other features of child-training are also said to be of significance. One is the way in which they are literally put through the motions of etiquette, much as the Balinese children are, so that they become habituated to certain responses. The other, and perhaps the most significant, is the attitude of the home circle to unacceptable behaviour. The home in the early days was a safe, happy place, where love and approval were assumed. Then comes a change. The playful threat of abandonment, which used to be mere teasing, now assumes an aspect of real possibility. The whole family become 'a solid phalanx of accusation'. Ridicule and rejection are the weapons which Japanese culture uses to induce obedience to its rules. But a free area is allowed, at any rate to the men, in which they can enjoy all the pleasures of the flesh. Asceticism is not a feature of their character, its place is taken by discipline.

There is, therefore, an elaboration of the methods of self-discipline which have been developed in the east, without accepting their original purpose. Zen-Buddhism is the most carefully organized of these

---

[1] op. cit., p. 254.
[2] *Themes in Japanese Culture.* Transactions of the New York Academy of Science V., 1943, p. 106.

methods; it aims at achieving whole-hearted and spontaneous devotion to duty by eliminating the 'observing self', which criticizes and questions and thus impedes pure and direct action.

It is clear that the methods of child-training have had their effect, but it is equally clear that they are not the whole story. They fit into a structure which has been determined by other factors—historical and economic. Assuming the analyses to be correct, a comparison between German culture and Japanese culture is of interest. Both stress obedience to authority, duty, and respect for position. They are inculcated by quite different methods—and with different results. The German boy is strictly brought up and there is a continuity in his development. The Japanese boy is allowed considerable freedom, within a hierarchal framework which he must accept, but this means that devices have to be found to bring him into line when his real training begins.

Margaret Mead's study of the American character[1] was written to explain Americans to themselves and to us, so as to make the contacts which wartime alliance brings about as smooth as possible, and also to warn Americans that their 'way of life' depends upon conditions which are vanishing. She was followed by Gorer,[2] whose analysis is on much the same lines. Their clue to the American character is indicated by the titles of the leading chapters of their books. Margaret Mead gets going in the third chapter which she calls: 'We are All Third Generation'. Gorer's first chapter is on 'Europe and the Rejected Father'. The theme in both is the anxiety of the children of immigrants to be 'good Americans', which they cannot be if they follow the old folk-ways of their fathers. This is combined with the passionate desire of the parents that their children should succeed. This constellation of notions operates on the background of a tradition of liberty, self-reliance, enterprise and a frontier beyond which lie new worlds to conquer. The first result of the rejection of the father as the authority is that the mother takes his place, and the result of that is the development of what Gorer calls a 'predominantly feminine'[3] conscience. The rejection of Europe leads to the establishment of competitive achievement as a standard of success. You must visibly do better than others. 'Goals,' says Mead,[4] 'are not stated in class terms, but in pecking order terms and in terms of the outward and visible signs of success. To get ahead, to make good—these are the goals which are impressed on American children—to go some place else, get on with it, count your success by

---

[1] *The American Character*. Penguin.   [2] *The Americans*. Cresset Press, 1948.
[3] Gorer, G., op. cit., p. 39.   [4] Mead. *American Character*, p. 51.

the number of less handicapped that you have passed on the road.' So
that material success is 'good' which means that failure is 'bad'.

This involves a danger to which Mead calls attention. Now that
the frontier has been pushed to the Pacific, and in the face of recurrent
economic crises, will not the terms in which approval is phrased put a
painful pressure upon the younger generation?

However that may be, the framework outlined above: rejected
father, dominant mother, success measured by outward and visible
criteria, and the priority of the young as vindicators of parental short-
comings, does enable a number of other features of American life to
be fitted into an intelligible pattern. There is, for instance, the pre-
occupation of mothers with methods of child-rearing, schedules of
hours for feeding, methods of teaching, etc., so as to be certain that all
is done to give their offspring a flying start. Then there is the pre-
occupation of the young with popularity. They must receive *overt*
recognition, so that the signs of friendship, of love, are for the
American not a luxury but a necessity,[1] while the one thing to be
avoided at all costs is being thought a 'sissy' or a 'sucker'.

Again, the rejection of the father spreads itself to all authority, and
fits in with the political tradition which dates from the Declaration of
Independence. There must be authority; everyone cannot be top dog,
but the social distance can be lessened if you call the great by their
Christian names. When it comes to fighting, early training, according
to Mead,[2] plays its part. On the one hand, mother tells you to stick up
for yourself like a man, which links manliness with aggression, but
on the other hand, you mustn't start the scrap, so if you are spoiling for
a fight you go about with a 'chip on the shoulder' challenging anyone
to knock it off.

Finally, there is the famous boasting. Mead[3] quotes the contrast
drawn by Gregory Bateson between the English and American home
circle. In the former 'their view of exhibitionism versus spectatorship
it based on father hurrumpting to a juvenile audience'. He can afford
to play down. 'At the American breakfast table, the children perform
and father is the spectator.' The bigger father is, the bigger they have
to talk. Boasting turns out to be a compliment.

The study of national character does not only use assessment of traits,
and description of standards of conduct. There are numerous studies
of films and plays from this point of view.[4] Among them is a com-

---

[1] Gorer, G., op. cit., p. 101.   [2] op. cit., Chapter IX.
[3] op. cit., p. 99.
[4] cf. Klineberg. *Tensions Affecting National Understanding*, p. 49.

parison of the plots of American, French and English films by Martha Wolfenstein and Nathan Leites and a comparison of American and German plays by Donald V. McGranahan and Ivor Wayte.[1]

Conclusion. In the preceding chapter we took the 'culture pattern' as given, and considered some of the ways in which it moulds the newcomer, by making certain demands upon him, by offering him certain rewards, and by subjecting him to certain pressures. In this chapter we have turned to the analysis of the patterns themselves.

Every society has its unique 'pattern', and there is a school of thought, with a long history behind it, which so emphasizes the uniqueness of societies, that one might well despair of finding any general frames of reference which can be used in comparative study, whereby they can be 'understood'. One reason why we need not accept so extreme a view is that, if societies were absolutely unlike one another in all respects, we should not be able to see any meaning whatever in their different ways of life.

The 'Functionalists'—such as Malinowski and Radcliffe-Brown— come to our aid. At least every society *must* provide means of satisfying the basic needs of its members, and we can therefore explain many of their institutions in terms of the function they perform to this end. Furthermore a society is an *integrated* system of purposes, and therefore, in order that there should be a society at all, there must be what one might call 'integrative devices', methods to ensure the maximum order and harmony possible. The ways in which basic needs can be satisfied are innumerable; they are only limited by biological and physical circumstances. Once, however, a method has been chosen for the satisfaction of one set of needs, the methods chosen for the satisfaction of others must not involve relationships and principles, which are incompatible with it. These two principles—the need for the satisfaction of human desires, and the need for a harmonizing of the methods chosen —go far to render the variety of social experiments intelligible. The application of psycho-analytic concepts enables us to go further. Every society requires of its members that they accept its rules, and this means that they must submit to various forms of constraint; they have to give up the immediate satisfaction of a great many of their impulses. Now psycho-analysis has shown that there are characteristic trans-

---

[1] A Comparative Study of National Characteristics, in *Experiments in Social Process.* Ed. Miller, J. G. McGraw-Hill, 1950.

formations of desire, which occur when desire is frustrated, and therefore, when there is *systematic* frustration of certain desires—differing from community to community—we can understand many of the further details in such communities as being responses to this frustration.

We can, indeed, go further still. S. F. Nadel[1] has suggested that in the explanation of patterns of culture we can make use of three frames of reference, which overlap one another. There is the 'purposive' one, which is very like what has just been described—the interpretation of social patterns as integrated systems of purposes, which are intelligible because the basic purposes of man are the same the world over. To this he adds two more explanatory tools. Man is a coherently thinking creature, and he elaborates his culture in a logically coherent fashion. There is not only a factual compatibility between his methods of satisfying his needs, but there is an enveloping ideology, a system of ideas, moral principles, and beliefs, which are congruent with these methods. This is Nadel's 'logical' frame of reference, which further determines the details of the different patterns.

The third frame of reference involves a more daring hypothesis. Nadel suggests that we can understand a certain amount of the variety of cultures if we adopt Janet's theory of energy-distribution. This, as applied by Nadel, provides us with two principles: (1) the expenditure of energy may be *uniformly* at a high level, or at a low level; (2) a high expenditure of energy in one set of activities may involve a low expenditure in others. These two principles are, obviously, quite different and it must be admitted that Professor Nadel does not know when—or why—one principle is operative, and when the other.

However, supposing one found a culture with a *uniformly* energetic way of life, or one with a *uniformly* quiescent one, it might be that the predominant personalities of the former were prone to a generally high expenditure of energy, and the personalities of the latter prone to a generally low expenditure of energy. Such might be the case if one contrasted a 'warlike' culture with a pacifist one. Again, if one found a culture in which there were, say, a vigorous cult of warlike activities, accompanied by a quiescent form of religion, it might be that the second principle was operative.

It is clear that more research is needed before we accept or reject Nadel's hypothesis, but if such a hypothesis could be established, we should have a further instrument of explanation which would fill in a good many more 'gaps'.

[1] Nadel, S. F. op. cit., Chaps. xi, xii, xiii.

Of course, there is an irreducible factor of 'chance', in the guise of history and geography. By 'chance' is meant any explanatory factor which does not imply, and is not implied by, social-psychological principles. Such factors are geographical environment, and historical episodes. Geographical environment does not *imply* any sociological arrangement—there may not be any society. No social organization *implies* culture-contact with other societies, by way of conquest or trade. The *de facto* physical environment, however, will set limits to the choices the inhabitants have of making a living, and the unpredictable (from the point of view of the society in question) historical episodes of culture-contact will materially alter the way of life on which the 'contact' impinges.

Another irreducible factor is provided by what we have called the 'innovators'. The result is: given the geographical situation, certain ways of life are rendered highly improbable, and certain ones very likely. *Which* particular way of life emerges is, at least partly, due to the creative ingenuity of the individuals concerned. Once a start has been made, then social-psychological rules come into play. The basic needs will have to be catered for, unsatisfied desires will have their characteristic repercussions, and logical principles will set bounds to sheer inconsequence. It may be, as Nadel suggests, that the innate constitution of the participants, in terms of their liability to one form of energy expenditure, as opposed to another, may play their part.

To this we must add two further points. The first is that, when any society has catered for the material needs of its members in a fairly routine fashion, energy is freed for a fuller development of human potentialities. The second is that we must be careful, as social psychologists, not to over-emphasize the orderliness of the social process. It is not a 'tidy' affair, even in the simplest society. The social structure we construct, and the social-psychological principles we abstract, must be thought of as flexible frame-works and general tendencies. What actually happens, within these frame-works and subject to these tendencies, always involves an 'untidy' clash of personalities, a conflict of ambitions, personal choices, and unexpected decisions. In a sense we operate on two levels. On one level we formulate ideal structures and principles, on the other we come down to real-life situations. The latter are unintelligible without the former, but concentration on the former must not allow us to forget the spontaneous element in the latter.[1]

[1] cf. Firth, R. *Elements of Social Organization.* Watts, 1951.

PART III

APPLICATIONS

CHAPTER XI

APPLIED SOCIAL PSYCHOLOGY

IN this chapter some of the fields in which social psychological considerations find application are discussed. Before turning our attention to them, however, it may be convenient to summarize the general issues with which the social psychologist is concerned.

These may be divided into two 'levels': on the one hand there are fundamental matters concerning individual personality as such, on the other hand there are matters concerning the individual, as we ordinarily think of him, and the relations he has with his fellow men. Doubtless these two topics will eventually be woven into a coherent body of knowledge, but even so it will always be possible to discuss certain problems—such, for instance, as the importance of the group in industry—in terms of the models we use in everyday life without paying attention to the 'deeper' question of the emergence of personalities out of the social contacts in infancy. The emergence of personality out of the matrix of social intercourse can be taken for granted, and with the 'personality-model' as our unit we can proceed to talk about the part which is played by satisfactory social relationships in providing incentives to action and a sense of security in life. In what follows we shall start with a few remarks about the 'deeper' issues, and then go on to topics which can be handled with more commonsensical concepts.

Philosophical Applications. The 'deeper' question, which touches on problems traditionally thought of as 'philosophical' has nevertheless certain practical aspects. We have to admit that what we think of as an individual human being, with his capacity for thought and communication, with his ideals, principles and beliefs, with his perception of the world, in which he selects certain stimuli as significant and in which other stimuli are 'unnoticed', is a social product in the sense that he only 'has' these characteristics by virtue of his intercourse with other organisms who have gone through the same shaping process as he went through when he was an infant in arms.

We have to go further than this and admit with Mead that his very sense of 'I' and the correlative senses of 'you', 'he', 'she', 'we' and 'they' come into existence through this same social process. Whether it is convenient to phrase the matter as Mead does in terms of 'taking on the role of the other' is a matter for further consideration. We have already suggested[1] that the notion of the 'generalized other' is extremely obscure, and it must be admitted that no satisfactory formulation of the 'individualizing' process has yet been put forward.

One virtue of Mead's account is that he leaves a loophole for creative judgment, and any future formulation will have to do the same. We must, as it were, have it both ways. The 'personality' is a construct by means of which we register consistent systems of response associated with the same organism. We endow it with a sense of 'I' and 'we' after the manner of our own internal experience. Most of these systems of response have been socially conditioned—that is what we mean when we say that 'personality' is a social product. From time to time, however, a decision is made, a moral judgment is pronounced, or a conclusion is drawn, which cannot be explained without residue in terms of prior social conditioning. We think of our model as 'containing' an independent 'self' which makes these decisions, pronounces the judgments and draws the conclusion. Professor Ryle[2] has shown that such a model has serious inconveniences if it is taken too seriously. There is no doubt about it, but at the same time, whatever model we do make will have to find a place for individual responses which are not merely the result of social training.

These considerations have a practical relevance to certain ethical problems. This is not the place to discuss ethical questions in any detail, but we must consider briefly the sort of contribution the social psychologist can make to their solution. Ethics is concerned with the good and the right, and since ethical theories deal with the good and the right with respect to human experience and action, the ethical theorist must make some assumption about 'human nature'. Indeed ethical theories differ from one another with respect to these assumptions.

[1] p. 132. [2] *The Concept of Mind.* Hutchinson, 1950.

If we assume that human nature can only be understood when it is related to a wider destiny, either in relation to God's purpose or in relation to a spiritual condition, so much more 'real' than everyday life, that everyday life pales into an illusion, it is difficult to see how social psychology can be of much importance.

If, on the other hand, we take the humbler and more plausible line, that human nature can only be understood in terms of life as we know it, then such knowledge of human nature as scientific study can provide is clearly of the utmost importance. If, again, we take the so-called 'humanistic' view that what is 'good' is roughly analogous to what is 'healthy', then a study of the variety of solutions to the problems of social life, which are to be found from one culture to another, is obviously relevant to the question: what kind of society is most conducive to the 'best'—or most 'healthy'—life for its participants?

It is here that the problems of the emergence of personality out of social intercourse come in. We very often think of the 'best' social pattern as that which is most conducive to the richest development of the individuals concerned. We have, of course, to tidy up any formulation we may make by introducing such safe-guards as that the development of one individual must not grossly impede the development of another. We may also quarrel about whether, say, an artist should be allowed freer range than his fellows because of the contribution he makes to the culture as a whole, or even because his experiences are intrinsically more valuable than those of other people not similarly endowed. Into such questions it is no business of ours to enter. The point which has to be made, in the light of our discussion of the nature of human personality, is that this simple phrasing of the ethical question is unsatisfactory.

If we think of the 'development of the personality as a whole' or use some such phrase, we are thinking in terms of a 'personality' resident in the new-born babe, the development of which can be hindered or facilitated by the social pattern with which it is confronted. But we have seen that there is no 'personality' whatever at the outset. Personality in the sense of a coherent method of living and experiencing is created by society; it is not there from the beginning, ready made and only awaiting the opportunity to expand.

Observations show that in every society there are rules, and that these get incorporated in the structure of its members, so that some standards of conduct will be almost inevitably acquired in social training. (We need not concern ourselves here with the social deviants.)

One very obvious course, which is often taken, is to say that moral issues are simply concerned with the rules of each society and to leave it at that: 'ethical relativism', in fact. This solution is hardly satisfactory, because we do seem to be able to judge—and agree in judging—one social pattern 'less good' than another. These criticisms appear to be based on a sense of justice and a disapproval of social disabilities. We criticize a society in which a few are able to enjoy an expansive range of experience at the expense of the many, and we criticize a society in which certain cultural features conspicuously prevent that enjoyment of life, which we observe to be possible under other conditions. We may accept that the Dobuans, who live their lives in an atmosphere of suspicion and anxiety, have a code of morality which is the 'right' code according to their lights, but we do not consider their lights particularly luminous.

The fact is that as we look about we get some idea of what human existence can be. We realize that it can be many things. We may go so far as to say that there are some experiences, such as aesthetic enjoyment and the pleasure of human friendship, which are overwhelmingly valuable to those who have experienced them, but which by no means come in the way of everyone. What, however, we notice most of all is that some culture patterns put such an inhibiting strain upon those who live them, that enjoyments are drastically curtailed and positive misery ensues.

If we can go so far as to say that human misery is to be deprecated, and that the interests of every member of a society ought to be considered, then we have at least a negative criterion with which to judge and condemn certain social régimes.

Positive criteria are more difficult to come by. So many cultural patterns may produce different forms of human health, that is to say human beings not suffering from any obvious disabilities, that it is almost impossible to put a case for any one of them as 'the best'. This brings us to the borders of ethical judgment and it is not our business to penetrate that difficult territory. Those who hold that there is some intrinsic value in certain states of mind will naturally prefer those régimes which produce organisms which 'have' those states of mind, and will appeal to the social psychologist to tell them how to arrange matters so that such states of mind are likely to occur. It is not the social psychologist's business to make the value judgments; he merely supplies the recipe—if he can.

The social psychologist certainly can be of some use. The comparative study of societies for example seems to show that certain methods of child-rearing are prejudicial to the production of secure and happy personalities, while there may be a range of alternative methods, each of which will produce its own type, and none of which are harmful, so that it is not easy to choose between them. Again, certain politico-economic régimes seem to have obvious disadvantages, but there may well be a variety of régimes, each of which brings out its own range of human excellences, and none of which have any particular ill effects. Thus far we may support the adherents of relativism.

If we think of social environments as *creating* personalities, rather than of the social environment as being the soil in which a single type of human being is attempting to grow, and being helped or hindered in the process, we can envisage a variety of 'basic personalities' all different and all equally acceptable. In the political field, one cannot help thinking that if politicians were to pay more attention to the actual personalities created by the cultures in which they play a dominant role, and if they paid more attention to the removal of conditions which clearly make for what all would consider to be unhealthy, they would have less time to spare for quarrelling about different theories of government, which are often based upon an out-of-date concept of 'human nature'.

The danger of this position is that it appears to play into the hands of those enemies of the people who say: 'Why try to interfere with the so-called oppressed classes? They are quite happy as they are, knowing no different.' This argument is used time and again to support the most monstrous tyrannies. The answer is perfectly clear. We know from observation the enormously wide range of human excellence which societies can create, and within that range many types and combinations are acceptable. We also know perfectly well that the personalities created by oppressive and exploitative régimes are not up to any acceptable standard whatever. We should no more take the allegation of happiness—an allegation which is all too often patently false—as a conclusive objection to any attempt to better things, than we should be prepared to accept the alleged contentment of a cretin as an argument against treating him with thyroid extract. Human happiness is a tricky guide, and pleasure a trickier one. Both may attend states of affairs which we should all agree to call pathological. We have to use—and in everyday life we do—some standard of *unhealthiness* below which personality-creation must be condemned. Social psychology, it is claimed, throws a light upon such pathogenic conditions.

Above this standard people and peoples may be left to their own creative devices.

General Issues. As we emerge from the deeper issues we have been considering into the more congenial atmosphere of everyday life, we pass through an intermediate range of topics, which are matters of current discussion. If, as is suggested, we ought to think of the individual personality as, in some sense, a cultural precipitate, we shall expect that as the individual disengages himself from the matrix which has created him, he will have acquired certain standards of conduct, and certain motives for action which are characteristic of the *milieu* which produced him. Because of these cultural markings we can, with due caution, speak of a 'national' or 'tribal' character, in the construction of which individual idiosyncrasies disappear.

We also notice certain trends of social conduct which persist in spite of the fact that individual persons may (*a*) be unaware of them, and (*b*) act in disaccord with them. There are, for example, those sociological regularities which form part of the study of economics. We may be told, for instance, that if we put more money in people's purses and no more goods in the shops, the prices of such goods as there are will go up. No claimant for higher wages desires this, and yet this unintended result of a lot of human intentions just comes about. Are we to suppose that there are certain super-human laws which it is the business of economists to discover, and which human beings are bound to obey, in the same sort of way that they are bound at their peril to obey the laws of gravitation or electricity?

Such a supposition is entirely unnecessary. The rule is a kind of probability prediction about the likely behaviour of enormous numbers of individual human beings, as buyers and sellers. It is based upon certain very plausible assumptions about human conduct and *such of its motivations as are relevant*. It allows for certain individuals not behaving as expected, because they get lost in the masses who do behave as expected. It takes no account of a great many individual motives because they are irrelevant to the general issue. A man who has earned more money is likely to be prepared to pay more for a pair of socks. Whether he buys them for himself, or for his Uncle Charlie is irrelevant; what matters is that he is prepared to pay more for them. If, by some miracle, everyone were suddenly quite convinced that he really would be bound for Eternal Damnation if he paid more than five shillings for a pair of socks, then however much money he had in his purse he would rather go bare-foot than pay more.

The point is more realistically illustrated if we consider any form of piece-rate payment. You might expect, on certain obvious hypotheses about 'human nature', that if by doing more work a man could earn more, then paying him by the piece would ensure the highest output of which he is capable. Even if we leave aside strategical questions about increased output leading to a lowering of the rate paid for the job, the general rule need not hold. If the operative has a certain fixed standard of life at which he aims, he will quite likely try to earn enough to achieve it, and then stop. The donkey, in fact, may have a taste for small carrots.

This shows that economic rules which concern human conduct are ultimately based upon assumptions about what influences the behaviour of individual men and women with respect to the rule propounded. In so far as these assumptions are correct for a sufficiently large number of persons in a culture, the rule will hold; if the assumptions are not correct, the 'rule' will be falsified.

The fact that economic rules of behaviour are statistical predictions about the conduct of millions of human beings is clear enough. There is, however, a political field in which an analogous problem of individual versus mass conduct is discussed. It is said that classes of people who have certain economico-social privileges will act in such a way as to defend those privileges, *even though they are unaware of so doing*. Such a statement again hints at super-individual rules which govern individual conduct. Again such 'idealism' is to be deprecated— particularly when it comes from those who claim to be, in some sense, 'materialists'.

We are told that when considering political conduct, and even aesthetic taste, we ought to think in terms of 'classes', and that the motives of individuals are not only irrelevant, but inaccessible. There is undoubtedly some truth in this, but it is explicable in terms of many individuals being conditioned in the same way, and we need not let ourselves in for any super-individual 'force' whatever. Individuals created by social contact with people who enjoy a socially privileged position will acquire similar preferences, standards, assumptions about the rights of their position, and cultural tastes. Supposing the position of all members of such a class is threatened. This means, in the first place, that large numbers of members of another class, which is now on the way to being an opponent class, are asking awkward questions, making protests, listening to people telling them how ill they are treated, and so forth.

The privileged class feels itself attacked. This means that individual members find that their individual expectations are thwarted in innumerable ways, each one of them feeling the pressure from his own particular position. Communication among them will spread the news that they, as a group, are threatened, and each, according to the way in which he feels the threat to himself, and envisages the threat to the class as a whole, is likely to react defensively. The individual motives for any reaction which is called forth in any particular situation may certainly be inaccessible, and even if we think we know why the person acted as he did, his motives may or may not be largely irrelevant to the class-struggle. Members of classes engaged in the 'class-struggle' seldom think in terms of the class-struggle, any more than members of the public who find prices rising think in terms of inflation.

All that the notion of behaviour 'as a class' requires is that the conduct of the majority of its members in relevant situations should be such as to be in fact likely to safeguard their social interests. This is brought about by individual social conditioning, and no 'social force', or evolutionary urge need be held responsible. Man is a moral animal in the sense that he phrases his ambitions in moral terms. In any development in social economic history the innovators will think of themselves as apostles of a new vision, and the old guard will conceive of themselves as protectors of the right. The culture of a privileged class, therefore, will include moral justification of their privileges. When they act in a way which is obviously in defence of those privileges, they will phrase their action to themselves and to others in terms of a defence of the right, and so far as the class struggle is concerned their conscious motive is irrelevant.

Thus, just as in the case of economic generalizations there may be sufficient uniformity of conduct relevant to any generalization to allow us to dispense with a great many individual motives in our formulation, so where there is class conflict, there may be sufficient uniformity of conduct to enable us to ignore the particular motives in the minds of the actors. In the ultimate analysis, however, we have nothing but individuals interacting in both cases. What the economist and the political sociologist do is pick out certain uniformities of conduct which interest them and treat the various accompaniments of such conduct as irrelevant.

Application to Special Fields. When we come to the application of social psychology to the practical problems of everyday life the issues are quite straightforward. It is broadly true to say that one single principle is involved. This principle is the importance for a sense of security and happiness, of harmonious personal relations. Very broadly speaking, it appears to be the case, in our culture at any rate, that if for some reason or other people have met with rebuffs, slights, oppressive treatment, unkindness, or lack of consideration, they will tend to respond to other people with hostility, suspicion, withdrawal, and compensatory devices. They will not work their hardest, they will not behave properly, they will be miserable, and possibly develop pathological symptoms as a safeguard. If, on the other hand, their desire for a sense of worth is satisfied, they will be secure enough to respond to other people with friendliness and tolerance, they will be ready to co-operate, they will behave decently, and live in healthy and happy relationship with their fellow men. This puts the matter in a rather extreme form, but such is the general attitude of social psychologists when they approach practical problems.

It is, perhaps, hardly necessary to point out that the social treatment which any person has experienced and is experiencing must always be viewed from his or her point of view. To the spectator a man may be 'well-treated' and yet not, as they say, 'respond'; on the other hand a child may be strictly disciplined and yet not experience any ill effects. In the first case past experience may have engendered an attitude of suspicion, in the second the child may welcome consistent treatment, provided its obedience is rewarded by affection. Thus, in any given case-history one is concerned more with the way in which personal relations appear to the individual in question than with the intentions and attitudes of the other people with whom he is concerned.

The principle which has been outlined above can be applied diagnostically and therapeutically. When something is found to be wrong, one of the things we may look for is unsatisfactory social relations in the present. If our problem concerns large numbers of people, it may be impossible to delve into the past history of each in order to find out why the existing social relations are unsatisfying; we must be content to see whether the existing situation can be improved. If the problem concerns individual cases, we may be able to find out why an undesirable attitude has developed by an analysis of the past pressures which are responsible for it. Which of these lines is taken will, of course, depend upon the nature of the problem, the facilities provided for investigation, and the possibilities of making the changes which are deemed desirable.

A further point to be made is that the application of social psychology to social problems may be 'wide' or 'narrow'. The social impact upon a person is both direct and indirect. In so far as he or she is influenced (or has been influenced) by actual direct social contacts we may apply our knowledge to a diagnosis of the effects of such social intercourse, and consider ways in which the situation could be improved. On the other hand we may turn our attention to the wider issue—to the general culture in which such social situations and relationships arise. Thus there will be 'radicals' and 'tinkerers': those who say that it is no use 'tinkering' with specific social contexts—a factory, a school, a home, etc.—one must change the whole pattern of society in which these ill-adjusted groups are allowed; and those who take the line that we must do something here and now and that we cannot afford to await the Millennium.

In what follows an attempt will be made to indicate the sort of way in which social psychological considerations have been applied in industry, in psycho-pathology and in the study of delinquency.

Industry. In industry, a key position is occupied by the celebrated experiments which were carried out at the Hawthorne plant of the Western Electric Company in America.[1]

The investigation started in 1924–26 with a study of effects of different forms of lighting on output—a routine investigation for industrial psychologists. Control groups and experimental groups were duly compared, but the results were not at all what was expected. The output of the test group went up, but not closely correlated with changes in the lighting, and, more disturbing, the output of the control group went up as well, with no change in lighting at all. 'This', as a writer to the *Readers' Digest* of April, 1941, remarks, 'was completely screwy. But screwier results were to follow. Light for the test-group was decreased below that of the control group. Its output went up again. So did that of the control group! What, in Heaven's name, was going on?'[2]

---

[1] cf. *Management and the Worker*. Roethlisberger, F. J. and Dickson, W. J. Harvard Press, 1939. *Leadership in A Free Society*. Whitehead, T. N. Oxford Press, 1937. A good short account of the series of experiments is to be found in *The Making of Scientific Management*. Vol. III. *The Hawthorne Investigations*. Urwick, L. and Brech, E. F. L. *Management Publication Trusts*, 1948.

[2] Quoted. Urwick L. and Brech, E. F. L. op. cit., p. 15.

These paradoxical results led to the 'Hawthorne Experiment' proper, and it lasted from 1926 to 1932. In the research as a whole, three groups who were closely observed, are of special interest.

The 'Relay Assembly' group of five girls were set to do their work in a special room. They had to assemble telephone relay units and they were paid on a group piece-rate basis. Their output rose. Variation in rest-pauses and hours worked did not seem to make very much difference. What seemed to matter was: 'The absence of constraint by supervision, consultation and participation in decisions, freedom of conversation and interpersonal contacts, a sense of importance or recognition, and the establishment of a full and satisfying motive.'[1] The latter, the new motive, is interpreted to be the contribution to knowledge in which they felt they were participating. A sense of responsibility was engendered, and it appeared that though the girls were encouraged to work 'just as they felt', they did in fact work harder without feeling any pressure. A further curious fact emerges when the variations in output of the girls are inter-correlated. At the beginning there was but little correlation, but as the team became more harmonized the inter-correlations of their rates of output became remarkable.[2]

The second group which claims attention was made up of five girls engaged in Mica splitting, a skilled job. Their output rose, but apparently not so conspicuously as did that of the Relay Assembly Group. There were, however, differences. The Relay Assembly Group formed, as has been said, a harmonious team, and this revealed itself in informal social activities during leisure hours. There was nothing of this with the Mica splitters. The Relay Assembly test room was a group story; the Mica splitting test room was a story of individuals. The significant difference in their condition was that the girls engaged in Mica splitting were paid at individual piece-work rates. This may well not have been the whole story, of course. It is, perhaps, significant that in the photographs one sees the Relay Assembly Group sitting side by side at a long bench, while the Mica splitting group are so placed that three sit at one table, while the other two sit behind them at another. Towards the end of the experimental study of both groups the output fell. In both cases the operators were nervous about their futures. This had nothing to do with the experiment, it was due to the threat of unemployment and transference to another job on account of changes in the external circumstances. The investigators make the

[1] ibid., p. 51.   [2] Whitehead, T. N. op. cit., p. 45.

point that reason should prompt them to work as hard as they could while the going was good, so that if they are turned off, as they fear, they will have something to fall back on. This, however, is the reverse of what they actually do; the financial motive, in its pure rational simplicity, is not the only factor operating.

The third group which was specially studied was a group of nine wire men, three solderers and two inspectors who were engaged in Bank-wiring, a job which involved the participation of them all, so that the rate of work of each was controlled by the operations of some-one else. There were several such groups in the whole Department, and payment was on a Departmental piece-work basis. Here the situation was very different from that of the other two groups. The output remained astonishingly constant. The group as a whole, fearing that piece-rates might be lowered if they produced too much, and that they might be criticized if they produced too little, set themselves a target and preserved an even rate by employing the sanction of abuse against anyone who worked too fast or too slow. Another feature of this interconnected group was that it had a status hierarchy of its own which showed itself in the way they treated one another, and also a friendship system which cut across the hierarchy and divided the whole group into two for informal activities.[1]

The study of these groups revealed, among other things, the im-portance of supervision, and the attitude of the workers to 'manage-ment' in general. This led to a large-scale interviewing programme which covered almost the whole plant.

The results of this inquiry are, in a sense, not surprising. What is more surprising is, perhaps, that no serious attention had been paid to the social aspects of industry before. Everyone knows, from his own experience, that work is less laborious if one is working with people one likes, for people who appreciate what one does, and for a result one deems worth while. Everyone knows, too, that it is almost im-possible to work with people, whether side by side or in co-operation, without one's relations with them making a difference. And yet a good deal of thinking about operations in industry has, in the past, been carried on as though such matters were irrelevant, on the grounds that each man and woman is solely interested in the pay-packet.

This, of course, does not mean that the pay-packet is not of major importance. It means, rather, that if one is considering incentives, and,

[1] For a detailed analysis of this group see Homans, George C. *Human Groups.* Harcourt Brace, 1950, Chaps. 3, 4, 5, 6.

more certainly, if one is considering happiness, other factors have to be taken into consideration. Among these other factors are the relationships between the worker and his fellows, and his attitude towards 'management'. So far as attitude towards other workers is concerned Wyatt and Langdon[1] found that one of the most important factors which made for satisfaction among operators engaged in the monotonous task of feeding machines was having companions near them that they liked.

From the Hawthorne investigation we can extract a variety of topics which are of social-psychological interest.

The Bank-wiring group, it will be remembered, had a social system of its own. In every industrial enterprise there is, of course, an official hierarchy and, according to W. B. D. Brown,[2] managing director of a bearing manufacturing company, it is of great importance that this should be as clear as possible, particularly if there are recognized methods of getting promotion.

This official hierarchy, however, is not the only one; there is often an unofficial status scheme in which, for a variety of reasons, jobs and persons are positioned. The Bank-wirers, for instance, seemed to be divided into 'connector wiremen' and 'selector wiremen', and the former thought themselves a cut above the latter, though there was no difference in skill between them. This, we are told, was due to the chance that in the Department the selector wiremen worked behind the connector wirers, and that part of the shop had lower prestige, because the newcomers started there and moved forward as they became proficient. This kind of chance-wise stratification—the importance of certain seats, certain positions, certain jobs and the like—combined with the official hierarchy makes an industrial enterprise a complicated system of status-positions. The degree to which they are significant may well depend upon the anxiety or security of their holders, but it is perfectly clear that the culture-pattern of any enterprise has to be carefully investigated before any changes are made.

Another factor we have seen to be significant is the method employed in supervision: the personality of the supervisor, his technique of persuasion and disciplining and so forth. In an investigation in Rowntree's Cocoa Works, York, it was found that 'next to wages [the influence of supervision] was the most forceful element in creating con-

---

[1] Ind. Health Res. Board. No. 32, 1938.
[2] 'Incentive within Industry.' *Occupational Psychology.* XIX, 1945, p. 82.

tentment and maintaining the level and consistency of production.'[1] The experiment of Lewin, Lippitt and White on the effects of different forms of leadership which have been described already[2] are relevant here, and attempts have been made to teach 'democratic' methods of foremanship.[3] We are warned, however, by Bradford and Lippitt[4] that in the training of a supervisor it is important for him to learn, not only what he ought to do or avoid doing, but also to ensure that he appreciates the effect of his action on the group. To this end Moreno's device of the socio-drama has been used.[5] In this technique the trainers play the part of supervisor and employee in turn.

A third topic raised, this time by its effect on the Relay Assembly Group, is the topic of participation, to which we may add the allied topic of consultation. These two topics are of very widespread importance. If we think of participation as working together with others towards an end, the effect of the group upon the individual member will be determined (1) by the degree to which he identifies himself with them (the degree to which he is 'ego-involved') (2) the standards and the 'tissue of expectations'[6] which characterize the group. These last are influenced by the 'intelligibility of the target, [the] assessability of progress, and [its] susceptibility to control'[7] together with the group's general attitude towards the worth-while-ness (economically and otherwise) of the job.

We have here a large number of variables, all of which help to determine the amount of effort a person is prepared to put forth. Furthermore the form taken by them will vary from one type of industrial situation to another. To consider them all in detail would mean writing a book about the 'Human Factor in Industry', but one or two points may be made here.

1. The degree to which a person identifies himself with the group raises the issue: 'which group?' A man may identify himself with the group with which he is actually working face-to-face; he may identify himself with 'the firm' or 'the industry'; he may identify himself with

---

[1] *Personal Management.* Northcott, C. H. Pitman, 1945, p. 207.

[2] p. 79.

[3] *Psychology in Industry.* Maier, R. J. Harrap, 1947, p. 98.

[4] *Supervisory Training for Group Leadership.* Publ. Research Centre for Group Dynamics 1945. cf. Krech and Crutchfield. op. cit., p. 431.

[5] cf. Lippitt, R. *The Psycho drama in Leadership Training Sociometry,* 6, 1943. [The word 'socio-drama' is used in the text because the actors play *social roles* rather than parts which represent personal difficulties.]

[6] Mace, C. A. 'Satisfaction in Work.' *Occup. Psych.* XXII, 1948, p. 13.

[7] Mace, C. A. 'Advance in the Theory and Practice of Incentives.' *Occup. Psych.* XXIV. 1950, p. 239.

the whole community for whose benefit the firm is deemed to exist; or he may identify himself with all these.

At the face-to-face level of identification, the experiments of Bavelas are relevant. He has shown reason to accept Lewin's principle of the importance of group decision[1] as applicable to industry. In the sewing plant of the Harwood Manufacturing Corporation it was found that after group decision to do so, a higher target could be achieved. This result, however, seems to have been in part due to the charms of Bavelas because when French[2] tried the same thing it did not come off until he had learnt the technique of 'democratic' leadership. However, even if leadership is required to 'fix' a group decision, the fact that it is made in a group would seem to be of major importance in the sense that it 'commits' its members.

The 'ego-involvement' in the face-to-face group, whether based upon spontaneous liking or mere incorporation, by no means insures the sense of participation in the larger unit of 'the firm'. The Bank-wiring group proves that. The individual's identification with 'the firm' depends among other things upon his knowledge about the part his own activities play in the whole concern, and various devices of instruction and decentralization have been developed to give the individual operator a sense of his function. In the Bata shoemaking firm in Czechoslovakia, for instance, there was an elaborate division of processes so that each shop had to 'buy' its own raw material and 'sell' its products to the shop doing the next process. Such a scheme, it was hoped, would give more interest in the enterprise as a whole to the individual worker.[3] Other devices are: profit sharing, the provision of 'welfare' facilities, the encouragement of sports and entertainments and so on.

Again, identification in the firm does not ensure 'ego-involvement' in the needs of the community at large. To this end are employed various methods of information, propaganda, the romanticizing of nationalized industry, the public recognition of good service (as in the U.S.S.R.) and (also in the U.S.S.R.) public disapproval of dissentients.

The individual operator, then, may identify himself with all or any of these groups. So may the face-to-face group with whom he is working. They may identify themselves with the interest of the firm,

---

[1] cf. Lewin, K. 'Frontiers in Group Dynamics'. *Human Relation* I., 1947, p. 35.

[2] French, J. R. P. Jun. *Field Experiments. Changing Group Activity in Experiments in Social Process.* Ed. Miller, J. G. McGraw-Hill, 1950. cf. Maier, R. J. op cit., p. 264.

[3] Dubreuil. *L'Exemple de Bata.* Paris, 1936. cf. Friedmann, G. *Problèmes Humains du Machinisme Industriel.* Gallinard, 1946, p. 309f.

or they may not (the Bank-wirers did not). They may identify them-selves with the community at large, or they may not.

2. The 'tissue of expectations', to use Mace's useful phrase, by which an individual is influenced is liable to be stronger when it con-cerns the expectations of the face-to-face group, than when the expecta-tions are those of representatives of 'the firm' or 'the country'. The expectations of all these systems may, of course, reinforce one another, but this is by no means always the case, and when it is not the case it is difficult—as every reader of old-fashioned schoolboy stories will remember—for the individual to hold out against the 'ethics' of his immediate fellows. This being so, the scientific study of working groups is of the utmost importance, because one of the most powerful sources of incentive to work is the expectations of the people you are working with. As Mace puts it: 'In the past the control of human energies has been thought of either as control *from above* or as control *from within*. To foster codes and standards in a cohesive working group is to involve the principle of control *from around*'[1] (his italics).

3. One of the ways in which an attempt is made to bring working groups into closer participation with wider interests, so that the ex-pectations they will have of one another will be more in accord with the requirements of the larger groups, is of course the establishment of joint consultation. So effective is this scheme in all fields of modern Russian politico-economy, that discussion settles almost all local issues, leaving only large-scale planning to be done by the central authority. The general principles of joint consultation in its widest sense are that policy should be discussed and explained before it is put into operation, that no change should be made without consultation, that the griev-ances of the workers should have fair hearing, that rates, pay and methods of payment should be freely argued out by 'management' and employees, and that, in general, the employees should be 'brought into the picture' at every level.

A variety of methods are in existence in this country, in America, in France[2] and elsewhere, and various studies, such as that of Lester Coch, and French[3] on the beneficial effects of consultation on change of job, have been made. However, the mere introduction of joint-consulta-tion in one form or another is not enough. The mutual suspicions are not swept away just because a group of workmen and managerial

---

[1] *Occup. Psych.* XXII, 1948, p. 15.
[2] cf. the account of Gérard Bardet's factory in Friedmann. op. cit., p. 315.
[3] 'Overcoming Resistance to Change.' *Human Relations*, 1, 1948, 512-532.

officials sit round a table, smoking each other's cigarettes, and going through the motions of hearty goodwill.

One of the troubles is that attitudes of suspicion, antagonism, and anxiety may be there, without the workers participating in the discussion being fully aware of it, and even cynicism on 'the other side', when it is there, may also be but half conscious. These unconscious undercurrents are constantly upsetting calculations in the industrial field. Time and again experience has shown that a complaint or a request has as its 'latent content' something other than its 'real content'. Thus various changes or amenities may be asked for and granted, and then, to the exasperation of 'management', no use is made of them. One can only suppose, and this can sometimes be verified, that the complaint made masks a trouble of which the complainant may be hardly aware, and that the request for something which is not used when it is granted, is really a kind of unconscious 'try-out' of managerial goodwill.

One attempt has been made to exorcise these undercurrents, which bedevil joint consultations, by bringing them to the surface as and when they manifest themselves to the percipient eye of the therapeutist. This is the subject-matter of a preliminary report by Elliott Jacques[1] on his work, as a member of the Tavistock Institute of Human Relations, at the Glacier Metal Company. The position of the therapeutical observer is delicate because his neutrality has to be established, and of course he may be the target for displaced hostility. The technique was to comment on and interpret to the committee members the significance of their remarks, their emotional displays, their criticisms, and their constant habit of moving from the actual topic they were supposed to be discussing, which was a change from piece-rates to hourly rates of pay. The meetings of the various committees, each of which had a practical issue to discuss, became in effect (though not explicitly) psycho-dramas in which the emotional undercurrents came to the surface and were duly interpreted. The results of this technique are, at the time of writing, unknown, but if it can make the work of committees not only smoother but also shorter, the Tavistock Institute of Human Relations will have done a service to Industry in particular, and to mankind in general.

4. A final point remains to be mentioned. The social-psychological problems in industry vary from factory to factory, and what applies

---

[1] *Human Relations*, III, 1950, p. 223. For another study of joint consultation cf. Scott, W. H. *Joint Consultation in a Liverpool Manufacturing Firm*. Univ. Press, Liverpool, 1950.

in one context does not necessarily apply in another. This is even more evident when we compare one type of industry with another. In a factory all—or most—operatives are working in large or small rooms; the size of the units, and the size of the rooms are clearly relevant to the possibilities of social intercourse, but there are many factors common to all factory situations. The problems are entirely different when one passes from factories to, say, transport or to the extractive industries.

In a coal-mine, for instance, where coal is got under mechanized conditions, by the 'long wall' system, the social psychological problems are almost insoluble. Under 'hand-got' conditions the work was done by small teams, who completed the whole operation. Under a mechanized shift-system this is not the case. The process of coal-getting is divided into two parts—cutting and filling. The 'fillers' work their stint on a long coal-face, each independent of his fellows. They are dependent on the skill of the 'cutters' and 'gummers' (whose job it is to clear the region of the cut). The 'fillers' are also confronted by unpredictable faults and other geological irregularities. Team-work, which might lessen the sense of frustration, is impossible, and so the frustration tends to give rise to hostility, which is directed against the cutting shift, or against 'the system'. The 'cutters' and 'gummers', also do not form a team, and are liable to feel resentment at the criticism of the 'fillers'. Undoubtedly a good deal of the unrest in the coalfields may be traced to the socially unsatisfying conditions of work.[1]

The word 'industry' covers a heterogeneous collection of social situations, and each has to be dealt with on its own merits.

Psychological Medicine. The application of social psychology to the field of psycho-pathology is twofold: (1) etiological (2) therapeutic.

(1) The whole body of psycho-analytic doctrine, whether orthodox or deviant, is *au fond* a branch of social psychology in the sense that most mental disease is primarily caused, according to such hypotheses, by social relations in infancy rather than by physiological determination, bacterial infection, or constitutional peculiarities, though these latter may play their part. In this book, however, no attempt will be made to give an account of psycho-analysis and its derivatives, and having stated what may be regarded as an exorbitant claim, we will turn to wider issues, which no one is likely to dispute.

---

[1] Trist, E. L. and Bamforth, K. W. Some Social and Psychological Consequences of the Longwall Method of Coal-getting. *Human Relations*, 1951. IV, 3.

If we regard the personality as a creation of the cultural matrix, then 'abnormal' personalities are as much produced by their social setting as 'normal' ones. This notion can be pressed further. If we abolish the distinction between the 'mind' and the body'—or, rather, if we put that model aside—and think of the organism as a whole, we realize that it is not only in its 'mental' or 'psychological' aspects that it is culturally shaped but in many of its physiological aspects as well. Its digestive system, its eliminative system, its sexual system, and, indeed, its muscular system are all modified by the training it receives, so that, as Lawrence K. Frank puts it, 'the infant surrenders his physiological autonomy to cultural control.'[1] Culture in fact must be thought of 'as operating within human organisms where it has been established in their very organic structure, functioning and behaviour.'[2]

Now emotional responses such as those of anxiety and anger involve large-scale physiological disturbance, and therefore cultural pressure which arouses anxiety or aggression may be expected to give rise, under certain circumstances, to bodily symptoms. Thus the incidence of what are known as psycho-somatic diseases such as peptic ulcer, asthma, hypertension, Graves' disease, is indirectly determined by the culture-pattern. Furthermore since the essential physiological processes of eating and eliminating are the processes round which so much infant care and training are centred, we shall expect that physiological symptoms associated with them will vary in nature and significance from one culture to another. Mead, for instance, points out that according to Alexander constipation may be a symbolic gesture representing the formula: 'I do not need to take or receive, therefore I do not need to give.' Such an hypothesis implies a certain attitude toward the products of defecation.

Now it appears that the Manus are also particular about this subject and drill their children to defecate once and only once a day so that they grow up expressing a general character formula, such as, 'I am a good person because I defecate every day and confine myself to one difficult and constipated stool.'[3] Now whether we accept Alexander's analysis or not, the point is that any somatic symptom will have whatever

---

[1] 'Cultural control and Physiological Autonomy.' Frank, L. K. in Kluchohn. *Personality*, p. 114. cf. Mead, M.: 'Every socialized individual is ... so profoundly moulded by his culture that the most fundamental life processes will have systematically different patterns even though these patterns may all lie within the margin of safety for human functioning.' 'The Concept of Culture and the Psychosomatic Appeal', in Haring, D. G. *Personal Character and Cultural Milieu*. Syracuse Univ. Press, 1949, p. 534.

[2] ibid., p. 115.

[3] In Haring, op. cit., p. 531.

meaning it has determined by the relevant cultural principles with which it is associated.

Thus every culture will put its own peculiar strain on those who act it out, the result of such strains may be specific in their symptomatology to any given culture, and the culture itself may provide what one might call 'a language' for the expression of the maladjustments to which it gives rise.

Here we have to pause, because it will be seen that the whole problem of 'normality' versus 'abnormality' looms ahead. 'Cultural anthropology,' says Sapir,[1] 'has the healthiest of all scepticisms about the validity, the concept, "normal behaviour".' This is perfectly true, but it prompts dangerous thoughts. We are familiar with cases in which what we think of as 'abnormal' is 'normal' elsewhere, and others in which what we think of as 'normal' is 'abnormal' elsewhere. To many American Indians it is 'normal' to have visions; with us the patient who has visions is clapped into a Mental Hospital with 'schizophrenia' on his dossier. The Haida chief whose relative has died suspects supernatural persecution; with us he would be labelled 'paranoic' and sent for 'treatment'. So one could go on with the 'insult complex' of the Kwakiutl and the 'phobias' of the Dobuans.

Does this means that the concept of 'abnormality' is purely relative? By no means. The American Indian who has his vision is culturally expected to have one, the bereaved Haida chief is culturally expected to suspect a hostile cause, the Kwakiutl lives in a world of detractors, and they meet their situations accordingly. With us, however, visions are no longer expected, medical science has taught us why people die, and we are not surrounded by people who ill-wish us. We live in a different world.

The question really is: given the same syndrome, can we say that in one case it is 'abnormal' or 'neurotic', in another case it is 'normal'? Karen Horney suggests two criteria. 'There are two characteristics,' she says, 'which one may discern in all neuroses . . . a certain rigidity in reaction and a discrepancy between potentialities and accomplishments.'[2] In other words: 'It is not the mechanism that is abnormal, it is its function which determines its abnormality.'[3] If the symptom or mechanism is an accepted and expected way of behaving

---

[1] *Selected Writings of Edward Sapir.* Ed. Mardelbaum, D. G. California Univ. Press. 1949, p. 514.

[2] *The Neurotic Personality of Our Times.* Kegan Paul, 1937, p. 22.

[3] Wegrocki, Henry J. 'A Critique of Cultural and Statistical Concepts of Abnormality', in Kluckhohn, C. ed. *Personality*, p. 56.

it is 'normal' for that culture. If it is a method of resolving intro-psychic conflicts then, though it may be similar in many ways to the 'normal' in some culture or other, it is 'abnormal' or 'pathological'. It is this function that gives the symptom its 'rigidity', and it is because of the conflict at its roots that there is a depletion of the patient's powers.

The other situation in which what is 'normal' for us is 'abnormal' elsewhere presents no problem if we distinguish under 'abnormality' between the 'pathological' and the 'deviant'. The forceful character may find the role of younger son in the Tanala culture irksome. As a younger son, his behaviour will doubtless be deprecated, but he need not necessarily develop a neurosis. Similarly with the elaborate peace-fulness of the Zuni and the Hopi, the violent energetic person may be looked upon as extremely odd. He is 'statistically abnormal', but unless his conduct is the result of inner conflicts he is not 'pathologically abnormal' at all.

Now since the culture shapes the whole personality—mind and body—so profoundly we shall expect to find familiar pathological symptoms cropping up under unusual circumstances, because the pressures will be different from those to which we are accustomed; we shall also expect a variation in the incidence of neurosis from culture to culture; and finally we shall expect unusual symptom complexes.

With regard to the last, we hear of the so-called 'Arctic hysteria' in Siberia and what is known as 'lattah' in Malay. These complaints are similar in their symptoms, which include a marked imitativeness (echolalia and echopraxia) together with the shouting of obscenities and feelings of anxiety. Women appear to be the principal victims. Men, on the other hand, are the victims of the type of seizure known as 'amok', which also occurs in Malay. A mad rage, and hallucination of being attacked by men or animals, often occurring on the loss of something valuable, appear to be its symptoms.[1] Finally we may mention the 'windigo' psychosis, found among the Cree Indians in which a man may believe himself to be transposed into a 'windigo', a cannibalistic being, and may either go through the motion of eating flesh or actually do so.[2] These are only three examples of unusual symptomatology and there are many others. One may suppose that the general theory of intro-psychic conflicts is applicable to all such cases; the problem is to discover what the conflicts are, and why they

---

[1] cf. Klineberg, O. *Race Differences.* Harper, 1935, p. 297. And Wegrocki, op. cit., p.556.
[2] cf. Klineberg, O. *Social Psychology*, p. 518.

produce these specific manifestations. It would seem plausible to suppose that the beliefs of the society (e.g. in the case of the 'windigo psychosis') and also the very existence of a typical symptom-complex in a culture (in the case of 'amok') play their part in providing a 'language' in which conflicts express themselves.

When we turn to the incidence of pathological conditions we are up against two difficulties: in primitive societies which have no records, it may not be easy to find out the facts, and in countries with records, it is always difficult to be sure about conformity in diagnosis and hospitalization, when we compare one set of statistics with another. All the same, certain pronouncements have been made. Malinowski,[1] for example, tells us that the Trobriand Islanders had no hysteria or obsession-neurosis, while their neighbours on the Amphlett Islands were almost a community of neurasthenics. The former have few bars to sexual intercourse and sexual play, whereas the latter are very strict about sexual matters. Again we are told that schizophrenia is unknown among the Bantu, and it has been suggested that this is because the social structure is such that everyone has a definite place in which he can feel secure.[2]

Social change, too, when it is sudden and far-reaching may produce pathological effects. In China, it seems, the change from the old family pattern to one more resembling the West presents difficulties, and there is some evidence of pathological results.[3] More startling is the 'Vailala madness', a kind of mass hysteria, with giddiness, loss of control, and verbigeration, which swept through the Gulf Division of Papua in 1919–21 and has been put down to the 'effects of contact with and subjugation by a superior people'.[4]

Coming closer to our own culture the view has been expressed that all our quota of mental illness, with the exception, perhaps, of senile decay is due to defects in our pattern of life. Trigant Burrow,[5] for example, is one of the leading exponents of this view. For him, the fault lies mainly in our individualism, or, rather, in our isolationism. We have over-developed the 'private' and lost touch with the 'phylic'. Karen Horney in a book significantly called *The Neurotic Personality of our Time*, to which reference has already been made above, accuses the

[1] *Sex and Repression in Savage Society.* London, 1927.
[2] cf. Ogburn, W. F. and Nimkoff, M. F. *Handbook of Sociology. Kegan* Paul, 1947, p. 151.
[3] cf. Klineberg, O. *Social Psychology*, p. 512.
[4] Williams, F. E. 'The Vailala Madness in Retrospect' in *Essays Presented to C. G. Selizum.* Ed. Evans Pritchard, E. E. Kegan Paul, 1934, p. 377.
[5] *Social Basis of Consciousness* 1927. *Neurosis of Man* 1949.

contradictions of American life. There is the contradiction 'between competition and success on the one hand, and brotherly love and humility on the other'; there is the contradiction 'between the stimulation of our needs and our factual frustrations in satisfying them' and finally there is the contradiction 'between the alleged freedom of the individual and his factual limitation'.[1] 'All these factors together—competition and its potential hostilities between fellow-beings, fears, diminished self-esteem—result psychologically in the individual feeling that he is isolated.'[2]

Finally we may mention the views of Dr. J. L. Halliday.[3] He has stated the relationship between psycho-genic maladies—he is mainly concerned with psycho-somatic ones—and society in forceful terms. 'A group which is able to produce and also to reproduce (i.e. maintain or increase its social goods) is attractive and integrated (i.e. is socially healthy) and its members reflect its social health by being emotionally integrated (i.e. psychologically healthy). If, however, the psychological bonds of a community become weakened (whether as a result of "causes" from without or within) the group loses its coherence, becomes repellent, suffers dispersal, and ceases to be able to fulfil its particular social function; that is, it no longer produces "social goods", but "social evils". Such a group may be described as a disintegrated (i.e. socially unhealthy) or as a sick community or sick society, and its members reflect its social ill-health by being emotionally disintegrated (i.e. psychologically unhealthy).'[4] Psychological sickness is thus an index of social sickness, and Halliday produces statistics of psycho-somatic disease in Scotland as evidence of our social decline. Since the latter part of the last century, the family pattern has broken up, religious beliefs no longer hold us together, and our economic life is a battle-ground rather than a co-operative effort. The result is bewilderment, frustration, isolation, a sense of pointlessness, and a rise in the psychopathic rate.

Such views, of course, are supported from time to time by negative evidence. We have already mentioned the comparative rarity of mental disease in primitive societies which are more integrated than we are. Ogburn and Nimkoff refer[5] to a study of a group of five communities of varying cultural complexity in the Blue Ridge Mountains of Virginia. One of them, Colvin Hollow, was almost isolated from

---

[1] op. cit., pp. 288, 289.   [2] ibid., p. 286.
[3] *Psychosocial Medicine. A Study of the Sick Society.* Heinemann, 1949.
[4] op. cit., p. 147.   [5] op. cit., p. 156.

the outside world. The inhabitants could not read or write, and they had not even heard of ex-President Hoover. They were self-supporting, satisfied—knowing no better—and neurosis was unknown. As the investigation passed from this simple paradise through the neighbouring communities to 'civilization' they found that as they got nearer, the evidences of neurosis became more and more apparent.

So much for simplicity. But complexity is not of necessity ruinous. No one could call the U.S.S.R. 'simple', and at least one writer, Frankwood Williams[1] claims that the incidence of mental disease has declined with the removal of these 'anxiety pressures' that are characteristic of the capitalist countries. He admits that accurate statistics were not available when he visited Russia, and now the political climate is such that unhappily an atmosphere of suspicion is engendered by any observation to the credit of the régime. At the same time it must be agreed that in so far as a sense of collective purpose, and an absence of economic anxiety, are characteristic of the Soviet way of life, a decline in psychological disease is what one would expect.

An alternative explanation is that the Russian family, in which the infant is indiscriminately cared for by a number of adults, is not conducive to the establishment of a strong super-ego. This would mean that the *internal* conflicts would not bulk so large as the ones between the individual and his group. This might lead to hostility being directed *outwards* in the form of criminality, rather than *inwards*, giving rise to neuroses.

(2) So far we have considered the social psychological aspect of the etiology of mental disease. The application of social psychology to psycho-therapy is of a different order. Of course the views outlined above carry therapeutic implications: cure the sick society and you cure its members. But we must now consider a somewhat narrower field of inquiry: the use of small groups as a method of treatment.

It was noticed by two French psychiatrists that the patients in a large ward at the Salpetrière seemed in better trim than the private patients, and in 1904 they published a book called *Isolement et Psychotherapie.* They did not, however, make any practical use of this discovery. In 1905 in Boston Dr. J. H. Pratt found that when he gave instructions to tubercular patients in groups, the very fact that they met in groups seemed to have a beneficial effect. This time the principle of group-treatment was consciously exploited, but not for mental patients. It

[1] Williams, F. *Russia, Youth and the Present-Day World.* New York, 1934.

was Moreno, whose sociometric methods have been described,[1] who first used group acting as a therapeutic device in Vienna in 1911, and later he took his psycho-drama to the United States.

The 'psycho-drama' is a device for inducing spontaneity and insight by getting patients to act out their troubles on a stage. It is distinguished from the so-called 'socio-drama', which came later, by the fact that in the latter it is social roles that are acted out rather than personal difficulties. At about the same time in 1909 and later in 1912 L. C. Marsh was trying out methods of large-scale group therapy based on revivalist meetings and community singing, and in 1919 Edward W. Lazell was discovering the beneficial effects of lectures on psycho-analysis given to patients in a mental hospital.

In this brief account of the pioneers of group-therapy[2] several features may be noted which were developed by those who came after them. There is the general therapeutic value of any kind of social participation, noted in the wards of the Salpetrière and among the tubercular patients. This is widely recognized and in various ways social participation, so far as is possible, is encouraged in many institutions for the treatment of mental diseases.

S. H. Foulkes, for example, at the Northfield Military Hospital during the last war, introduced a measure of self-government among the patients with beneficial effects.[3] Clubs, dances, a newspaper, and the like were organized and run by the patients, who in this way were drawn into responsible positions, given an interest in the running of their affairs, and made to feel that their efforts counted for something in a common enterprise.

At Rampton State Hospital, the inmates of which suffer from severe behaviour disorders, it has been found that organized team games such as football are of educative value, in the case of boys who suffer from serious mental defects. Their intellectual disabilities are improved by their participation in a game which has certain formal characteristics—the goal they must attack, the goal they must defend, and so forth—and the very participation in a team gives them practice in social co-operation. The last factor is even more evident in the games of hockey which have been introduced among the women patients. Girls, whose behaviour disorders and temperamental instability manifest themselves from time to time in severe emotional outbursts, will play hockey with

[1] p. 34.
[2] Taken from Klapman, J. W. *Group Psychotherapy.* Heinemann, 1948, Chap. I.
[3] *Introduction to Group Analytic Psychotherapy.* Heinemann, 1948.

full regard to the sporting proprieties of the game, and there is much evidence that this experience of co-operation has a therapeutic effect on their everyday conduct. This ameliorative influence is enhanced by the socializing effect of contact with outside teams, whom they entertain, while their self-control is increased by the social requirement of abiding by the decision of the referee in cases of dispute.[1]

The work of Moreno[2] on the psycho-drama has been developed and the technique is employed by several therapists. The 'stage' need not be a formal structure, but in some institutions a formal stage is erected on which patients act out their personal problems, or take part in drama specially prepared for them, in which some key person 'acts in a sense as a psychological *agent provocateur*.'[3] The acting out of a situation is diagnostically valuable, it may give the patient insight into his troubles, and it affords an opportunity of expressing himself freely (*abreaction*).

The combination of emotional self-expression and collective participation is doubtless responsible for the beneficial effects of Marsh's mass methods in which as many as 500 patients might form the group. In its narrower application groups are very much smaller, consisting of about eight or ten persons, though occasionally larger groups will be found.

What they do will depend partly on who they are, and partly on the theoretical view of the therapist. S. R. Slavson,[4] for example, employed group therapy in connection with the Jewish Board of Guardians in New York. He was dealing with children, and so discussion or lecturing was out of the question. In his view the children came into his care because they had not experienced the 'unconditional love' which they need from their parents, and so the atmosphere of the group had to be completely permissive in order to 'counteract the inhibitive and restraining pressures in the child's past experience'.[5] The children were provided with games and material for making things and the adult watched their conduct in an attitude of benevolent neutrality, noting symptomatic behaviour for subsequent discussion.

Such a method is applicable to children, but with adults something else is required. Here there are differences in technique. Foulkes[6]

---

[1] I owe this information to the kindness of the Medical Superintendent of Rampton State Hospital, who was good enough to arrange a visit during which both the methods of treatment mentioned above were observed.

[2] Moreno, J. L. *Psycho-drama*.

[3] Klapman. op. cit., p. 127.

[4] *An Introduction to Group Therapy*. Commonwealth Fund, 1943.

[5] op. cit., p. 7.

[6] op. cit., p. 70 (see description of a session. ibid., p. 75 f.)

would appear to favour 'no set topics' and 'free floating discussion'. Klapman, on the other hand agrees with Sherman, who treated merchant seamen during the last war, that 'the power of the intellect has not received sufficient respect in psycho-therapy', and both these practitioners used explanatory methods of an information-giving kind. Indeed, Klapman's detailed syllabus of a series of Twenty-four lectures delivered to patients in a mental hospital is a formidable affair.[1] The re-education he aims at should not only be 'effective re-education', it must be 'orientation' as well, thus providing the patient with the tools for 'reality-testing' as well as an insight into his emotional disturbance.

One of the most obvious advantages of group-therapy is, of course, that it saves time, and—from the patients' point of view—money. Klapman, however, insists that this is by no means its only advantage; it is no *pis aller*. The fact that the patient is in a group at all has an ameliorative effect. Furthermore this effect is not only apparent among psycho-neurotics, psychotics respond to it too. 'The schizophrene,' says Klapman, 'longs for human contact and understanding but is afraid to admit it even to himself.'[2] This means that some patients may be accessible to group-therapy, who are not so accessible to individual treatment. Another advantage, closely connected with the very membership of a group, is that the patient realizes that he is not the only sufferer, and that other people have just the same kind of trouble that he has, a realization that diminishes his sense of isolation and cut-off-ness.

Another of Klapman's arguments in favour of group-therapy which is also voiced by Sherman is that the individual analysis involves a social situation, a group of two, which may well deal with certain sides of a patient's nature and experience, but is too narrow to deal with them all, so that, as Sherman puts it: 'All those problems and conflicts which come roughly within the domain of the social super-ego do not seem to be properly worked out.'[3]

It is no part of the thesis of those psycho-therapists who practise group methods that such methods should replace individual analyses. The two techniques are complementary rather than alternative. Much that emerges in a group session will be worked out in individual sessions, and the releases achieved in the individual session bear fruit when the patient meets his fellow members in the group.

[1] Klapman. op. cit., Chapter X.
[2] op. cit., p. 77.
[3] Quoted. Klapman. op. cit., p. 87.

Delinquency. The social psychological aspects of the enormous topic of delinquency can be considered much in the same way as was adopted in the above passages about psychological medicine. There is an etiological aspect and a therapeutic aspect.

(1) It is obvious enough that crime is a social concept. The accepted pattern of behaviour in any society, its beliefs, its attitude towards responsibility, and its established method of dealing with injuries, all contribute to its criminology. There are, doubtless, certain codes of conduct which are demanded of any group if it is to continue in existence, but at the same time there are actions which are 'criminal' in some societies and not in others.

Again, if there is a current belief in the powers of men to work evil magic on their fellows, what we might consider to be an 'act of God' may well be attributed to the malevolence of a human enemy. In some primitive societies the idea of personal responsibility is not an essential part of their attitude towards injuries. Attention would seem to be concentrated upon the readjustment of a disturbed balance, rather than upon the punishment of the evildoer. Thus, for instance, among the Tlingit, if a man of high rank is murdered, then a man of equal rank from any class to which the murderer belongs, must die.[1] The injury in such cases must be compensated for by an equivalent damage in person or cash, so that honour is satisfied and indignation assuaged.

In modern civilized societies there is on the whole a greater similarity in what is regarded as a crime, though, as we might expect, in the field of sexual conduct there are many different rules, and of recent years politics have reappeared as a differential source of criminal categories.

Another way in which cultural differences play their part in criminology is illustrated by American evidence of the results of culture contact. It appears that numbers of Mexicans were convicted in New York State for carrying concealed weapons, a habit which was usual in their own country. Another case of the distressing persistence of old habits is provided by Hungarians in Detroit who 'transferred to coal-stealing from the railroad their old attitude towards the stealing of wood from a nobleman's estate'.[2] This latter example raises an important general issue.

The statute-book crimes almost always exceed in range what we might call the socially-disapproved crimes, either in a society at large (cf. prohibition in America) or in a sub-culture of a society. In trying

[1] Klineberg, O. *Social Psychology*, p. 539.   [2] Klineberg, O. ibid., p. 536.

to disentangle the 'causes' of crime it is important to consider not only the attitude of the criminal to the sort of thing he has done, but also the attitude of the society with whom he mixes to that sort of thing.

Another piece of information we receive from America is that criminal conduct can be modified by general cultural assimilation. E. H. Sutherland[1] tells us that in Massachusetts in 1915 a classification of Italians, committed for crimes of violence, in terms of those 'born in Italy' and 'native born' in the U.S.A. show that the former out-number the latter in a ratio of about 9:1. Similarly Irish immigrants go in more for homicide than for gambling, while the second generation Irish conform to the American pattern, and go in for gambling more than for homicide.

Turning from these sub-cultural details to general problems of the responsibility of a society for the criminals it creates, we find ourselves confronted with such an enormous mass of material in the form of evidence and theory that it is out of the question to attempt any kind of summary. Once the hypothesis of hereditary tendencies to crime has been abandoned, social conditions stand in the dock. Frustration, poverty, city-life, broken-homes, lack of parental discipline, and the alleged general decline of morality are accused, to say nothing of the influence attributed to war and revolution. Obviously societies make their criminals by requiring their members to do things they don't want to do, by forbidding them to do things they do want to do, by putting special pressure upon certain sections of the community, and by a failure to devise effective disciplinary techniques.

Such general observations, however, even when backed up by statistical evidence are not of very great value unless they are supported by more detailed studies. Many people are frustrated and do not turn into criminals. Most people manage to bear frustration with no ill effects. The interesting question is whether those who find their frustrations unbearable can be divided into two *constitutionally* different groups: those who turn their aggression on to themselves and become neurotic, and those who turn it outwards and become criminals, or whether the 'intro-punitives' and 'extra-punitives' are socially deter-mined.

A similar question, as yet unanswerable, is: are the so-called 'psycho-pathic personalities' the victims of circumstances or innately incapable of developing self-control? They form the 'hard core' of the delinquent

[1] *Principles of Criminology.* Philadelphia, 1934.

population, because they seem inaccessible to any kind of influence, and further legislation may have to require their segregation until we discover methods of dealing with them.

Poverty, again, has notoriously its honest victims, though obviously in a competitive and mobile culture it puts a greater strain upon them than is the case in a culture in which everyone has the same standard of life, or one in which the poor accept their position and look upon luxuries as 'not for the likes of us'.

Shaw and his collaborators[1] found that the majority of the juvenile delinquents in Chicago came from the centre of the city, and that the number diminished as one proceeded through the various zones towards the periphery. In New York there are various 'delinquency centres'. In London Sir Cyril Burt[2] showed a high correlation (.77) between delinquency and density of population. Such ecological studies are important. An inspection of the delinquency maps prepared by the Nottinghamshire County Council reveals the curious way in which juvenile delinquency 'coagulates' in certain small areas—it may be street or groups of houses. At the same time there is the question: why not elsewhere? And in the towns: why not everyone in the contaminated area?

'Broken Homes', lack of parental discipline are fashionable delinquents as causative of delinquency. But, again, there are many 'broken homes', and many inadequate parents whose offspring are perfectly adequate citizens.

If we are to further our knowledge about delinquency at least three lines of inquiry have to be opened up. In the first place, and this applies more especially to juvenile delinquency, we need a more refined scale of 'criminality'. In this country under the heading: 'indictable offences' are to be found various juristically determined categories, and when an urchin of ten has accepted parts of a stolen bicycle he comes under one of these, and joins the statistical roll of serious offenders, together with the dull-witted boy of twelve who assisted in the offence of 'carnal knowledge'. It is, of course, very shocking even at the age of ten to be a 'receiver', and some cognizance has to be taken of it, but one cannot help thinking that the two cases may not be of equal prognostic value. However that may be with these (actual) cases, the problem remains: which of the delinquents are 'serious' cases, and which are not? and this cannot be decided on juridical standards.

---

[1] Shaw, C. R. *et al. Delinquency Areas.* Chicago, 1929.
[2] *The Young Delinquent.* Univ. of London Press, 1925, p. 77.

The second topic for inquiry is: what are the accepted standards of the sub-group to which the delinquent belongs? If he is brought up with middle-class standards, his conduct may mean one thing, while if he is brought up in a world which distinguishes between the 'wide' and the 'mugs' to the detriment of the latter, it may mean something quite different.

The third line of attack is implicit in the other two. The delinquent after all, whether a juvenile or an 'old lag', is an individual product of his social environment. We want to know why *he* has done whatever he has done. This brings us to the significance of case-histories. Everyone is a product of the society to which he belongs, but everyone is a *unique* product.

In Healy and Bronner's[1] study of delinquency it was found that in families in which at least one child was delinquent and at least one not delinquent, the former felt a sense of deprivation and rejection, and on the whole the latter did not.

More detailed case-studies have been carried out in this country by John Bowlby and D. H. Stott, both of whom stress the significance of personal relations among the factors causing delinquency. Bowlby[2] studied the cases of forty-four thieves who had been sent for treatment to the London Child Guidance Clinic, and he used as a control group forty-four patients who did not steal. One fact that emerged was that seventeen of the thieves had suffered prolonged separation from their mothers, while only two of the control group had had that experience. The rest had unsatisfactory mothers, but much the same was also true of the controls. This looks as though 'prolonged separations are a specific and very frequent cause of chronic delinquency',[3] and this is borne out by the fact that the habitual offenders had experienced separation more than the less serious ones. Furthermore the largest group (fourteen) of thieves who could be classed together manifested a personality type, called by Bowlby 'affectionless', and of these, twelve had suffered separation. The hypothesis which emerges is that separation deprives the child of the love relationship out of which the super-ego is built, and/or kills such love as has been developed by engendering rage and hate.

Such findings are not in disaccord with those of Stott,[4] though he goes much further into the 'meaning' of delinquency for his 102 youths

[1] *New Light on Delinquency and its Treatment*. Yale Univ. Press, 1936.
[2] *Forty-four Juvenile Thieves*. Baillière, Tindall and Cox, 1946.
[3] op. cit., p. 55.
[4] *Delinquency and Human Nature*. Carnegie Trust, 1950.

in an approved school. His principal thesis is 'that delinquent break-down is an escape from an emotional situation which, for the particular individual with the various conditionings of his background, becomes at least temporarily unbearable.'[1] The emotional situations which are so painful are, broadly speaking, those in which the individual's need for love and social security (in the inter-personal and not the economic sense) is unsatisfied.

Such situations, when they reach an intolerable phase, may be 'met' in five main ways—distinguishable, but not mutually exclusive. The boy may try to get out of his difficulty by 'avoidance excitement', that is to say, by plunging into a life of excitement in order to divert his attention from his anxieties. On the other hand, he may try and get his own back by going to the bad: 'That'll learn 'em.' A third, and somewhat similar reaction, is to try to get attention by delinquency, which may, of course, have the additional motive of retaliation combined with it. It is, however, different from pure retaliation, and more a matter of testing out his parents' affection. The fourth of Stott's motives is simply to get away from the situation at any cost, and he calls attention to the curious way in which some of the boys committed a crime at the school on the eve of their release, which looks as though they did not 'really' want to go back to a situation from which they had escaped. Furthermore in many of the cases where the removal motive was strong there was a past history of unsuccessful attempts to leave home in a perfectly respectable way, such as going to sea and the like. The last of the motives enumerated is 'inferiority compensation' which was often found in combination with one or more of the others.

Such studies as these show that broad statistical research into delinquency, whether juvenile or adult, is of very limited value unless it is combined with an inquiry into the way in which the factors which are brought out by large-scale study affect the individual victim. At the same time large-scale studies, based on case-histories are needed in order to find out how widespread are the experiences which seem significant in individual cases.

It might be thought that once the scientific study of delinquency had got under weigh, it would proceed apace and change our whole attitude towards the treatment of criminals. There are, however, two difficulties. In the first place, of course, enough has been said above to show that the discovery of cause-factors is no easy matter, and the

[1] op. cit., p. 11.

inference which can be drawn from ascertained cause-factors to appropriate methods of treatment is even more difficult. There are those, however, who say that there is another and more sinister difficulty which has to be overcome. Paul Reiwald, for instance, a Swiss criminologist, agrees with Alexander and Staub[1] that the punishment of the criminal has an unconscious meaning for the upright. Reiwald[2] brings evidence to show how irrational is the treatment of criminals, and the attitude towards crimes in general, in a large variety of countries. The number of dangerous criminals is small, but our reaction to their misdeeds is disproportionately violent. We know that brutality brutalizes, but we are constantly demanding penalties which have already proved useless.

These and other irrationalities he explains—and so do Alexander and Staub—in psycho-analytic terms. The righteous do not find righteousness easy to keep up. The criminal in their secret eyes has done what they long to do, but their own unruly selves would be even more difficult to keep in order if he got away with it. Thus crime and punishment fulfil a double function. On the one hand we have the vicarious pleasure of crime, and so far we identify ourselves with the criminal; on the other hand we see to it that conscience has its way by demanding punishment for his guilt, and so far we identify ourselves with that father-substitute, the judge. By this argument, not only is our irrationality explained, but we must infer that the criminal plays an essential role in society.

Such a view may seem hard to swallow, but at the same time it must be admitted that many of us are at once fascinated by crime, and relieved when it meets with its due retribution, and that the resistance put up in legal circles against a scientific approach to delinquency is not easily explained. There is no doubt that undercurrents of desire and guilt play their part in our attitude towards criminology, and that we have to take account of such undercurrents if any progress is to be made.

(2) Progress, however, is made here and there. Just as improved social relations in face-to-face groups were found salutary in dealing with mental illness, so attempts are made to induct the anti-social into an environment in which he will find social conduct more rewarding than the reverse. Experimentation in this field has obvious difficulties. We pay, it may be said, to be protected from criminals, and it is not

---

[1] 'Der Verbrecher und Seine Richter.' *Internat. Psycho-an. Verlag*, 1929.
[2] *Society and its Criminals*. Heinemann, 1949.

part of the bargain that prisoners should be given such freedom that they can prey upon us from the very prison-houses in which they have been incarcerated. And yet if it is true that delinquency arises from love-less human relations, and a lack of practice in the social virtue of responsibility, it would seem rather silly to reinforce the lovelessness by harsh treatment, and to perpetuate old habits by never giving the delinquent a chance to learn and practise new ones. Happily, in this country at any rate, the Home Office is prepared to take the courageous line, and the consequent risks. And, further, it must be granted that, in spite of Reiwald's analysis of the public mind, the 'public' are not seriously disturbed.

Social psychological considerations have made their mark in many Approved Schools, in the whole Borstal system, in some Prisons (such as Maidstone) and in the experimental 'open prisons' at Sudbury and Redhill where an attempt is being made to evolve a communal life based upon trust and responsibility.

There have also been experiments which are, in a sense, more experimental.

In the year following the First World War, August Aichorn was in charge of a '*Fursorgerziehungsanstalt*', a kind of Approved School, at Oberhollabrunn near Vienna. He had absorbed psycho-analytic teaching and determined to apply it to his charges. This meant the manipulation of the transference relationship and in order to establish this the inmates had to be on good terms with the staff who looked after them. This, in its turn, meant mild and friendly treatment rather than severe discipline. The children were divided into groups of twenty-five and in the early stages the membership of each group was dictated by the chances of committal. Gradually, however, those who were uncomfortable in the groups to which they had been assigned moved out to find more congenial friends and so the institution settled down into a harmonious grouping in which, interestingly enough, each group contained members whose problems were similar—e.g. intellectual defect, mild social defects, more serious social defects and so forth.[1]

Twelve youths, however, fitted in nowhere: they were too aggressive. It is concerning their treatment that Aichorn's experiment claims special attention. Violence, in his view, springs from frustration and lovelessness. To counter it with repressive measures is not only to per-

[1] Aichorn, A. '*Verwahrloste Jugend*.' *Intnat. Psycho-an. Verlag*, 1925. Lecture 7. (Translated: *Wayward Youth*. Viking Press, 1936.)

petuate the cause but, in a sense, to play the game of violence itself, because in the past aggression has met with punishment and therefore may be said to have an excuse. You respond with aggression to the outside world which thwarts you and denies you love; the outside world hits back and this confirms you in your hostile attitude. What then, was to be done?

He put all the twelve 'aggressives' into the same hut and let them run riot. They were in nominal charge of himself and two women teachers, who were almost driven out of their minds. No interference was allowed except to save life. They broke the windows, they refused to sit at table and gnawed their food in corners of the room. They threw things at the teachers and ceaselessly fought among themselves for about three months. During this time, however, a change in their conduct was observed. They became more and more violent, but gradually, according to Aichorn's estimation, the violence was directed not so much at its overt object as at inducing punishment, or some kind of retaliation from the staff.

In each case a crisis came with some conspicuous act, of which Aichorn gives an example where one boy seized a bread knife and rushed at another crying: 'You cur, I'll cut your throat.' Aichorn, with some courage, stood by apparently unmoved. The boy flung the knife on the floor and burst into floods of angry tears. This crisis was followed by a period of emotional attachment to the women teachers, and gradually that gave way to the formation of a consolidated group. As may be supposed Aichorn's interpretation of the final phase is in terms of Freud's theory that groups are bound together by the mutual identification of their members in their common attachment to the same objective.

Much the same technique of non-interference was practised by W. David Wills in his two experiments at 'Hawkspur' and 'Barns'. The former was a 'Q camp' established in 1936 by the Society of Friends for unruly adolescents. Two principles governed the enterprise. The first, in Wills' own words, runs as follows: 'The task of those who are attempting to get the offender to fit into his environment is first to abandon the fruitless attempt to force *our* discipline upon him. Thus to devise a means by which he can formulate a system of his own which is not unacceptable to society.'[1] The second was: being free and having to discipline oneself is a burden, which means that group life and the

---

[1] *The Hawkspur Experiment.* Allen and Unwin, 1941, p. 38.

acceptance of rules is rewarding. The technique employed to promote a less hostile and more co-operative attitude to society was a system of self-government which passed through many phases of harshness and mildness until a harmonious adjustment of individual claims to social needs was established.

At 'Barns' in Peeblesshire the same kind of permissive régime was tried out with success on younger children who could not be placed satisfactorily in the wartime evacuation scheme. Again, as with Aichorn's experiment with his 'aggressives', there was a period of mounting violence when 'crockery would be dashed on to stone floors, games destroyed, furniture broken, stones hurled through the windows',[1] mainly to find 'punishment point'. Again, when it did not come, it was possible to establish some kind of order.

Such experiments as these obviously need considerable courage both on the part of authorities who are responsible for public safety, and on the part of the experimenter and his staff who carry them out. It is quite clear that only from such bold experimentation shall we learn more about the possibilities of social education.

It will be seen from these few examples that social psychology has a twofold application to social questions. In the first place it may throw some light upon the workings of society in its wide sense, in the second place it may be applied to narrower practical problems. In the field of politics for instance the study of public opinion and prejudice is important, so is the study of the way in which members of one group tend to use other groups as projecting grounds for their animosities and vices. In the field of education changes in the class structure and in social needs are relevant, as also are investigations into generally accepted methods of discipline.

On the more practical side our knowledge about political affairs may be enhanced by the study of small face-to-face groups, and in education this is even more obvious.

In general, the main principles of application are the need for social security in the psychological sense, and the fact that most people enjoy co-operation in harmonious relation with their fellows. At the same time it would appear to be needful for human progress, for the manifestation of human value, and for the enrichment of human experience, that individual differences should not be submerged in an undifferentiated morass of group uniformity. Of course the time when large-

[1] *The Barns Experiment*. Wills, W. David. Allen and Unwin, 1945.

scale application of social psychology is possible lies far ahead—we know too little. If it is true, as has been suggested that society *creates* its members, we must hope that, if ever the time comes for societies to create them scientifically, *all* the potentialities of human existence which are compatible with a stable society will be catered for.

INDEX